Dead, White and Blue

Contributions to Zombie Studies

White Zombie: Anatomy of a Horror Film. Gary D. Rhodes. 2001

The Zombie Movie Encyclopedia. Peter Dendle. 2001

American Zombie Gothic: The Rise and Fall (and Rise) of the Walking Dead in Popular Culture. Kyle William Bishop. 2010

Back from the Dead: Remakes of the Romero Zombie Films as Markers of Their Times. Kevin J. Wetmore, Jr. 2011

Generation Zombie: Essays on the Living Dead in Modern Culture. Edited by Stephanie Boluk and Wylie Lenz. 2011

Race, Oppression and the Zombie: Essays on Cross-Cultural Appropriations of the Caribbean Tradition. Edited by Christopher M. Moreman and Cory James Rushton. 2011

Zombies Are Us: Essays on the Humanity of the Walking Dead. Edited by Christopher M. Moreman and Cory James Rushton. 2011

The Zombie Movie Encyclopedia, Volume 2: 2000–2010. Peter Dendle. 2012

Great Zombies in History. Edited by Joe Sergi. 2013 (graphic novel)

Unraveling Resident Evil: *Essays on the Complex Universe of the Games and Films*. Edited by Nadine Farghaly. 2014

"We're All Infected": Essays on AMC's The Walking Dead *and the Fate of the Human*. Edited by Dawn Keetley. 2014

Zombies and Sexuality: Essays on Desire and the Living Dead. Edited by Shaka McGlotten and Steve Jones. 2014

…But If a Zombie Apocalypse Did *Occur: Essays on Medical, Military, Governmental, Ethical, Economic and Other Implications*. Edited by Amy L. Thompson and Antonio S. Thompson. 2015

How Zombies Conquered Popular Culture: The Multifarious Walking Dead in the 21st Century. Kyle William Bishop. 2015

Zombifying a Nation: Race, Gender and the Haitian Loas on Screen. Toni Pressley-Sanon. 2016

Living with Zombies: Society in Apocalypse in Film, Literature and Other Media. Chase Pielak and Alexander H. Cohen. 2017

Romancing the Zombie: Essays on the Undead as Significant "Other." Edited by Ashley Szanter and Jessica K. Richards. 2017

The Written Dead: Essays on the Literary Zombie. Edited by Kyle William Bishop and Angela Tenga. 2017

The Collected Sonnets of William Shakespeare, Zombie. William Shakespeare and Chase Pielak. 2018

Dharma of the Dead: Zombies, Mortality and Buddhist Philosophy. Christopher M. Moreman. 2018

The Politics of Race, Gender and Sexuality in The Walking Dead: *Essays on the Television Series and Comics*. Edited by Elizabeth Erwin and Dawn Keetley. 2018

The Subversive Zombie: Social Protest and Gender in Undead Cinema and Television. Elizabeth Aiossa. 2018

Parenting in the Zombie Apocalypse: The Psychology of Raising Children in a Time of Horror. Steven J. Kirsh. 2019

Beyond the Living Dead: Essays on the Romero Legacy. Edited by Bruce Peabody and Gloria Pastorino. 2021

Reading the Great American Zombie: The Living Dead in Literature. T. May Stone. 2022

Faith and the Zombie: Critical Essays on the End of the World and Beyond. Edited by Simon Bacon. 2023

Dead, White and Blue: The Zombie and American National Identity. Aaron W Clayton. 2023

Dead, White and Blue
The Zombie and American National Identity

AARON W CLAYTON

CONTRIBUTIONS TO ZOMBIE STUDIES

McFarland & Company, Inc., Publishers
Jefferson, North Carolina

This book has undergone peer review.

ISBN (print) 978-1-4766-8493-2
ISBN (ebook) 978-1-4766-5027-2

LIBRARY OF CONGRESS AND BRITISH LIBRARY
CATALOGUING DATA ARE AVAILABLE

Library of Congress Control Number 2023018575

© 2023 Aaron W Clayton. All rights reserved

No part of this book may be reproduced or transmitted in any form or by any means, electronic or mechanical, including photocopying or recording, or by any information storage and retrieval system, without permission in writing from the publisher.

Front cover image © streetart project/Shutterstock

Printed in the United States of America

*McFarland & Company, Inc., Publishers
Box 611, Jefferson, North Carolina 28640
www.mcfarlandpub.com*

For two wonder women,
Amy and Ellie.
Being part of your lives is an honor.

Acknowledgments

There are so many people that supported me. Starting at the beginning, I wish to thank Libby Tucker for guiding me throughout the entire project and my field exam advisors and the members of my dissertation committee—Praseeda Gopinath, Douglas Holmes, Michael Sharp, and William Spanos.

The sabbatical from Frederick Community College enabled me to resurrect my dissertation and transform it into this book. I received invaluable support from the staff and administrators at the FCC library including Patty Furry-Hovde, Patty Hude, Janet Kalinowski, and Colleen McKnight. I also wish to thank all the other librarians and archivists who shared their expertise and resources: Kevin Thomas (FDR Presidential Library and Museum); Karen Preis (McCracken Research Library); Matt Gorzalski (Morris Library); Wade Popp, Gene Morris, and Carmel Wilkes (National Archives); Nailah Holmes (New York Public Library); and Robin Vance (Washington County Public Library).

I wish to thank my editors Layla Milholen and Kyle Bishop for believing in me and graciously tolerating my spectacularly slow progress as well as the two anonymous readers whose encouragement and criticism helped immensely. I am grateful for everyone on Team Aaron—Robin Abell, Christina Cook, Bryan Hiatt, Anne Hofmann, and the many who attended my Disney *Zombies* viewing parties.

I am thankful for my parents and my daughter Ellie. Above all others, I thank my essential juice of pineapple, Amy. You are listed under all the subject headings in the card catalog of my heart.

An early version of Chapter Five previously appeared as "The Magic Island of Seabrook High: Disney Retcons the Civil Rights Movement in *High School Musical* Descendant *Zombies*" in *Social Order and Authority in Disney and Pixar Films* edited by Kellie Deys and Denise F. Parrillo and published by Rowman & Littlefield, all rights reserved. I wish to thank Rachel Twombly at Rowman & Littlefield for granting me permission to reprint that text here.

Contents

Acknowledgments vi

Preface 1

Introduction 7

CHAPTER ONE
Myths of Colonial America 19

CHAPTER TWO
Lakota Ghost Dance and the Imaginary Frontier 35

CHAPTER THREE
Caribbean and Gothic Origins of the American Zombie 57

CHAPTER FOUR
Social Critique and the Modern Zombie 85

CHAPTER FIVE
Civil Rights Movement Retold in Disney *Zombies* 114

CHAPTER SIX
Destiny Manifested in *Westworld*'s Philosophical Zombies 132

Conclusion 161

Chapter Notes 165

Bibliography 183

Index 195

Preface

After the release of his novel *There There*, Tommy Orange appeared as a keynote speaker at the NCTE annual convention in December of 2019 advocating for the teaching of more books by indigenous authors in public schools. He observed, "I don't think I was ever handed a book because a teacher thought I would connect with it." His remarks were not intended as a criticism of the educators he encountered but the failure of our schools, our school libraries, and our communities for not demanding more books with diverse characters written and illustrated by diverse creators. The argument is familiar and sobering given the historical and political moment. For the public-school educators in Orange's audience like my wife, a high school English teacher turned elementary school librarian, his words were equally affirming and frustrating. As a woman who has dedicated her life to the teaching of reading, she regularly served on textbook adoption committees fulfilling her self-imposed obligation to give students books where they can see themselves, books written in their native tongue. She accomplished a lot of good but not without resistance from the administration and calls for censorship from our community.

Unbeknownst to anyone, Orange's address occurred at the midpoint between the first publication of the 1619 Project and the murder of George Floyd. In local town halls and national platforms, these two events continue to be invoked paradoxically by parties across the political spectrum as metonyms of the social ills that afflict the nation. For some, the prominence of the 1619 Project illustrates the injustice of recognizing a singular national narrative. For others, it signals a need to restrict the free speech of educators. Similarly, George Floyd's murder is interpreted as symbolic of contradictory failures in the justice system. Considered alongside Orange's keynote, the responses to these events point to an uneven consensus about the identity and historicization of the U.S. as a nation.

Like my wife, I too have obligations to my students. As a community college professor, I rarely encounter students who enroll in an American studies course because they are eager to dig into colonial pamphlets or religious meditations. The students we serve need us to offer transferable courses that also fulfill a graduation requirement. This often limits me to teaching the survey courses like Early American Literature. Like my colleagues, I turn to popular culture, the shows students watch on Netflix and Disney+, not only to engage them but also to help them develop awareness of their own situatedness as citizens of a nation. Some days that means exploring racial bias in an episode of *Z Nation* that reimagines the narrative of *The Adventures of Huckleberry Finn* in a zombie wasteland. Other days it means discussing *The Book of Boba Fett* to examine how a Star Wars television series unapologetically reasserts the myth of the disappearing Indian by recasting James Fenimore Cooper's Natty Bumppo as Boba Fett among the noble savage Tusken raiders.

As I intend to show, popular culture is a powerful entry point into literature and a site where the myth of national identity is communicated and negotiated. Zombies, in particular, prove useful as a subject matter for two reasons. Personhood is central to many contemporary and emerging social justice questions including race, disability, immigration, abortion, and artificial intelligence, and zombies complicate and provoke arguments about what constitutes personhood in the narratives they inhabit. Moreover, the post-apocalyptic setting that often accompanies these creatures provides an occasion for writers to narrativize national history, posit counterfactuals, and imagine futurisms. My hope is to help other educators and scholars interested in popular culture by contextualizing an analysis of zombies with a genealogy of the American self.

Chapter Trailers

The opening chapter, "Myths of Colonial America," follows two lines of inquiry investigating the self-conception of British explorers and colonists and the socio-cultural relations that informed various iterations of national identity. First, I rely on the work of Americanist scholars such as Perry Miller and Sacvan Bercovitch whose canonical texts fashioned the field of American studies and are responsible for bringing critical attention to two fundamental ingredients of this study, the "Errand into the Wilderness" and the American jeremiad. Alongside Miller and Bercovitch, I turn to Richard Slotkin's cultural criticism that investigates the historical conditions informing the mythopoetic constitution of national identity while recognizing the regionalization of that myth across the continent. The other line of inquiry turns to the political, social, and economic philosophy that catalyzed the Revolutionary War and the Constitution of the United States. Influenced by Baron de Montesquieu, John Locke, and

Jean Jacques Rousseau, who quite rightly understood the imbrication of government, economics, and the individual even when they misunderstood its outcomes, the framers of the constitution inscribed private property and American individualism into the cornerstone of government and established the notion of the individual as synecdoche for country.

The second chapter, "Lakota Ghost Dance and the Imaginary Frontier," looks at two sites where U.S. history is produced within the *village* of national myth, the World's Columbian Exposition of 1893 and James Mooney's ethnography about the Lakota Ghost Dance of 1890. This choice of sites has the double function of illustrating the deployment of myth and introducing historical content invoked by contemporary works that I analyze in later chapters. Again, the object is not to set right the historical account. In both cases, that work continues to be done by scholars who are better equipped for that task. Instead, I sift through the artifacts of our shared memory to understand how these apologetic histories mediate the colonial impulses of the national consciousness, acknowledging that these artifacts are not stable concrete objects but are themselves products of a social and cultural heritage. A century of historical investigation and revision leaves behind a record of how that history is presented and adapted to suit interminable purposes. The subject of study for the chapter is the historiography of these events.

Opening with the 1893 fair, I discuss Frederick Jackson Turner, whose frontier thesis indemnified national memory against exogenous and endogenous threats through consensus politics. He saw himself uniquely positioned to synthesize the Social Darwinism of Herbert Spencer with the cultural and geographic history of our nation, producing a mythological narrative that reciprocally informed and was informed by its object. The occasion for Turner's paper was the closing of the frontier. Popular histories literally and figuratively marked this event with the supposed termination of the American Indian and the Lakota Ghost Dance religion at the massacre of Wounded Knee. By examining the ethnography that Mooney wrote to, at least in part, disabuse misrepresentations and falsehoods circulated by military officials and journalists concerning ghost dancers and the massacre, we expose the difficulties in arbitrating the truthfulness of any one account. The chapter concludes by returning to the Columbian Exposition to witness William Cody's historicization of the frontier in his titillating show Buffalo Bill's Wild West. Where Turner's paper molded representations of the frontier for generations of scholars, Cody's performances mirrored his influence upon the general public.

Despite Turner's fears, the U.S. government did not close the frontier in 1890; it merely relocated it to our neighbors in the Pacific Ocean and the

Caribbean. The colonial impulse to preserve Western culture from the negative influence of the inhabitants of this new frontier shaped the national perception of Haitians when U.S. Marines disembarked to occupy their nation in 1915. In "Caribbean and Gothic Origins of the American Zombie," I analyze the fiction and film as well as the anthropological investigations that issue from interest in this overseas frontier and its belief in zombies. I begin by examining the literary antecedents of these works by turning to the frontier fiction of Cooper and the gothic pulp of H.P. Lovecraft. Their writing discloses the semiological signifiers that initial nonfiction and fiction about Haiti would be fashioned to inhabit. Despite its lack of authenticity, William Seabrook's travelogue *The Magic Island* identified characteristics that would become integral to popular and scholarly representations of zombies, including their mindless, slave-like nature, their shuffling gait, and the connection between salt and savagery. More notably, *The Magic Island* offered the first book-length demonstration of the colonial attitude that sought to interpellate Haitian folklore within the national consciousness. The success of his book revealed or perhaps created an audience greedy to learn more about our "cannibal cousins."[1] The remainder of the chapter examines works that follow Seabrook's travelogue including Victor Halperin's film *White Zombie* as well as anthropological studies by Zora Neale Hurston, Melville Herskovits, and Maya Deren. All of them bear the marks of Seabrook's influence, and, in fact, most dare to own it.

Prompted by scientific advances in evolutionary biology and nuclear physics and the detachment of the frontier from a particularized geographic space, the zombie of fiction and film from the 1950s to the end of the millennium underwent a series of transformations. By analyzing the emergence and development of the modern zombie, "Social Critique and the Modern Zombie" seeks to understand how zombie narratives use the post-apocalyptic setting as a site for examining and negotiating the social conditions of modernity. Building on the scholarship of Darren Reed and Ruth Penfold-Mounce, I survey the post-apocalyptic texts that preceded George Romero's *Living Dead* series and analyze two of Romero's films that codify the representation of the modern zombie. The chapter concludes by investigating how zombie television shows fetishize survivalism and posit the self-reliant hero as the specular image of national identity. In series like *Z Nation* and *Fear the Walking Dead*, the post-apocalyptic landscape allows for the rebirth or reimagination of social and political institutions. Although I considered including these series in the final section, I concentrate on *The Walking Dead* because it singularly unites questions of indigenous personhood within a narrative that memorializes U.S. history while imagining the conditions for building a new nation. The malleability of zombie narratives reveals a double move that distinguishes the Hollywood zombie from its Haitian counterpart and simultaneously discharges the function of the possession ritual in Vodou by creating a space where such critiques can exist. Yet the potential for social critique does not ensure its efficacy. The self-awareness inscribed in social-science fiction proves both useful and problematic. The deployment of social critique reveals itself as the exemplar par excellence of what Bercovitch designates the ritual of dissent—the practice by which "social change is ritually controlled through dissent."[2] Marked by a specious opposition to society, the nature of dissent is in fact strictly governed by the subject of its critique. By employing colonial tropes of the frontier, the zombie as a figure of social-science fiction remains embedded in the very discourse it decries.

The question of how the national consciousness mythologizes its own history takes center stage in the narrative analyzed in the next chapter, "Civil Rights Movement Retold in Disney *Zombies*." The film recapitulates the civil rights movement and whitewashes national memory of colonialism, slavery, and discrimination. In her seminal work on cultural criticism of Disney films, Justyna Fruzinska observes, "It seems that Americans are particularly fond of making anti-imperialist films that should redeem them from their own imperial foreign policy and guilt complex."[3] Set in a fictionalized present-day, the bubblegum couture and literal wall of segregation that divides the town between "normals" and "zombies" make clear the connection to civil rights. If that alone was not sufficient, the zombies' urbanwear uniform, hip-hop choreography, rap songs, and regulated arm bracelets that control their savagery exaggerates the racial signification of zombies as black to the point of exhaustion. By leveraging his physical prowess for a spot on the football team, the zombie protagonist wins games for the local high school to qualify for permission to assimilate. The chapter concludes by emphasizing how the film mythologizes national memory and affirms the belief that individuals determine the identity of the nation. As the film demonstrates, the success of this process manifests in practical terms by accepting zombies as normals want them to be, not as they are.

The final chapter, "Destiny Manifested in *Westworld*'s Philosophical Zombies," is a close analysis of the HBO television series *Westworld* which takes the concept of remembering history to a whole new level. Set in a near but unspecified future, all but a few of the narratives take place in the theme parks and adjunct structures owned by Delos Destinations. The parks are themed by historical events and populated by period specific hosts. Hosts are the chosen term for robots or androids that Ned Block would describe as superficial functional isomorphs, where in this particular context superficial = external, functional = dispositional qualities, and isomorph = human.⁴ The hosts are essentially robots that are human in appearance and behavior. Like *The Walking Dead*, *Westworld* occupies the genre of social-science fiction that allows the writers and producers to explore themes of consciousness and free will. Although this lends itself easily to investigating the notion of philosophical zombies, more relevant to this book is the setting. The Westworld park is a simulacre of the American frontier, a kind of living museum of national memory. A character of particular interest is Akecheta, a host that is a member of an unnamed tribe who speaks Lakota and is costumed in garments typical of indigenous peoples from that region. As the barriers between real and fiction, human and machine are blurred, Akecheta experiences visions of his past lives as a host. He forms a renegade Ghost Nation tribe that seeks to revive their dead ancestors, an allusion to the Lakota ghost dancers massacred at Wounded Knee. As such, this particular narrative of *Westworld* also re-enacts the national memory of colonialism, rewriting Indian removal and the Trail of Tears into a narrative that absolves colonial guilt.

Examining the production of national myth within its historical, economic, and political context bears the risk of presenting myth as singular and inevitable through explicitly stated causal connections. In consideration of such risk, these chapters show that myth of national identity is neither singular nor inevitable but a composite of competing myths that emerge from various interested parties that seek to present a particular and totalizing myth that posits the past as homogenous with the present, removing contradiction and reifying social order. This semiological inquiry into zombies discloses that the myth of national identity particularized by the United States is founded on the principles of individualism and private property and rewrites collective memory to palliate and justify the past and present acts of colonialism that constitute its existence.

Introduction

> *The knowledge of the existence of the Devil Baby burst upon the residents of Hull-House one day when three Italian women, with an excited rush through the door, demanded that he be shown to them. No amount of denial convinced them that he was not there, for they knew exactly what he was like, with his cloven hoofs, his pointed ears and diminutive tail; moreover, the Devil Baby had been able to speak as soon as he was born and was most shockingly profane.*—JANE ADDAMS, "The Devil Baby at Hull House," in *The Atlantic*

> *These records also afford glimpses into a past so vast that the present generation seems to float upon its surface as thin as a sheet of light which momentarily covers the ocean and moves in response to the black waters beneath it.*—JANE ADDAMS, *The Long Road of Woman's Memory*

Devil Babies "R" U.S.

The mysterious Devil Baby materialized in Jane Addams' Hull House during the summer of 1913. That Addams flatly denied its existence only confirmed the suspicions of those determined to believe in it. Persons young and old, wealthy and poor, educated and illiterate made the pilgrimage to witness the Devil Baby, and their accounts constitute Addams' *The Long Road of Woman's Memory*, a composite work of memoir, ethnography, and social philosophy. While Addams limits her examination to the responses of elderly women, the Baby's appeal attracted persons from all walks of life.[1] The readiness of a civilized twentieth-century society to entertain the possibility of a Devil Baby with his "cloven hoofs, his pointed ears and diminutive tail"[2] may surprise some, but American folklore is shot through with antecedents. In his novel *The Scarlet Letter*, Nathaniel Hawthorne describes Pearl, the "demon offspring" of Hester Prynne, as "imp," "elf-child," and "emblem and product of sin."[3] Cotton Mather's record of the Salem witch trials contains testimony from Mary Short that depicts a "Divel" with "one Cloven-foot."[4] Tempting as it may be to dismiss the cultural genealogy of the Devil Baby, the accounts from *Long Road* confirm that the image bore more than mere physical resemblance to these predecessors. Like Prynne's "retribution" and "angel of judgement,"[5] many read the Devil Baby as the incarnation of the sins of the parents. For a woman who endured physical abuse from her husband and son, "the ugliness was born in the boy as the marks of the Devil was born in the poor child up-stairs."[6] For others it "put into their hands the sort of material with which they were accustomed to deal."[7] The Devil Baby was simply the most recent iteration of a myth that had evolved over generations. Reflecting on a speech by Addams titled "Immigrant Woman as She Adjusts Herself to American Life," Marilyn Fischer explains that "Addams interpreted the devil baby tales, not as evidence of superstitions held by ignorant, backward folks, but as a form of moral instruction that had evolved and been refined through a long historical development."[8] Addams' particular interest in immigrant women does not belie the fact that the story resonated across socio-economic and racial boundaries as she herself observed. Moreover, *Long Road* similarly uses the Devil Baby as an entry point for a meditation on the social function of memory and its plasticity.

For many of the visitors to Hull House, trauma was a common if not commonplace experience. According to Addams, the "sifting and reconciling power of Memory"[9] made life livable for these women. It allowed "the inconsistencies and perplexities of life to be brought under this appeasing Memory with its ultimate power to increase the elements of beauty and significance and to reduce, if not to eliminate, all sense of resentment."[10] What unites these accounts is the aporetical deployment of the Devil Baby as a signifier that was simultaneously empty and full. Empty in the sense that it was a vehicle or container for signification, full that it offered particularized meaning for each visitor. Similarly, these accounts led Addams to recognize the interplay of the personal and the social. She writes, "And yet, curiously enough, I found that the two functions of Memory first, its important role in interpreting and appeasing life for the individual, and second its activity as a selective agency in social reorganization were not mutually exclusive, and at moments seemed to support each other."[11] Such a reading of memory reveals its mythopoetic function. While memory "softened outlines of the past,"[12] its narrativization engenders meaning and as Addams rightly observes shapes future actions. But Addams is not satisfied with such a conservative view of memory: "At moments, however, baffled desires, sharp cries of pain, echoes of justices unfulfilled, the original material from which such tales are fashioned, would defy Memory's appeasing power and break through the rigid restraints imposed by all Art, even that unconscious of itself."[13] Whether or not readers choose to recognize the imbrication of psychoanalysis or social philosophy in her

Introduction 9

work, the salience of Addams' prose is nonetheless compelling. That she contradictorily asserts memory is conservative and progressive speaks to the precision of her analysis and not to its horizons. To summarize, memory, like myth, is both personal and social. It conceals and unconceals contradiction, just as it simultaneously offers and rejects resolution. And to paraphrase Addams somewhat indecorously, it puts into the hands of poststructuralists the sort of material with which they are accustomed to deal.

It is not my intention to begin with this example to claim that the Devil Baby is a zombie. The Devil Baby is not a zombie. Neither is the object of this book to locate the origins of the zombie as others have already done such as Kyle William Bishop and Sara Juliet Lauro. But like the Devil Baby, the zombie is the material of myth. Furthermore, both are the material of a particular myth, the myth of American national identity. That the Devil Baby serves a similar function reveals the exigency for unearthing its genealogy. By practicing her method of sympathetic understanding, Addams uncovers the racial and gender violence experienced by immigrant women. By comparison, deconstructing the deployment of the Hollywood zombie uncovers the foundation of colonial violence upon which the United States was built. As Roland Barthes observes, "Myth does not deny things, on the contrary, its function is to talk about them; simply, it purifies them, it makes them innocent, it gives them a natural and eternal justification, it gives them a clarity which is not that of an explanation but that of a statement of fact."[14] Thus, analysis is always possible because myth's task is to obscure and naturalize but not negate historical violence. As such, the text of myth is a window through which the past can be recovered. The object of this book, then, is a semiotic analysis of the zombie as it is located within the myth of national identity. Because such analysis demands a genealogy, I must also confront the problem of historiography and poststructuralism. Therefore, central to this investigation is a repudiation of monolithic history by demonstrating how our national consciousness sustains its homogenous and timeless appearance. Additionally, I must explore the capacity of national identity to reveal itself as *how it always has been and will be* even as the myth routinely adapts to retain the appearance of universality through ritual performances. By studying its genealogy, I do not intend to argue for the inevitability of its particularization. Its existence comes under attack through rupture and unconcealment of contradiction and by its relation to other myths. The historical and ideological horizons that I identify in writers should not be misunderstood as denunciation of their work but acknowledgment that every act of social criticism is historically bound. To engage this very same problem, Clifford Geertz turns to semiology.[15] It is in this spirit that I invoke

Geertz's eminent pronouncement to amend my own thesis: "The locus of the study is not the object of the study. Anthropologists don't study villages [...]; they study *in* villages."[16] Thus, the zombie is my Devil Baby, and national identity is my village.

Defining National Identity

The zombie is deeply entrenched in a discourse of national identity that simultaneously affirms collectivity and individualism. It (re-)presents the occasion for self-reliance, the value of self-determination both individual and national, the unequivocating justice of meritocracy, the threatening savagery (and allure) of the colonial other, and the backdrop of mindless consumption from which the individual can distinguish him or herself.[17] We might even be tempted to read the post-apocalyptic landscape of the zombie as a restaging of Walden Pond, thus reading Rick Grimes and Daryl Dixon of *The Walking Dead* as modern incarnations of Henry David Thoreau who journeyed into the woods "to live deep and suck out all the marrow of life" on his quest for self-discovery.[18] But American national identity, like the zombie, did not spontaneously erupt on a blank canvas, nor is it constituted by a fixed set of ideals or an ineluctable Puritan ideology. Rather it is a heterogenous and mutable plurality formed from a discourse that is both immanent and historical. Paradoxically, we perceive national identity as timeless and universal even as each constituent maintains a unique conceptualization unto themselves. Understanding what it means and how it mobilizes our thoughts and actions requires something other than Thoreau's mode of empirical inquiry. In fact, Friedrich Nietzsche cautions that "direct self-observation is not nearly sufficient for us to know ourselves." He continues: "we require history, for the past continues to flow within us in a hundred waves; we ourselves are, indeed, nothing but that which at every moment we experience of this continued flowing."[19] These words may seem to propose a strong determinism, but in fact Nietzsche offers genealogical analysis to demystify the past and liberate individuals from its hegemony. The path to understanding national and individual identity, the path to self-determination, involves synchronic study of the present and diachronic study through time. Genealogical inquiry for Nietzsche should not, however, be confused with searching for an origin to reveal an unalterable ideal essence or *das Ding an sich*, the thing-in-itself, as Immanuel Kant would say. Even though Nietzsche believed it possible to trace a concept to its origin, he did not consider the origin essential to its nature. Rather he states, "To glorify the origin—that is the metaphysical aftershoot that breaks out when we meditate on history and makes us believe that what stands at the beginning of all things is also what is most valuable and essential."[20] For Nietzsche, the recovery of an origin is significant if only for its part in the fulfillment of his genealogical project. What this suggests is that like ideology, national identity changes over time, but even as that change occurs, prior historical meanings are not fully negated. They are carried with it. Disentangling the accumulation, or as Antonio Gramsci says, "sedimentation," allows for the removal of hegemony from ideology.[21]

For these reasons, attempting to elaborate a definition of American identity is troubling yet necessary work. America is a nation, a culture, a people, and two continents. A naturalized immigrant of the United States and a citizen of Brazil have equal claim to identify as American. The effort in the 1960s and 1970s to rename indigenous peoples of the continent formerly called *Indians* with the more judicious appellation *Native American* underscores the complexity of the task. The change in nomenclature which, perhaps innocently, uses the European name for the continent signals unaffected sympathy and hubris. In contrast to other nations, Eric Hobsbawm asserts "the concept of Americanism as an act of *choice*—the decision to learn English, to apply for citizenship—and a choice of specific beliefs, acts and modes of behaviour implied the corresponding concept of 'un–Americanism.'" He goes on to say, "In countries defining nationality existentially there could be unpatriotic Englishmen or Frenchmen, but their status as Englishmen and Frenchmen could not be in doubt. [...] Yet in the U.S.A., as in Germany, the 'un–American' or 'vaterlandslose' person threw doubt on his or her actual status as member of the nation."[22] Such a narrow definition may appear short-sighted and even objectionable. But this particular invocation of *American* most interests me and therefore anchors the analysis in this book precisely because of how it proscribes what and who is *un–American*. Such investigation informs how we understand contemporary politics in the form of policy debates on citizenship status and the right to education and healthcare. It informs conversations on racial equity where, as Ta-Nehisi Coates observes, "an opioid epidemic is greeted with a call for treatment and sympathy [...] while a crack epidemic is greeted with a call for mandatory minimums and scorn."[23] These dialogues pivot on disparate visions of American identity where even minor fluctuations in the popularity of certain definitions result in broad policy decisions that impact the lives of many. If given the opportunity, Hobsbawm might amend his decision to include Germany. In an interview with Katrin Bennhold of the *New York Times*, Claudia Roth, Vice President, Deputy Speaker of the German Parliament, interrogates herself by asking and responding to several questions: "Can I love Germany? I would never say this. Can I be proud being a German? Never, I would never say

I'm very proud. German flag? No, this was never, ever. I'm a German, yes. I do not hide. But proud? No, I'm a German with all responsibilities."[24] By comparison, it is difficult to imagine any elected U.S. president or congressperson making a similar statement.

Methods

As early as Fredric Jameson's 1984 article "Postmodernism" and Michael Hardt and Antonio Negri's *Empire*,[25] contemporary continental philosophy has trended toward questioning or forgoing national in favor of transnational investigations. I concede to the allegation that national histories regularly overlook the marginalized and implicitly or even explicitly purport a linear and inevitable trajectory of progress. Moreover, as Jameson and Hardt and Negri have shown, the myopia of national critiques often renders them blind to the increasingly determining economic force of multinational capitalism. However, this does not mean the end of nationhood, nor does it render the discourse of national identity impotent. Étienne Balibar contends, "It is a pretty safe bet that criticism of other people's nationalism, in the name of our own capacity to transcend it or the idea that we have already moved beyond it, is only another figure of nationalism."[26] Balibar is arguing that embracing the pretense of having overcome the hegemony of national ideology is as equally problematic as examining it in isolation. Accepting Balibar's claim ushers in an era where the national and post-national must be examined as a dialectic. What is at stake is not the nation-form as a model for understanding political structures but rather our capacity to recognize the bio-political power of national identity. As such, how we represent our collective identity to ourselves is the subject of investigation for this book. And nationalism, for better or worse, is central to that.

By the same token, any investigation that asks to be taken seriously must preserve its integrity by avoiding evaluative conceptions in the categorical sense as well as in specific instances. Clifford Geertz's response to how academics often portray ideology is particularly poignant. He writes, "the conception of ideology now regnant in the social sciences is a thoroughly evaluative (that is, pejorative) one."[27] Even if national identity were revealed to be univocally evil, exposing it as such would not undo the violence it has caused nor provide sufficient insight to prevent further violence under a different guise. That such an essentialist view of national identity is bankrupt almost goes without saying. On the other hand, the justificatory function of national identity in the face of internal and external oppression cannot be ignored. The way forward is an autocritical humanism that examines national identity as a mode rather than a fixed object. While many legitimate academic endeavors may seek to uncover the consequences of such violence, this project seeks to recognize the deployment of power in the past, enabling a consciousness that frees individuals to act for themselves.

Therefore, I do not set out to (merely) uncover a subtext, a central purpose or meaning that subsumes media that constitute or perform national identity. That the authors I examine, whether they be historians or artists, may have a particular interest is relevant, but it does not follow that such interests exclusively determine their work's collective interpretation nor is a singular interpretation imaginable. Instead, I am interested in what the text and subtext do in light of recognizing national identity as a generative discourse. In his study of science, Michel Foucault draws attention to the discursive foundation of epistemology, displacing the history of science previously conceived of as the accumulation of knowledge with a genealogy of the language ordained to classify it. He writes, "Hence the possibility of writing a history of freedom and slavery based upon languages, or even a history of opinions, prejudices, superstitions, and beliefs of all kinds, since what is written on these subjects is always of less value as evidence than are the world themselves. [...] It is in them that what we imagine becomes what we know, and, on the other hand, that what we know becomes what we represent to ourselves every day."[28]

The difficulty incumbent with such an approach is the temptation to shift focus from uncovering the subtext of an individual work to simply uncovering a history of discursive power. Identifying, defending, or even rejecting a fixed identity telescoped through national history to the present misunderstands the work at hand. Following from Foucault's logic, the documentation of a nation's history produces the language with which the nation is represented to itself. Significantly, the components of discourse including language, rhetorical gestures, and narrative modes are used unevenly throughout that history and often in contradictory ways. Symbols generated for a particular purpose are redeployed in a separate context with entirely new meanings. Moreover, history reveals politicians arguing over the provenance of their intellectual inheritance demonstrates that constructing a singular genealogy is not possible.[29] Cataloging the deployment or even the abuses resulting from a particular discourse may provide valuable warnings but is insufficient on its own.

One way of understanding this is to look at Edward Said's formulation of humanism. For Said, a scholar of comparative literature, the work of humanism was close reading. He writes, "Thus a close reading of a literary text—a novel, poem, essay, or drama, say—in effect will gradually locate the text in its time as part of a whole network of relationships whose outlines and influence play an informing role *in* the text."[30] By situating the text within this constellation of political, geographic, racial, social, and economic relations, Said positions his humanism in the tradition of Nietzsche and Foucault. Only from this perspective are we able to comprehend his rallying cry "to understand human history as a continuous process of self-understanding and self-realization."[31] On the surface, this seemingly individual and existential turn may appear antithetical, like we have somehow reappeared alongside Thoreau. But where Thoreau emigrates from society to test his mettle against nature and find out what he is made of,[32] Said examines human history to understand how we are shaped by it. Fused with Said's humanist imperative is an unmistakable pedagogical component. The work is conducted by and for the individual, but when presented as a mode of inquiry, the work can be shared with and modeled for others. Importantly, the quotation above is from an essay (née lecture) concerning the "intellectual and scholar-teacher of the humanities in today's turbulent world."[33] No doubt this opens Said's project to the criticism that any education risks and likely necessitates re-enacting the same violence that he vociferously argues against. Perhaps anticipating such a critique Said adds that he believes "it is possible to be critical of humanism in the name of humanism" and concludes by defining this work as "a means of questioning, upsetting, and reformulating so much of what is presented to us as commodified, packaged, uncontroversial, and uncritically codified certainties."[34] This articulates what I referred to earlier as an autocritical humanism, which by definition acknowledges its limits and situatedness. It is therefore an individual act that occurs simultaneously across a public sphere. Paraphrasing Said's words, it is the whole consort dancing together contrapuntally.

Project and Destiny

National identity not only discloses how a nation is represented to itself in the present, but it is also the lens through which the past is perceived. Balibar explains succinctly, "The history of nations, beginning with our own, is always already presented to us in the form of a narrative which attributes to these entities the continuity of a subject." He continues by describing this narrative as "an invariant substance" that "consists in believing that the process of development from which we select aspects retrospectively, so as to see ourselves as the culmination of that process, was the only one possible, that is, it represented a destiny. Project and destiny are the two symmetrical figures of the illusion of national identity."[35] As such, the present and future course of a nation always already reveals itself (or refigures itself) as the inevitable, ineluctable, and univocal fulfillment of the project set forth by its architects. Moreover, the particular character and meaning and indeed the project itself is an invention of the present. Although this vision may be illusory, it is one that bears real value, unifies disparate communities, and mobilizes political and social action. In the final year of his presidency, Donald Trump held a press conference on the 1619 Project, an initiative by the *New York Times* with the self-described "[aim] to reframe the country's history by placing the consequences of slavery and the contributions of black Americans at the very center of our national narrative."[36] Trump characterized it as "anti-American propaganda" and condemned its inclusion in public school curricula. He further stated that "the only path to national unity is through our shared identity as Americans. That is why it is so urgent that we finally restore patriotic education to our schools."[37] While a U.S. president during a re-election campaign may be predisposed to detect imagined threats to democracy, the example illustrates the imbrication of national identity and history. Furthermore, this particular instance exposes that history is not only constituted retrospectively by determining what is included but also by what is left out. Ernest Renan famously observes, "To forget and—I will venture to say—to get one's history wrong, are essential factors in the making of a nation; and thus the advance of historical studies is often a danger to nationality."[38] Humanism and in particular postcolonial theory provides us with the tools for retrieving the content of these silences. Said once wrote, "There was never a history that could not to some degree be recovered and compassionately understood in all its suffering and accomplishment. Conversely, there was never a shameful secret injustice or a cruel collective punishment or a manifestly imperial plan for domination that could not be exposed, explained, and criticized."[39] If we are to succeed at understanding how national identity shapes our conception of history, then uncovering what has been silenced is part of that work.

To fully understand project and destiny in terms of national identity, Said as well as literary critics Sacvan Bercovitch and William Spanos turn to Erich Auerbach's etymology of *figura* and his historical exposition of biblical exegesis in *Mimesis*. It is also a worthwhile detour for this chapter because any study of national identity in American literature will inevitably encounter this legacy of *figura*, and this affords me the opportunity uncover its various meanings and dispel some of the ambiguity surrounding Auerbach's use of it. In his essay "Figura," Auerbach provides an exhaustive etymology of the term from its first known appearance in the second century BCE. Far from identifying a singular meaning, Auerbach traces *figura* through a variety of transformations and then concentrates his analysis on its use by Tertullian. In this period, the Christian church sought to reinterpret the Hebrew Bible as a prefiguration of the New Testament. As James Porter elegantly explains, "Figural reading had to wrest the Hebrew Bible, first out of the hands of its detractors who sought 'to drain it of its meaning,' then out the hands of the Jews, and finally out of history."[40] Porter's words highlight the aim of Auerbach's examination. While many writers at that time chose to interpret the Old Testament as purely allegorical, Tertullian "expressly denied that the literal and historical validity of the Old Testament was diminished by the figural interpretation."[41] Auerbach goes on to illustrate that Tertullian repeatedly emphasizes that *figura* unites two, very real, historical events, one past and one present, while also pointing toward a future. This creates a tension that is grounded in historical reality and outside of time, what Auerbach calls "omnitemporalness."[42] Likewise there is a tension between concrete reality and allegorical truth, a truth that is continually reimagined as each successive moment of the present gives way to the next. As an example, he quotes at length a passage from Tertullian's *Adversus Marcionem* that interprets Moses' naming of Joshua who would lead the Israelites into the promised land as foreshadowing of Jesus leading the elect to heaven.[43] Although figural interpretation was by no means universal amongst Christians, Auerbach confirms its prominence in the church and points to the Pauline epistles as evidence. It was this same mode of interpretation that Augustine would repeatedly employ to draw attention to certain historical events recorded in the Old Testament that could be re-figured to anticipate the present and future. As such, this approach looks less like an interpretation of the past and more like thrusting on the past a desired meaning to create the semblance of continuity that sets a course from the past through the present to the future. This is done without questioning the facticity of the past so much as rummaging through it to identify the events that can be molded to foreshadow the desired future. For Auerbach, this mode of interpretation is no longer employed in Europe post–sixteenth century and gave way to tragic realism.[44] Nevertheless, the scholars mentioned above quite rightly recuperate the concept to describe the function of national identity.

Because this investigation is primarily though not exclusively confined to literary interpretation, it is important to acknowledge the notions of project and destiny are not limited to these fields. In the context of the sciences, this can be broadly understood, borrowing from Martin Heidegger in his questioning of onto-theology, as the deification of *causa sui*.[45] More recently and perhaps more relevant, this concept is elaborated on by Johannes Fabian as the secularization of Judeo-Christian time. Much like Auerbach, Fabian identifies a significant development in what he calls "universal Time" via a reaction to the unresolvable conflict of biblical chronology and the increasing acceptance of a far more extensive geological time in the scientific community enabled by Charles Darwin. Yet for Fabian, "the true reason why biblical chronology had to be abandoned was that it did not contain the *right kind of Time*."[46] Fabian contends that biblical time was linear and marked by progress of events. He states, "it was chronicle as well as chronology."[47] Thus, it was teleological. Geological time supplanted sacred time because the "essentially discontinuous and fragmentary geological and paleontological record" could not be misconstrued into a linear teleological project.[48] For Fabian, social evolutionists recovered Judeo-Christian time by divorcing it from geological time and spatializing it. Rather than limiting time to a monolithic telos, it could be visually represented or imagined by the metaphor of a tree. What social evolutionists such as Herbert Spencer conceived of as primitive civilizations were no longer discontinuous aporia that contradicted the linear and innately progressive trajectory of evolution but instead branches of single tree whose vertical height was delayed by outward growth. Spatializing time resolved internal contradictions while preserving the notion of inherent and eternal progress. Thus, the notion of perfectibility derives from the secularization of Judeo-Christian temporality. Consequently, while not abandoning teleology, it allows institutions to instead cast emphasis on entelechy, an idealization of the present moment as a continuous move toward ineluctable fulfillment.

CHAPTER ONE

Myths of Colonial America

> *At any given time, the living see themselves in the midday of history. They are obliged to prepare a banquet for the past. The historian is the herald who invites the dead to the table.*—WALTER BENJAMIN, *The Arcades Project*
>
> *Thus in the beginning all the World was* America.—JOHN LOCKE, *Second Treatise*

This Unexamined American Life

Before exploring the history of American national identity, I would like to pause for a moment to offer an illustration that demonstrates the practical implications of this discussion. The United States values equality and applies it to all persons regardless of race, gender, and sexual orientation. After events such as the murders of George Floyd and Breonna Taylor, there were numerous calls for the nation to "live up to the Declaration of Independence" from across the political spectrum. Public discourse pivots to conversations that work toward a building consensus about how contemporary events relate to the past and the future. Figural interpretation allows the words "all men are created equal" to signal the unfulfilled yet ineluctable destiny of the nation. For example, in 2012 the presidential candidate Michelle Bachmann claimed that the founding fathers "worked tirelessly to end slavery." The heightened attention of a presidential campaign bid incited a flurry of defenders and attackers, but the emphasis was centered, and perhaps rightly so, on the facticity of her comments. Notwithstanding the inaccuracies of her word choice, her comments illustrate a narrative that the nation wants to believe. Consequently, those who rushed to her defense did so by tweaking her argument to match the facts as opposed to dismissing the narrative she sought to portray,[1] a narrative that notably was endorsed by the very president who abolished slavery, Abraham Lincoln.[2] Again, I want to be careful not to frame this as a critique of Bachmann, the architects of the U.S., or Lincoln, nor do I suggest that we must dismiss their accomplishments. Rather, I do so to break free from the notion that national identity is universal and homogenous across time. That the seeds sown by the founders have grown into this tree that reaches ever closer toward perfectibility. Figural interpretation such as this thrusts meaning upon historical events that were not endowed with such lofty ideals or at least ideals that were not in fact shared by all. Moreover, it relies on the very sort of glorification of origins that Nietzsche critiqued.

As it is my solemn duty as literary critic, I propose using a rudimentary understanding of psychoanalysis to further this discussion of examining how American identity portrays itself. Invoking the concept of individuation, it is possible to say that American identity is produced by the act of disavowal, but it is also constituted by the content of what is disavowed. Scholars have argued that it presents as a tension existing between two poles. While I am not comfortable asserting that such a tension is unique to the U.S., I can point to scholarship in various fields that affirms the claim that it is at least representative of it. In some instances, this emerges as an outright rejection of both poles. Early colonists defined themselves against the so-called savagery of indigenous peoples by trumpeting the progress of civilization yet simultaneously delivered exhortations on the valetudinarianism of Europe. To make the case for Daniel Boone as the archetype for the American hero, Richard Slotkin shares a unique and poignant example regarding religious practices that proves relevant here. The blood myths and rituals of indigenous peoples bore a striking similarity to the Catholic Eucharist where through transubstantiation bread and wine was transformed into Christ's body and blood. According to Slotkin, participating in this sacrament "under the ministrations of individuals as corrupt as the parish clergy, seemed to the Puritans an offense to reason and logic." He concludes, "Puritanism was founded on opposition to blood myth and blood ritual and on repression of those dark, passionate human impulses that such myth and ritual reflect."[3] For early Puritan colonists, the eucharist was a ritual that individualized acceptance of the social order they sought to reject. Repudiation of all blood rituals collapsed the personal and social, pagan and Catholic, sacred and profane, physical and spiritual, European and savage. Later chapters of this book will explore films like George Romero's *Dawn of the Dead* where the zombie simultaneously occupies both ends of the spectrum as mindless consumers produced by overcivilization and savage cannibals.

No doubt many contemporary historians rightly bristle at my inclusion of Puritans as indicative of colonial attitudes, so I offer two additional examples to demonstrate that this is not merely limited to a select group of individuals. In her landmark study *Manliness and Civilization*, Gail

Bederman charmingly describes Theodore Roosevelt's "time-traveling vacation" after his presidency to "share the bloody pastimes of his primitive ancestors" in Africa. It provided him the opportunity "to reexperience their pure, essential masculinity," which was "in contrast to the overcivilized present, threatened by decadent effeminacy."[4] While I admit choosing this example for Bederman's salutary wit, it points to a broader pattern explored in her book disclosing how American masculinity hinges on sustaining a balance between the primal natives and the degeneracy of overcivilization. Although there are other examples to consider, the final selection highlights the hierarchical character of the diffusion of information in the colonies. As Sandra Gustafson reveals in her study *Eloquence Is Power*, ambivalent attitudes about the balance between written and oral text as forms of legitimate and official communication shaped the constitution. Revolutionary agitators railed against the print texts that came down to them as English writs. These forms of legislation allowed the British aristocracy to maintain anonymity while exerting their authority from afar. Yet these same individuals were equally leery of unruly mobs and the oral traditions of their indigenous neighbors. This tension produced a heterogenous mixture of cultural practices such as announcing official communication to *the beating of a drum*, the reprinting of oral sermons, and inaugurating a long history of memorial speeches. The most notable immediate consequence was the creation of the public gallery, which gave people access to the political debates of their elected leaders. Gustafson even points to the adoption of Baron de Montesquieu's bicameral legislature comprised of a demotic House of Representatives and a Senate of landed aristocracy as a safeguard embodying this dynamic. These examples supersede my initial assertion that American national identity is a double negation and reveal it as a double affirmation. The unsettled tension between these two poles makes it possible for the colonists and contemporary American citizens to imagine the supposed New World as an empty virgin continent free for the taking even as it was purchased from its indigenous inhabitants by fiat and blood.

So far, I have sought to articulate a rudimentary schema of national identity and briefly introduced the unique tensions that characterize America's representation of itself. I have also argued that with self-identification, national identity becomes a lens through which individual citizens understand their history and themselves. This lens involves narrativization or emplotment that thrusts external meaning on concrete historical events and produces belief in the project and destiny of the nation. Therefore, we must investigate the history of this discourse, not to locate or determine its true content but to understand how it is constructed using a humanist mode of inquiry that acknowledges its own limits and situatedness. In particular, we will examine various permutations of the tensions described above as well as narrative modes, rhetorical structures, and symbolic figures. I will invoke these collectively as the discourse of national identity. However, I move hesitantly into this next step because the scholars who have done the most work in this regard have attributed the American national character with a primarily or even singular Puritan heritage. I refer of course to the intellectual tradition of Perry Miller and Sacvan Bercovitch. Perhaps it is ironic or perhaps it is the hubris of humanism that Bercovitch, who utilizes Auerbach's notion of figural interpretation, has been repeatedly critiqued under the same auspices. While I do believe their work deserves a more nuanced appraisal that it often receives, I do not want to misconstrue myself as an apologist. More than anything else, the horizons of their work highlight the unequivocal situatedness of all humanist inquiry. It is only right that the limits of Bercovitch are revealed. For that same reason, I hope that my work is not taken as complete but can be expanded on and overcome. Rather than take up arms in this debate, I seek to demonstrate that the discourse elaborated by Bercovitch was as widespread as he asserts but that it was not uniquely Puritan. Moreover, even this discourse could not be conceived as homogenous; the particular narrative structures and rhetorical gestures that I discuss were regularly employed beyond the limits of Puritan influence.

An (Im-)Puritan Legacy

The Puritan legacy has been long overshadowed, not without controversy, by Miller's seminal works: *Orthodoxy in Massachusetts*, the two-volume *The New England Mind*, and the collected essays *Errand into the Wilderness*. The self-reflection and candor in the front matter of his books reveal an austere view of the intellectual that epitomizes his rigorous approach. Reflecting on a previous edition of *Orthodoxy*, Miller critiques the naiveté of his former self who included a lengthy bibliography to, in his words, "show off my erudition" which he adds is an incentive that is "fortunately [...] no longer operative."[5] Without that distraction, he instructs the reader to do their own homework and study the academic journals themselves. In his preface to *Errand*, he shares his disapproval for the tendency in American scholarship to "idolize the footnote" and asserts that such annotations are for monographs not argument.[6] Following from this attitude, he was always forthright about his aims. In *The New England Mind* he described Puritanism as "the most coherent and most powerful single factor in the early history of America" and states that he "took the liberty of treating the whole literature as though it were the product of a single intelligence, and I have appropriated illustrations from whichever authors happen to express a point most conveniently."[7] The conviction of his argument, which conflicts with contemporary recognition of the inherent problems of such univocal histories, often belies his commitment to research.

For Miller, the characteristic form of Puritan rhetoric, at least initially, was the jeremiad, a Judeo-Christian rhetorical mode that involved castigating the community by enumerating all its sins. Despite its seeming pessimism, Miller argues that even John Winthrop's 1630 sermon "A Modell of Christian Charity" was, in fact, a motivating harangue. He states, "If you read them all through, the total effect, curiously enough, is not all depressing: you come to the paradoxical realization that they do not bespeak a despairing frame of mind. There is something of a ritualistic incantation about them; whatever they may signify in the realm of theology, in that of psychology they are purgations of soul; they do not discourage but actually encourage the community to persist in its heinous conduct."[8] While Miller believed the Puritan declension detailed in *New England Mind* meant the disappearance of the jeremiad as America turned its gaze to the frontier, perceiving this to be the end of story misunderstands Miller's argument. The jeremiad was simply a vehicle or rhetorical strategy. He proceeds by revealing the ideology of imperialism underlying the artifice of a Puritan dispensation that gives way to the errand. I use the phrase ideological imperialism because as Miller saw it, the rhetoric of the jeremiad typified in Winthrop was to set a community trajectory toward perfection that would be the model for other civilizations around the world. Intrinsic in this vision was not, according to Miller, a geographic expansionism but an ontological one. The errand could persist beyond the wilderness of New England into the frontier because as Miller states that "errand" and "wilderness" were only ever "figures of speech."[9] Insofar, he critiques Frederick Jackson Turner's frontier thesis as a means of providing a clarifying parallel. Just as the ideological imperialism of the jeremiad persisted beyond the Puritan declension by means of the myth of the frontier, so Turner's closing of the frontier is not the end of the errand.[10] For Miller, the trajectory of perfectibility, the myth of "unchecked progress" telescoped through the nineteenth century in the form of social evolution and industrial expansion.[11] The errand persisted even as the wilderness transformed through various geographic and allegorical iterations, now locatable in the frontier of science. He writes "the American nineteenth century proclaimed that the meaning of America's errand into the wilderness had disclosed itself as an errand without an end."[12]

Bercovitch appends Miller by doing away with his equivocating use of the term errand and offers the formula jeremiad = internal decay and frontier = external threat and site of progress. Furthermore, Bercovitch reads these as semiological figures that constitute a ritual of national identity. To combat the threat of internal decay, the nation engages with the savage other on the frontier. If this sounds familiar, it is regnant in the example of Roosevelt. As Bercovitch explains, this ritual goes by many names "Puritan errand, national mission, manifest destiny, the dream."[13] In this sense Bercovitch asserts that expansionism identified by Miller was not only ideological but also geographic. He clarifies, at least for me, the complexity of the tension between the individual and the community through this notion of what he terms "representative selfhood."[14] The example of Roosevelt is again quite useful. Each citizen is at once an individual and specular image of the nation. This further elaborates what Hobsbawm meant by saying being American is a choice. To be American, one must participate in the ritual of national identity. In narrative form, we have the romantic hero in conflict with society, individuating him-/her-self from it by journeying into the wilderness. But we also have the heroes' return. Whatever change occurred in the hero during their adventure must be approved or authorized by the consensus of the community. Thus, from these scholars we have a trove of symbols that are not quite symbols but *figura*.[15] While Miller argued, perhaps not loudly enough, that the errand was not unique to New England, Bercovitch yoked these symbols to a Puritan origin, an argument that could not persist in a postmodern climate where linear historical narratives are suspect.[16]

In the 1980s, this tradition of Puritan scholarship underwent its own declension, the result of academic reevaluation which can be distilled into three critiques.[17] The first is that a Puritan origin does not account for the diverse colonial demographics. Many other groups migrated to the colonies often in far greater numbers.[18] Even within New England, the colonists did not universally practice congregationalism. Church historians Roger Finke and Rodney Stark estimate a 17 percent adherence rate for New England in 1776. By comparing this to recorded figures of births, they offer the provocative observation that single women in New England were more likely to engage in premarital intercourse than church functions.[19] The second problem is that of continuity. This is the most baffling aspect of Bercovitch's approach. He employs Auerbach's notion of *figura* to reveal how Puritan rhetoric reimagines historical events to accommodate their ideological project. And yet by locating a singular origin point from which develops the rhetoric and symbology of American national identity, Bercovitch is in fact imposing his own figural interpretation upon history. An explanation for his seemingly contradictory move may lie in the muddled and contradictory interpretations of Auerbach's work that pervaded literary and theological journals in the years preceding the publication of

Bercovitch's first book, *The Puritan Origins of the American Self*. James Porter observes that in the introduction to *Mimesis* Edward Said misapprehends Auerbach in a similar fashion. He writes, "To claim, as Edward Said [...], that biblical background meanings 'can only be recovered by a very particular act of interpretation,' one that Auerbach 'described as figural interpretation,' is to get hold of the matter from the wrong end. Figural readings do not 'recover' meaning from the Hebrew Bible; they foist meaning on what was never meant to be grasped."[20] Like Said, Bercovitch employs figural interpretation to replace the Puritan meaning of events with his own. There can be little certainty about the source of this confusion, but it is possible that Bercovitch learned of figural interpretation by reading Said who began publishing on Auerbach as early as 1968, seven years prior Bercovitch's *Puritan Origins*.[21]

Thirdly, the scholarship assumes a homogenous Puritanism that simply did not exist.[22] Bercovitch, particularly in his later work, challenges this final critique by asserting that his interest was not in the content but in the rhetoric of Puritanism. While these critiques repudiate a Puritan legacy, they also clear space for inquiry that is no longer bound to a favored origin story whether it be a Great Migration or the extension of a British tradition. What we have today is not the inevitable development of a singular tradition of thought, but the accumulation of competing and contradictory discourses that cannot be fully synthesized yet share commonalities. That the discourse is not homogenous or universal does not preclude individuals or communities from imagining a homogenous and universal national self. Therefore, the more interesting questions concerning the origin of American national identity are these: how and why did the narrative of a small minority of migrants become and persist as the representative origin story for an entire nation? and what can that tell us about how national identity is constructed today?

One explanation is that the colonists and early Americans had few ready-made alternatives to choose from. As Virginia DeJohn Anderson observes, "New Englanders were the only colonists in British America self-conscious enough to locate the origins of their society in a 'Great Migration.'"[23] New England produced two of the most widely read narratives of migration, Winthrop's *History of New England* and Cotton Mather's *Magnalia*. Even in the eighteenth century, historians John Oldmixon and Daniel Neal, who were critical of the inaccuracies in Mather's *Magnalia*, still depended heavily on it for their source material.[24] Moreover, *Magnalia* and other works by Mather would continue to be read by generations of leading political and literary figures including Benjamin Franklin, Ralph Waldo Emerson, and Nathaniel Hawthorne.[25] Harriet Beecher Stowe's reminiscence of Mather is quoted by her son: "But there was one of my father's books that proved a mine of wealth to me. It was a happy hour when he brought home and set up in his bookcase Cotton Mather's 'Magnalia,' in a new edition of two volumes. What wonderful stories those! Stories too about my own country. Stories that made me feel the very ground I trod on to be consecrated by some special dealing of God's Providence."[26] Stowe's fondness not only reveals her high esteem for Mather but also makes clear the interrelation of nation and project.

The hierarchical structure of communication may have also been a contributing factor. In the colonies, communication was primarily disseminated by sermons and public notices. The latter, according to Richard Brown, "were short, straightforward, and either highly functional or ceremonial in nature" leading him to conclude that the "sermon was the sole form of legitimate public address."[27] Often these religious orations would announce and offer reflection on current events. As evidenced by Brown's study of Samuel Sewall, the preachers or clergy were in similar circles as elected leaders. Thus, preachers or clergy were privy to communication and events and would be the first to disseminate that information to the public.[28] Harry Stout argues that this "unique social structure of interlocking institutions governed by a single nucleus of covenanted saints [...] Endowed the sermon with unprecedented range and influence." He goes on to add that "sermons were authority incarnate."[29] These observations, however, tread very close to, if not fully embrace the narrative of a linear Puritan pedigree that I hope to avoid espousing. I include these to simply show that government and church were interwoven and the discourse of each, including that of how colonists viewed themselves and their history, was symbiotic. Even an audacious claim such as Stout's does not preclude the fact that the individuals delivering sermons were not birthed in a vacuum but were situated in a historical moment where a Puritan inheritance numbered among the numerous forces at work. Thus, I have two examples to share. The first is Benjamin Church's account of King Philip's War, which illustrates the heterogeneity and tension among the New England Puritans. The second example offers an alternative perspective from outside the Puritan community. Although each serve different ends, both share the rhetoric that would later characterize the discourse of national identity.

Pumetacom

Originally published in 1716, *Entertaining Passages* is Benjamin Church's account, dictated to his son Thomas, of his involvement in the armed conflict between the colonists and Pumetacom, also known by his adopted English name as King Philip. Under the leadership of the sachem Massasoit, the Wampanoags maintained a positive relationship with the Puritans and the New England settlers since their arrival in Plymouth in 1620. Pumetacom, the son of Massasoit, inherited his father's position as well as his deteriorating relationship with the colonists. There are conflicting accounts of the events that precipitated the outbreak. Plymouth colonists tried and convicted three Wampanoags for murder. They were publicly executed for an incident that only involved Wampanoags and occurred on Wampanoag soil. In response to this violation of sovereignty, Pumetacom began raiding numerous New England towns.[30] Without help from Europe, the colonists were left to fend for themselves. The value of Church's chronicle rests in its function as a document of popular narrative. In it we see notable similarities with Puritan rhetoric but also differences, both of which would become instituted in the discourse of national identity.

What initially marks Church's narrative is a tension between an obligation to his community and his refusal to identify with them. He takes pains to show that his participation in the war was neither motivated by a pursuit of individual honor, glory, or adventure, nor reflective of his interactions with the Wampanoags. By his own accord Church "gain'd a good acquaintance with the Natives: got much into their favour, and was in a little time in great esteem among them."[31] Instead, he joins in a response to a call, much like Winthrop's jeremiad, to defend the nearby towns by Governor Bradford.[32] Thus, the conflict belonged to the other colonists. Moreover, after each expedition, he looks forward to returning home only to be immediately called back up to fight.[33] Because my interest is in the rhetoric and semiology of his narrative, there is no need to place trust in the accuracy of his sentiments or the dependability of his representations. On the contrary, reading authenticity as artifice reveals his belief that readers would more readily accept and prefer a protagonist that prioritizes his community than one directed foremost by his own interests.

Even more interesting are his repeated efforts to differentiate himself from the actions of the other colonists. These range from descriptions of tactical failures and incompetence such as soldiers giving away their position, falling asleep on watch, and killing a prisoner who might have provided valuable information to more egregious moral failures.[34] On one occasion 180 Wampanoags surrendered "on terms promised by Capt. Eels." Although there is no indication what those terms were, Church states that if these terms had been upheld it would have gone a long way toward bringing a swift conclusion to the war. As it stood, the captives were brought to Plymouth, sold as slaves, and shipped out of the colony.[35] Church expresses similar disgust at the conclusion of the war when he learns that the colonists beheaded "the last of Philips friends" including the great Wampanoag warrior Annawon.³⁶ Church's reactions highlight a tension between the individual and the community that recurs throughout the discourse of national identity. Even though his disapproval appears to run counter to the belief and importance of community espoused by Winthrop, his continued service reveals that community is a value that each person must uphold individually. Moreover, his criticism can be read as its own jeremiad, where his military prowess and achievements as well as the positive reception of his account attest to the adoption of his transvaluation.

The result is a romantic narrative that differs from European tradition. On his errand or hero's journey, Church learns from his encounters with the enemy and trains the soldiers under his command to employ their tactics. These include reloading rifles at staggered intervals, returning by different routes to avoid ambush, posting two scouts ahead of the main force, deploying soldiers outside garrisons, and scattering their positions to avoid presenting the enemy with a single target in a tight formation.³⁷ Learning from the Wampanoag warriors has two outcomes in terms of its mythopoetic function. It crystallizes the ritual of *becoming Indian* and it provides Church the opportunity to prove himself superior to the Wampanoags at *being Indian*. This approach to warfare prefigures the self-described use of so-called *Indian tactics* by the United States military throughout its history beginning with the General Nathanael Greene in the Revolutionary War and continuing to the present. The crossed arrows insignia assigned to the First Special Services force during World War II was originally used to designate U.S. Army Indian Scouts as early as 1890. The crest is still used as a U.S. Army Special Forces regimental designator symbolizing covert and irregular operations.³⁸

Because Pumetacom's death at the hands of a praying Wampanoag proved too anticlimactic, Church extends the narrative to include a final confrontation that results in his single-handed capture of Annawon, Pumetacom's war chief. Indicating the manliness of his achievement, Church offers a phallic description of a gift he receives from Annawon after the capture. He writes that Annawon "pull'd out Philips belt curiously wrought with Wompom being Nine inches broad." Church's portrayal of this act—gifting Pumetacom's wampum belt—signifies that Annawon recognizes Church as the superior *Indian* warrior.³⁹ Juxtaposed alongside the praise Church receives from the colonists, these events secure Church's position as an emergent protonational self. He represents the genetic European refined by experience on the frontier, a synthesis of and superior to both. By serving the community, Church becomes a better individual. By remaining faithful to his individuality, he preserves and strengthens the community. Collectively these offer a narrative of progress and perfectibility.

Importantly, Church does not provide the only account of this conflict. His is just one of the competing representations produced at that time. By comparison, Increase Mather describes the death of Pumetacom as an act of "Divine Providence" in his 1676 account "A Brief History of the Warr with the Indians in New-England."[40] He frames the scene with a reference to Isaiah 33:1 by writing, "Thus when *Philip* had made an end to deal treacherously, his own Subjects dealt treacherously with him."[41] With this as frame, Mather discloses what he presents as the most notable fact of Pumetacom's death—that it came at the hands of a Wampanoag. He writes, "but as [Pumetacom] was coming out of the Swamp, an *English-man* and an *Indian* endeavoured to fire at him, the *English-man* missed of his aime, but the *Indian* shot him through the heart, so as that he fell down dead."[42] Rather than suggest one version more precisely represents national discourse, the differences in these accounts reveal the plasticity of mythopoetic representation. What remains constant across these accounts is the use of figural interpretation. For Mather the events signify divine retribution and the fulfillment of a spiritual *telos*. For Church it is the perfectibility and superiority of civilization.

Jamestown

Despite being the first permanent English settlement predating the arrival of the Mayflower by over a decade, Jamestown's place in national history is less of an origin story and more of an ambiguous entry in the early colonial mythos. The accounts of John Smith begin with "A True Relation" of the settlement recorded in a private letter that was edited and published by John Healey without Smith's permission. Like Church, Smith was not of noble stock typical of romantic heroes in the European tradition, and this fact provoked distrust and enmity among the pedigreed settlers. His obtuse chivalry put him at risk of execution on more than one occasion. However, it was these same qualities that characterized his contributions to the colony and assured his eventual election as their leader. Throughout the "The Proceedings," Smith cultivated the respect of his peers with his willingness to perform duties that other colonists, particularly those with aristocratic upbringing, neglected. According to his account, "The new President, and Martin, being little beloved, of weake judgement in dangers, and lesse industry in peace, committed the managing of all things abroad to captaine Smith: who by his owne example, good words, and faire promises, set some to mow, others to binde thatch, some to build houses, others to thatch them, himselfe alwaies bearing the greatest taske for his owne share, so that in short time, he provided most of them lodgings, neglecting any for himselfe."[43] Embedded within this account is a critique situated halfway between Church's negative appraisal and Winthrop's jeremiad by enumerating the decadence of aristocracy. In terms of the two poles that American identity is defined against, Smith produces the image of his self in relief. Notably, Smith's "The Proceedings" was published in 1612, eighteen years prior to Winthrop's sermon.

We also find evidence of the peculiar tension between the individual and community. Smith was the target of several plots and was falsely imprisoned for conspiring to murder the governing council on the voyage from England to Virginia. Because of an unusual order likely intended to preserve the authority of fleet commander Christopher Newport while the expedition was still at sea,[44] the identities of the council members who would govern the colony were sealed in a box until the fleet disembarked at Cape Hope. In a bizarre turn of events, Smith was listed among those named to the council he was accused of plotting to usurp.[45] After their arrival, conditions in Jamestown were difficult and the ill-suited settlers made multiple attempts to abandon the colony. These often occurred when Smith, who opposed returning to England, was away from the settlement procuring supplies. On one such occasion, Smith returned to discover "a dangerous conspiracy, for which Captaine Kendall as principal, was by a Jury condemned and shot to death."[46] What I find most interesting is Healey's editorial decision to retain these internal disputes in the narrative intended to bolster interest in the colonies. In later versions, Smith supplements these events with description of thwarting an attempt by John Ratcliffe, the president, to abandon the colony and return to England. Smith rationalizes the inclusion of Kendall's execution and Ratcliffe's mutiny with the following statement: "These brawles are so disgustfull, as some will say they were better forgotten, yet all men of good judgement will conclude, it were better their baseness should be manifest to the world, then the busines beare the scorne and shame of their excused disorders."[47] Smith's disavowal of Ratcliffe and his confederates prevents their actions from staining the reputation of the settlement. By taking up arms against the president, Smith recuperates the honor of the community. His independent spirit and commitment to the errand functions as a synecdoche for all of Jamestown. Such a move presages Winthrop's incantation of the city upon a hill. Retaining these incidents in the narrative advertises Smith as just the sort of man needed in Virginia. On the one hand this foreshadows American identity, but on the other it reveals that such individuals already existed in England.

Even as the account distinguishes Smith from the weaknesses of landed aristocracy, it asserts the superiority of civilization over the so-called *savages*. During another attempt to forage for supplies, Smith is taken captive by Opechancanough, the Pamunkey werowance. As the Pamunkey prepare to overwhelm Jamestown by force, they barter with Smith for intelligence. In an uncanny foreshadowing of John Locke's words that found their way into the Declaration of Independence, the Pamunkey ask Smith for this information in exchange for "life, libertie, land, and women."[48] Smith does not take the deal and instead wagers the fate of the Jamestown on a ruse. He writes instructions on a "Table booke" and convinces the Pamunkey to deliver the message to the settlement. Smith then informs the Pamunkey that Jamestown is well defended with "great gunnes" but willing to trade. To the disbelief of the Pamunkey, armed settlers emerge in a show of force at the exact time communicated in Smith's message and deliver supplies that evening at the appointed location "which they found accordingly, and [...] to the wonder of them all that heard it" and are persuaded to believe "that he could either divine, or the paper could speake."[49] The ruse does not secure Smith's release but it does avert the assault on Jamestown. Instead, Smith is taken to the Powhatan chief for his apocryphal encounter with the chief's daughter Pocahontas, who "got his head in her armes, and laid her owne upon his to save him from death."[50] Because modern readers are inclined to distrust the facticity of these incidents, I offer the reminder that for our purposes their integrity is of little importance. What matters is the function of these narrative elements, and any embellishment points to a desire to bolster the efficacy of their rhetorical effect. Like the gifts Annawon bestowed upon Church, having the "Indian princess" choose his life over her own symbolically confers on Smith the title of werowance. Paired with Smith's subsequent election as president of the colony in 1608, Smith emerges as an archetype of the American hero, recognized as chief by natives and British colonists alike.

His reign, however, is short-lived, and he soon returns to England to recover from a gunpowder explosion. Uncowed, Smith resumes his travels on the American continent by conducting further explorations to prepare for settlements in regions north of Virginia. Possibly because of his volatile nature, the Puritans did not choose to enlist Smith when he offered his services to help them settle New England. Yet his outsider status did not prevent him from leaving his mark on their narrative. He gave the region its name when he published his 1616 Map of New England. Moreover, it was Smith who first described Winthrop's six ships as "a great company of people of good ranke, zeale, meanes, and quality."[51] This utterance, I believe, led John Gorham Palfrey to introduce the talismanic phrase "the great emigration" to describe Winthrop's fleet in his *History of New England*.[52]

A Non-Puritan Legacy

Returning to the overall point I am trying to make, embedded in the most accessible and popular accounts of the British colonies were the rhetoric and symbols that would define the popular mythology of America's creation story. Dean Hammer argues that "by the eve of the American Revolution, a Puritan tradition had become a part of a broader national vocabulary." He describes this as "not a particular theology" but instead "a legacy of a Puritan founding—a myth of origins that gave sustenance to an early American search for identity."[53] It was a myth elaborated by John Adams in his four articles for the *Boston Gazette*, a response to the Stamp Act ten years before the start of the revolution.[54] While a case may be made that this legacy is in part due to the hierarchical communication structure of the time, such a case is not required. By way of the accounts already discussed, I contend that much of what is associated with the Puritan tradition in terms of the rhetoric and narrative of national identity, could be found outside of New England and prior to the so-called Great Migration. Healey's publication of Smith's private correspondence, in fact, suggests that the discourse is not even distinctly American.[55] By divorcing the rhetoric from exclusively Puritan genealogy, we can recuperate its significance and reconcile its diffusion (or lack thereof) across the disparate colonies.

While I do not want to spend much time repeating Slotkin's argument, in *Regeneration through Violence* he makes the case for Daniel Boone as the fulfillment of the archetypal American hero prefigured in the colonial era by accounts similar to those of Smith and Church. To be clear, I am not suggesting that we use figural interpretation to understand national history. Rather, I am attempting to demonstrate that the myth of national identity is a figural construction assembled with the rhetoric and symbols already present in these early texts. That the texts themselves or the discourse in which they are embedded are not uniquely American is beside the point. What matters is that these personal narratives are read across the nation as representative of American history and identity. I reference Slotkin's analysis of Boone because he carefully reveals how the myth of Boone was adapted to appeal to the heterogenous demographics of the United States. The rampant plagiarism of John Filson's stories led to Boone's regional versioning, where his identity and adventures were collectively misrecognized to reflect the diverging values of those disparate places. The result allowed for each region to herald Boone as a hero that was synecdochical for a homogenous national identity even as the particularization of that character was imagined differently from person to person.

A limitation of examining national identity as literary phenomena, notwithstanding the biographies and autobiographies already discussed, is the tendency to elide strictly political writings. The discourse of national identity does not restrict itself to the confines of compartmentalized academic fields, so neither should we allow ourselves to be bound by them. One advantage to the benighted canonization of Early American Literature is the necessarily elastic definition of what can be called literature born from the need to fill anthologies with something, even if that means the inclusion of congregationalist sermons. Among this expanded crop of American writing, we find Elisha Williams who illustrates the synthesis of Lockean and Puritan rhetoric. Hammer writes, "The orthodox Congregationalist Elisha Williams, writing in response to a Connecticut law banning itinerant preachers, argued that 'every Christian has a *Right of Judging for himself* what he is to believe and practice in Religion' according to the rule of Scripture."[56] Hammer continues, "Williams, in an argument that would be drawn on extensively by the patriot preachers, took his argument still further by tying a Lockean notion of the inalienability of property to the purpose of government as providing protections to this property. Since '*every Man* having a *Property* in his own *Person*, the *Labour of his Body* and *the Work of His Hands* are properly his own, to which no one has Right but himself,' so 'The great End of civil Government, is *the Preservation of their Persons, their Liberties and Estates, or their Property*.'"[57] Although this example frames Williams as integrating Locke within Puritan rhetoric, it points more broadly to the interpenetration of politics and religion, both of which contribute to the discourse of national identity. Lest we forget, Locke was not primarily a political theorist but an empiricist philosopher. The epigraph for this chapter should be understood in that context. As an empiricist, Locke perceived indigenous peoples as untainted by civilization. Just as Church learned how to become a better warrior from his Wampanoag enemies, Locke turned to the unmediated experience of "children, idiots, savages, and illiterate people, of being all others the least corrupted by custom, or borrowed opinions" and argued that "one might reasonably imagine that in their minds these innate notions should lie open fairly to every one's view."[58] Here we see what I have been calling the ritual of national identity revealed as an epistemological enterprise, not merely a phenomena limited to the construction of a collective self. It is a mode of hermeneutic inquiry that is both figuratively and literally enacted by the individual who leaves society to encounter the primitive on his errand into the wilderness and return with knowledge to improve the community. These examples illustrate that the project of national identity is an extensible structure that accommodates and informs the very notions of knowledge.

As I close, permit me to share one more, admittedly lengthy, quotation that reveals the interrelation of geography, politics, religion, and history within a narrativization of American identity. Beginning with an inaugural political oration on the one-year anniversary of the March 5, 1770, so-called Boston massacre, America established a tradition of commemoration. These events in part contributed to popularity of the Puritan origin story. The following is an excerpt from one such oration by Daniel Webster celebrating the bicentennial of the Pilgrims arrival at Plymouth. In it he goes beyond figural interpretation and in fact rewrites history by anachronistically proclaiming what the Puritans should have said when they arrived on that day two hundred years ago. Webster states, "'If God prosper us,' might have been the more appropriate language of our Fathers, when they landed upon this rock:—'if God prosper us, we shall here begin a work which shall last for ages; we shall plant here a new society, in the principles of the fullest liberty, and the purest religion: we shall subdue this wilderness which is before us; we shall fill this region of the great continent, which stretches almost from pole to pole, with civilization and Christianity; the temples of the true God shall rise, where now ascends the smoke of idolatrous sacrifice; fields and gardens, the flowers of summer, and the waving and golden harvest of autumn, shall extend over a thousand hills, and stretch along a thousand valleys, never yet, since the creation, reclaimed to the use of civilized man.'"[59] As we will see in the next chapter, commemoration such as this emerges as a liminal site for renegotiating the project of American destiny and identity. Considered together, these events are overwrought by contradiction and contesting ideologies. Individually they produce a space for reimagining the past, present, and future within an inexorable national trajectory.

Chapter Two

Lakota Ghost Dance and the Imaginary Frontier

There we are, finished; our victories—their bellies sticking up in the air—show their guts, our secret defeat.—Jean-Paul Sartre, *Black Orpheus*

Ghost dancers journeyed to heaven to save the earth they knew.
—John Kucich, *Ghostly Communion*

Frederick Jackson Turner

To begin this chapter, I turn to consider another commemoration, the World's Columbian Exposition of 1893. So much has been written about Frederick Jackson Turner's address and Buffalo Bill's Wild West, including examination of these performances in terms of national identity and mythmaking.[1] Nevertheless, there are additional reasons for returning to both in this context. By comparison, William Cody and Turner provide compatible representations of American history for popular and academic audiences that embody the rhetoric and symbolism discussed in the previous chapter. And rather than make additional claims about the prescience, durability, or extensible range of influence, I intend to show that these individuals expertly synthesized the semiological referents that were already existent. As Richard White notes, "Theodore Roosevelt rather begrudgingly credited Turner with 'having put into shape a good deal of thought that has been floating around rather loosely.'"[2] Although White does not reference Roosevelt's previous publication, his adverb implies shrewd awareness of Roosevelt's implication. Turner is often credited for declaring the close of the frontier in his Columbian Exposition address even though Roosevelt made a similar observation one year earlier. In a book review for *Atlantic Monthly*, Roosevelt wrote, "the frontier proper has come to an end." He continued, "The expression 'on the frontier,' which for more than a century of our national existence had a most definite and significant, is now meaningless, for the frontier itself no longer exists."[3] Reflecting on his career later in life, Turner acknowledged as much in his correspondence with William Dodd. He wrote, "I think the ideas underlying my 'Significance of the Frontier' would have been expressed in some form or other in any case. They were part of the growing American consciousness of itself. What I shall write of is rather the time and form of my own attempt to express them."[4] Turner's own words frame his contributions as consequential rather than highly original yet representative of the national consciousness. More to the point of this chapter, Turner theorizes and performs a new method of historiography that delineates his cleavage from contemporary scholars and acknowledges his intellectual genealogy. Thus, Turner's historiographic and historical address provides an index of how the nation viewed itself—past and present—in the years leading up to the U.S. occupation of Haiti and the arrival of the zombie.

First and foremost, Turner viewed himself as a teacher. He sought to shape the next generation of historians by training them to interpret the past within his narrative framework. In the preface to the 1899 reprint of "The Significance of the Frontier in American History," he explains that the new edition "may be helpful to teachers of American history"[5] and includes instructional strategies such as learning activities and discussion questions. The final item in the list epitomizes his object: "Particular topics, like slavery, the tariff, suffrage, internal improvements, the currency and banking, the land policy, diplomacy, etc., should be examined with reference to the influence upon them of these facts of expanding settlement."[6] From this we are meant to conclude that the propulsive machinery of American history is the advancing frontier line, which for Turner was coextensive with social evolution.

Although Turner may have been destined to be a historian, it was a destiny that took some time for him to realize. The journey that led him to discover his interest in history also shaped his understanding of it. His father, Andrew Jackson Turner, was the editor for a newspaper, the *Portage Wisconsin State Register*. This bore its mark on Turner's early professional career, and the "Class Book of the Class of 1884," the handwritten yearbook from his graduating year at the University of Wisconsin, identifies journalism as his future profession. As an undergraduate, Turner co-created and edited *Badger*, a weekly student newspaper. Prior to commencement, Turner followed in his father's footsteps and took a job as Madison correspondent for *Milwaukee Sentinel*, and in 1885 he took a position as legislative correspondent for the *Inter Ocean*, a national newspaper based in Chicago.[7] Despite the seemingly inevitable trajectory toward journalism, his heart was not in it. In the spring of 1885 Turner jumped at the opportunity to teach the last few weeks of undergraduate courses for William

Allen, his former professor, and then returned to campus in the fall as an instructor and graduate student in history.[8]

Turner kept a commonplace book which he used to record favorite quotations and errant thoughts about what he was reading. Although most of the writing is undated, there is a 40-page span bookended by dated entries, January 30, 1884, and May 2, 1885. Entries from this selected range were written during his brief career as a journalist prior to his return to the University of Wisconsin as a graduate student. In one passage, Turner bemoans his current profession and shares his yet unrealized vision for bringing Social Darwinism to the field of history. He writes,

> History must be read in the light of the development hypothesis. This method being applied [illegible] history brought more within the modern style of thought a multitude of such questions as that above, would be open to investigation and solution. Beginnings have been made at this as in Tylor's Primitive Culture, Maine['s] Ancient Law, Coulanges['] Ancient City and so on, but much yet remains to be done. From it will come a new sociology and religion. Indeed an intelligent understanding of the past by this key would give so many generalizations that the proper completion of such a work would inaugurate a new era. Sciences has of late years revolutionized zoology, biology, etc. It must now take up recorded history and do the same by it. This I would like to do my little to aid, but find not the time. It is a very egotistical idea that haunts me that if I were to drop my detestable dishing up of newspaper flippancy [I could] and [next page torn out].[9]

The passion of this journal entry is not exceptional but characteristic of his writing style. It signals Turner's overarching interest in the narrativization of history, specifically reframing that narrative in terms of Social Darwinism. The next page is suspiciously missing, and Turner resumes on the page that follows it with a reflection on interpreting history as a novel. Like Social Darwinism, this too is an idea that recurs throughout his commonplace books. From within the same span of undated entries he also writes, "The history of humanity has been a romance and a tragedy."[10] In this and similar passages, Turner redirects the attention of history from the second estate to the general public. Nevertheless, Turner's body politic is no less white than the European aristocracy against which he is contrasting this new historiography. Situated within the context of his commonplace book where he records his reading and rereading of Thomas Carlyle and even includes quotations valorizing presentism, we see a union of Turner's vision for narrativizing history with the evolutionary theory of Herbert Spencer. These writers gave Turner the pretext and discourse for framing the history of civilization as one of ineluctable progress.

What begins as private musings in his journal becomes the foundation of his essay "Problems in American History," the predecessor to his frontier thesis. In "Problems," Turner raises objections to framing American history as a narrative of slavery and abolition. He writes, "The struggle over slavery is a most important incident in our history, but it will be seen, as the meaning of events unfolds, that the real lines of American development, the forces dominating our character, are to be studied in the history of westward expansion." Turner accepts narrativization as a constituent of historiography but calls into question the particular character of the structure employed by his contemporaries. He continues,

> In a sense, American history up to our own day has been colonial history, the colonization of the Great West. This ever retreating frontier of free land is the key to American development. The work of the historian of the United States is to account for the predominant characteristics of the United States of today, by comparative and genetic study; to enable the present age to understand itself by understanding its development from the past. To state this is to show the inadequacy of our histories. American history needs a connected and unified account of the progress of civilization across this continent, with the attendant results. Until such a work is furnished we shall have no real national self-consciousness; when it is done, the significance of the discovery made by Columbus will begin to appear.[11]

Turner's linguisticity as evidenced by his inclusion of words like development, genetic, progress, civilization, and continent synthesizes history with disciplines of biology, sociology, and geography. His object is to produce a "national self-consciousness." Thus, for Turner history can be understood as the collection of examples that delineate the identity of a people by looking at where they have been and where they are going. Accurate interpretation of American history for Turner is concomitant with developing a national identity, and he concludes his introduction to "Problems" by invoking a figural interpretation of "the discovery made by Columbus." It is no surprise then that Turner would draw from "Problems" for the paper he delivered at the World's Columbian Exposition, a fair celebrating the quadricentennial of Columbus' arrival in the West Indies.

National History as Social Evolution

In "Problems" and "Significance," Turner summons the rhetoric of early colonists by defining the trajectory of civilization qua American history in relation to savagery and decadence. For Turner, progress was both literally and figuratively embodied by the advancing frontier line that divides savagery from civilization. Importantly, Turner asserts that this boundary is permeable, a quality that he views as essential to progress. In

"Problems," Turner asserts that "native populations" and "the location of Indian tribes ha[ve] been influential in determining the lines and character of the advance" and then adds that "the wilderness has been interpenetrated by lines of civilization."[12] Later in "Significance," Turner clarifies the meaning of this passage by stating that proximity with the other provides the necessary conditions for American development. He writes, "This perennial rebirth, this fluidity of American life, this expansion westward with its new opportunities, its continuous touch with the simplicity of primitive society, furnish the forces dominating American character" and concludes that "thus the advance of the frontier has meant a steady movement away from the influence of Europe, a steady growth of independence on American lines."[13] While it may be difficult to imagine John Winthrop or Cotton Mather uttering these words, it is not so different from the example set by Benjamin Church who attributed his victory over Pumetacom to his successful adoption of Wampanoag military tactics. Turner asks his audience to make this precise sort of comparison by adding, "And to study this advance, the men who grew up under these conditions, and the political, economic, and social results of it, is to study the really American part of our history."[14] Such an approach explicitly enables the identification of the individual with the national. Thus, the hero's journey finds its place in the rhetoric of American historiography. Taking into account Turner's belief that the subject of history is no longer the actions of the nobility but the everyman, each individual on the frontier could and did representationally enact the ritual of national identity. Developing a national self-consciousness prepared citizens with the tools to read their actions and their history as the fulfillment of a project that unified biological and social evolution with geographic and economic expansion. And although Turner presents this project as uniquely American, he also suggests that the history of America is the universal history of civilization. He writes,

> The United States lies like a huge page in the history of society. Line by line as we read from west to east we find the record of social evolution. It begins with the Indian and the hunter; it goes on to tell of the disintegration of savagery by the entrance of the trader, the pathfinder of civilization; we read the annals of the pastoral stage in ranch life; the exploitation of the soil by the raising of unrotated crops of corn and wheat in sparsely settled farming communities; the intensive culture of the denser farm settlement; and finally the manufacturing organization with city and factory system.[15]

Because, as Turner wrote earlier, "this ever retreating frontier of free land is the key to American development,"[16] the relation of society to the frontier not only maps the course of civilization but also functions as the catalyst for progress. It follows that the nation would require a limitless frontier to colonize to sustain its development.

Edward Said argued in *Orientalism* that imperial powers mobilized the "moral neutrality" of geography to map the world into civilized and uncivilized spaces. He attributed responsibility for this development to Britain citing George Curzon's 1912 address to the Royal Geographic Society, where Curzon described "geography as the handmaid of history."[17] Said recognized this use of geography as a "rationalization"[18] revealing it to be a post hoc apologetic. While that may have been an accurate assessment of Curzon who was at that time the former Viceroy of India, applying the same critique to Turner would be a disservice. Notwithstanding Turner's uncritical view of imperialism, geography was not an afterthought but an intellectual site or laboratory where historians could begin their work by drawing from various scientific disciplines. Despite these differences, Curzon all but names Turner as the reason for the rise in popularity of geography among historians. In a lecture delivered five years earlier, Curzon affirmed the origin story of the American self by stating, "Not till the mountains were left behind and the American pioneers began to push across the trackless plains, did America cease to be English and become American. In the forests and on the trails of the Frontier, amid the savagery of conflict, the labour of reclamation, and the ardours of the chase, the American nation was born." A few sentences later he paraphrases Turner:

> The panorama of characters and incidents, already becoming ancient history, passes in vivid procession before our eyes. First comes the trapper and the fur trader tracking his way into the Indian hunting-grounds and the virgin sanctuaries of animal life. Then the backwoodsman clears away the forests and plants his log hut in the clearings. There follow him in swift succession the rancher with his live-stock, the miner with his pick, the farmer with plough and seeds, and finally the urban dweller, the manufacturer, and the artisan.[19]

At least in this earlier speech, Curzon, like Turner, maintained that geography was not merely a palliative for the guilty conscience of the colonizer—it, of course, served this function—but also defined the "evolution of the national character as determined by its western march across the continent."[20]

What is additionally striking is how Curzon and Turner flatten the chronology of social evolution by listing regional occupations. Intentional or not, their words echo Walt Whitman's catalogue of American identity in "Song of Myself," a poem published in various iterations from 1855 to 1881. But unlike Whitman's explicit rejection of social hierarchy in his celebration of diversity, Curzon and Turner collapse time into space and thereby reframe difference as individual points on a singular continuum. In other words, they arrange what Whitman conceived of as heterogeneity into a linear chronology that stretches across the continent from the civilized metropole to the uncivilized frontier. It is as though they labeled each silhouette on the pictogram of human evolution with a different profession and called it a map of the United States. Doing so affirmed a homogenous American community where every individual participated in the ritual of creating the nation by holding space on the trajectory of social evolution. To revisit the past, one merely had to travel West to the frontier or, as we will soon see, attend Buffalo Bill's Wild West.

Ghost Dance Background

It may not be possible to claim that the Lakota Ghost Dance is the most maligned or misunderstood phenomena in U.S. history, but it is certainly one that accumulated more interest and research without demystifying what occurred. Consequently, the most authoritative texts are not ones that provide narratives but those that serve as annotated bibliographies such as Rani-Henrik Andersson's *The Lakota Ghost Dance of 1890* and Michael Hittman's *Wovoka and the Ghost Dance*. Like François Hartog's study of Herodotus, examining even a single reconstruction of these events reveals underlying ideological tensions in the author that in this case illustrate the pervasiveness of Turner's model of social and national history and the impact such thought had on how events of the present and past were interpreted by his contemporaries. Thus, we turn to James Mooney's *The Ghost-Dance Religion and the Sioux Outbreak of 1890.*

What we do know is that the Lakota Ghost Dance began as a prophecy from the Paiute medicine man Wovoka. Tribes from the surrounding regions sent representatives to learn from Wovoka about the prophecy and his teachings. From the Lakota, he received two delegations: Short Bull and Kicking Bear in 1889 and Good Thunder, Cloud Horse, Yellow Knife, and Short Bull in 1890.[21] By all reliable accounts, Wovoka's message was one of nonviolence. Along with instructions about ceremony, he taught, "You must not hurt anybody or do harm to anyone." Rather than encourage resistance, he encouraged followers to live peaceably with white settlers and even adopt their ways. He wrote, "Do not refuse to work for the whites and do not make any trouble with them until you leave them." According to Wovoka there was no need to retaliate or mourn when loved ones died, because—and this is the crux of his message—"the dead are all alive again. I do not know when they will be here; maybe this fall or in the spring. When the time comes there will be no more sickness and everyone will be young again."[22] He declared that if they observed these ways life would return to what it was before European contact. He predicted the removal of the colonizers, but he taught the practice of acculturation.

White settlers and the U.S. government did not appreciate the nuance and perceived ghost dancing as "savage fanaticism," a threat that would, if unchecked, become a violent resistance movement.[23] The fact is the Lakota Ghost Dance was a singular development that differed from the practices of other tribes who adopted Wovoka's teachings. It is possible that some of the participants wanted violence and may have used the Ghost Dance to achieve those ends.[24] It is also clear that the ghost dances did become more violent in the final months of 1890 and participants slaughtered cattle and raided farms because they needed food to continue dancing. However, characterizing the entire movement or even the Lakota Ghost Dance in particular as intent on violent resistance is inaccurate.[25] Lakota dancers ranged from nonprogressives that refused to embrace farming practices to progressives that accepted assimilation. Even some Christians participated in the dancing.[26]

This presents the first of two problems that writers face when historicizing the Ghost Dance—providing a behaviorist interpretation of the ceremony. Mooney, like other anthropologists, sought to understand and share with his readers why ghost dancing attracted so much interest and what participants hoped to accomplish. The second problem is constructing a causal chain of events. Whether a writer makes causality explicit or implicit, it shapes decisions about which related events warrant inclusion. How each historian addresses these problems results in wildly different narrativizations. Louis Warren *God's Red Son* portrays the Ghost Dance as an acculturation movement,[27] whereas the terminology offered by Joanna Rak allows for it to be read as contra-acculturation.[28] Mooney's rendering portrays it as an optimistic but inevitably doomed "revival nativism,"[29] what Anthony Wallace would later define as a "revitalization movement."[30] The history of these terms and the variations between them is complicated but important because the available discourse predisposes researchers to expect certain causes. Although Wallace never exclusively identified deprivation as a cause of revitalization,[31] it is a term that over time became indissolubly related to these movements. Michael Carroll attributed the widespread receptivity and adoption of ghost dancing at that time to deprivation by establishing a correlation between tribal dependence on the now extinct buffalo.[32] Kaye Brown refutes this claim citing Carroll's methodology and (mis)use of data.[33] To my knowledge, Russell Thornton provides the most authoritative insight into ghost dancing and deprivation. He cites demographic information and identifies two potentially meaningful factors—population decline and population size, stating that "inspections of the table cells show the Ghost Dance involvement of the small tribes, especially those with population declines, to have been almost total."[34] Essentially, small tribes with population declines were most likely to participate. Small tribes without population declines and large tribes regardless of population change were less likely to participate.

By anticipating deprivation, historians like Robert Utley uncritically accept the Lakota Ghost Dance and the massacre at Wounded Knee Creek as sequential steps in the *end of Indians narrative*. While Utley focuses less on the beliefs and practices of the Ghost Dance, he doubles down on portraying the massacre as the "military conquest" and "psychological conquest" that "destroyed them as a nation" in his aptly titled *The Last Days of the Sioux Nation*.[35] Utley goes so far as introduce his book by pointing to the Ghost Dance and subsequent massacre as events that signified the end of the frontier making Turner's utterance in "Significance" possible.[36] Far from being an outlier, twenty years after its initial publication, Utley's book remained the "definitive modern historical study" of these events and arguably still is.[37] Conversely, almost a century after Mooney wrote his ethnography, Raymond DeMallie confronts the problems in Utley's historiography and begins the work of decolonizing the dominant ghost dance narratives in his magisterial essay "The Lakota Ghost Dance: An Ethnohistorical Account." Explicitly mapping the Ghost Dance within Wallace's framework of five stages, Alice Beck Kehoe follows after DeMallie and situates the movement within a broader context of Lakota spiritual and cultural practices. Importantly, her work traces those developments into the present.[38] Mooney, Warren, Utley, and Kehoe are just a few Ghost Dance narratives. My purpose in singling out Mooney is to neither evaluate his legacy as a hero or villain of Lakota historiography, nor make definitive claims about the right interpretation. Instead, I examine Mooney to understand what the particularizations of his account reveal about narrativization in the wake of Turner's paper and in the political climate prior to the occupation of Haiti. Mooney produced ruptures in the pervasive ideology of Social Darwinism and in the field of anthropology, yet the allowances he made to ensure academic attention, his uneven rejection of the dominant trends in his field, or some combination of the two hamstrung the development of a counternarrative. Moreover, its structural ambiguity permitted his readership to uncritically interpret his ethnography as an affirmation of the *end of Indians* narrative despite his efforts to the contrary.

Ethnographic Structure

There is an ideological tension that runs throughout Mooney's ethnography that shows him simultaneously in agreement and at odds with Turner. The tension emerges from Mooney's recursive style of introducing an event in one chapter, exploring it in another, and summarizing it in a third, each time framing the subject differently. Michael Elliott argues that this "represents a careful strategy on Mooney's part to resist the evolutionary version of human history put forward by Lewis Henry Morgan and John Wesley Powell."[39] Elliott qualifies his reading by acknowledging that Mooney's strategy is not successful because it still interprets the events an inevitable tragedy. Although there is more room for nuance, his analysis is nonetheless reliable and offers valuable insight into the ideological landscape of anthropology that Mooney was resisting. For example, interpreting the Ghost Dance along the lines Morgan and Powell's acceptance of Social Darwinism would have resulted in reading native practices as static and unchanging, leaving room for only two responses to contact with civilization—assimilation or disappearance. Mooney unabashedly objects to such a reading in his opening paragraph when he states that his research "might be continued indefinitely, as the dance still exists (in 1896) and is developing new features at every performance."[40] This proposition is a casting down of gauntlets or hold my beer moment that presents the Lakota as not disappearing but evolving in a non-teleological fashion. Yet his next sentence, the final sentence of that paragraph, introduces the opposing and unresolved tension of his work. He writes, "The uprising among the Sioux in the meantime made necessary also the examination of a mass of documentary material in the files of the Indian Office and the War Department bearing on the outbreak, in addition to the study in the field of the strictly religious features of the dance."[41] Here we see that Mooney declares it impracticable to examine the Ghost Dance without also examining the massacre. The rationale is ambiguous, but Mooney's wording suggests that he reads the massacre as an indigenous uprising associated with "non-strictly religious features of the dance."[42] It is difficult to discern his meaning with more clarity because when Mooney redresses causality in subsequent chapters he vacillates between pointing to the mismanagement of the Indian agents and the rash actions of a few Lakota in the moments leading up to the massacre. Mooney eschews directly stating a causal relation between ghost dancing and the massacre but raises the connection referentially by quoting others such as the report by General Miles. For this reason, I view his recursive style as a strategy, purposeful or not, that allows Mooney to posit multiple (contradictory) versions of history.

Mooney divides his work into three parts: "Introduction," "The narrative," and "The Songs." The three-page introduction briefly overviews the chronology of Mooney's research and concludes with acknowledgments of his sources. The narrative, comprised of sixteen chapters, spans approximately two-thirds of the text and will be the focus of our analysis.

Although Mooney does not further subdivide these chapters into sections, he develops an implied structure that allows the reader to separate them into what I like to think of as three acts of a play that adheres loosely to the inverted U-shape of tragedy elaborated by Northrop Frye. The first ten chapters provide a history of indigenous acculturation to European contact and invoke the rising action. The next four chapters discuss specific instantiations and historical context of ghost dancing concluding with the massacre at Wounded Knee Creek, the climax of the narrative. And in the two final chapters, the denouement, Mooney relates the current state of ghost dancing and compares the ritual to other religions.

Equilibrium and Rising Action

The dramatic structure of tragedy in literature begins with an equilibrium that is immediately disrupted by conflict. For Mooney, the steady state is Turtle Island (the Americas) precontact, and to underscore this he titles the first chapter "Paradise Lost." In it we find Mooney at his most poetic and abstract. He describes precontact Americas as the "golden age, before Pandora's box was loosed."[43] By making comparison to Greek mythology as well as Hinduism and Christianity, Mooney insists that the Ghost Dance is not so different from other religions past and present, all of which include a prophet who foretells a return to a better time. It is an idea that he revisits in the final chapter and hints at a behaviorist determinism that informs his view of all religious practices. While this may simply be indicative of the distance at which Mooney holds religion, the effect circumvenes his rejection of Social Darwinism by asserting, quite explicitly, the Edenic character of precontact Americas. True to his recursive style, Mooney equivocates on the symbolic referent of this golden age. When he describes the arrival of the Spaniards he states, "The simple native welcomed the white strangers as the children or kindred of their long-lost benefactor, immortal beings whose near advent had been foretold by oracles and omens,"[44] implying that the golden age ended prior to the appearance of the white strangers. Yet after this opening chapter where Mooney construes Spanish conquest of the Aztecs to represent how all Europeans were received by indigenous tribes, the golden age referent consistently signifies precontact Americas.

Quite plainly, chapters two through eight retell a history of responses to English settlement by various tribes that delineate a loose history of the religious and cultural precursors to Wovoka's prophecy. Mooney begins this genealogy in chapter two by introducing Neolin, a Delaware prophet who as recorded in the "Pontiac Manuscript" commanded his followers to reject white men's ways, to "live as you did before you knew them [the French]."⁴⁵ The instructions continued, "Drive them [the English] away; wage war against them; I love them not; they are my enemies; they are your brothers' [the French] enemies. Send them back to the lands I have made for them. Let them remain there."⁴⁶ The chapter on Neolin is followed by a chapter on Tenskwatawa, a Shawnee prophet, who inaugurates what Mooney describes as the direct antecedent of the Ghost Dance ceremony. He writes, "enough is known to show that in its leading features the movement closely resembled the modern Ghost dance."⁴⁷ A second similarity is Tenskwatawa's attendant authentication as a prophet by accurately predicting an eclipse. Doubting Tenskwatawa's power over nature, Mooney adds, "By some means he had learned than an eclipse of the sun was to take place in the summer of 1806."⁴⁸ Mooney's inclusion of Tenskwatawa further develops his revitalization genealogy, but his editorialization serves as a reminder of his interpretative frame. This recounting of Ghost Dance predecessors continues through the next half-dozen chapters until Mooney introduces Wovoka and his revelation concurrent with the solar eclipse on January 1, 1889. In contradistinction to the wide paintbrush that Mooney uses in "Paradise Lost," these intervening chapters disclose the uneven and heterogenous development of cultural practices. Such a history defies the predominant anthropological thought that perceived indigenous cultures as invariable. Yet the narrow limits of Mooney's analysis leave him open to critique. Mooney's narrative structure exacerbates the tension introduced in his opening paragraph by depicting the precontact continent as a primitive paradisical stasis disrupted by colonization. Readers are left to puzzle for themselves the unanswered and unanswerable counter-factual—what if the Spanish never arrived? By tracing the development of a reactive ceremony, Mooney's history of indigenous culture points to a single agent of change, white people. The implication then is that the only history is the history of western civilization.

The biographical account of Wovoka and the Ghost Dance prophecy further illustrates Mooney's method of interweaving recursive narratives to provide multiple, often conflicting, accounts of the same events. According to Mooney, Wovoka was born 1856 and was the son of Tävibo.⁴⁹ This closely aligns with a birthdate "at or near the head of an 1860–1884 cohort," which Hittman proposes.⁵⁰ Mooney is ambivalent about whether or not his father was the prophet of the 1870 Ghost Dance among the Paiute or simply participated in it.⁵¹ Alternatively, Hittman makes the qualified assertion that "if he [Wovoka's father] were living in the Walker River area in 1869" then he would have at least participated in it.⁵² In his early years, Wovoka spent a considerable amount of time on the Wilson Ranch where he would have gotten another name, Jack Wilson.⁵³ With the help of a translator, Wovoka explained his vision to Mooney. Wovoka said, "When the sun died, I went up to heaven and saw God and all the people who had died a long time ago. God told me to come back and tell my people they must be good and love one another, and not fight, or steal, or lie. He gave me this dance to give to my people."[54] True to his disruptive style, Mooney only includes the statement in an epigraph for chapter nine. When he shares the narrative of his interview with Wovoka in the body of the chapter, he referentially calls forth the statement by requoting the first few words. He follows this narrative with a third retelling by paraphrasing the statement of a neighboring rancher. The presumably white rancher explained that Wovoka was sick with a severe fever when a solar eclipse occurred, which, according to Mooney, "seems to explain the whole matter."[55] He elaborates by writing,

> It was now, as Wovoka stated, "when the sun died," that he went to sleep in the daytime and was taken up to heaven. This means simply that the excitement and alarm produced by the eclipse, acting on a mind and body already enfeebled by sickness, resulted in delirium, in which he imagined himself to enter the portals of the spirit world. Constant dwelling on the subject in thought by day and in dreams by night would effect and perpetuate the exalted mental condition in which visions of the imagination would have all the seeming reality of actual occurrences. To those acquainted with the spiritual nature of Indians and their implicit faith in dreams all this is perfectly intelligible. His frequent trances would indicate also that, like so many other religious ecstatics, he is subject to cataleptic attacks.[56]

Difficult as it may be to keep our presentist impulses in check when reading these words, doing so reveals the perspicacity of Mooney's narrative style. By dislocating Wovoka's statement and by citationally invoking it with the phrase "when the sun died" in both the scene of the interview and his scientific rationalization, Mooney illuminates his situatedness as an ethnographer. To read Wovoka's full statement in the context of either version, the audience must interrupt their reading of Mooney's prose to flip back several pages and find the epigraph. The inclusion of his delirium rationalization does not belie the significance of this rhetorical move. The act of signification reveals the explanation as an imposition of the author on the text. Moreover, employing the same strategy for the interview demonstrates admission that any account, even when dictated (with a translator) to the author, entails interpretation, especially when those words relate an event three years prior that cannot be iterated without also calling forth the massacre.

Climax

Even though Mooney's narrative oscillates chronologically when reporting individual events, until this point each chapter marked a linear sequential step leading from the past to Wovoka's revelation. Chapters eleven through fourteen, which comprise the climax of the tragic narrative structure, break from this pattern and flatten time geographically like Turner. Because, as Turner showed, the frontier line extended to its western limit of the Pacific and the so-called savagery of indigenous peoples was circumscribed in reservations, Mooney's narrative moves spatially examining first the more restrained and thus more comprehensible ghost dancing west of the Rockies in chapter eleven to the co-occurring feverish instantiation east of the Rockies in chapter twelve. Although the stated purpose of chapter twelve is to describe the Ghost Dance among the Lakota and the two subsequent chapters discuss the arrest and death of Sitting Bull and the massacre at Wounded Knee Creek, Mooney nevertheless concludes this chapter with an explanation of the causes of the outbreak.[57] Superimposing these proceedings reaffirms the accepted belief that the conflict was indissolubly related to the dancing. More specifically, it reified the perception that the Ghost Dance could not be examined without acknowledging its inevitable trajectory that led to destruction of the Lakota. Second, in terms of narrative structure, it discloses that the massacre, not the Ghost Dance, is the climax of the book. Authors do not tease what comes next at the apex. That would draw the reader's attention away from rather than toward the focal point of the narrative. Discordant with the original title of his manuscript that only mentioned it appurtenantly, the conflict at Wounded Knee Creek was in fact the showpiece.[58]

At the end of chapter twelve, Mooney attributes the outbreak to three causes. These are as follows: "(1) unrest of the conservative element under the decay of the old life, (2) repeated neglect of promises made by the government, and (3) hunger."[59] These reasons are more notable for what is omitted rather than what is included. Mooney makes no mention of the purported topic of the chapter (and book for that matter), the Ghost Dance. To ensure this absence was acknowledged, Mooney went on to state "that it [the Ghost Dance] was not the cause of the outbreak is sufficiently proved by the fact that there was no serious trouble, excepting on the occasion of the attempt to arrest Sitting Bull, on any other of the Sioux reservations, and none at all among any of the other Ghost-dancing tribes from the Missouri to the Sierras."[60] In fact, Mooney went even further to claim that the actions of indigenous peoples did not cause the outbreak at all. He criminated the Indian agents put in charge by the government. He wrote that "the Ghost dance itself [...] was only a symptom and expression of the real causes of dissatisfaction and with such a man as McGillycuddy or McLaughlin in change at Pine Ridge there would have been no outbreak, in spite of broken promises and starvation [...]."[61] Mooney is walking a tight line here, and it is important to remember that his role is not to litigate the massacre. Nevertheless, his approach acknowledges the failures of U.S. government but does not hold them responsible for the atrocity. It condemns the mismanagement of a few bad actors. At this point, it may be possible to read this as a narrative sympathetic to the Lakota by eliminating their culpability in the outbreak. Therefore, we turn to the final clause omitted from the quotation above: "and the Indians could have been controlled until Congress rectified their mistakes." These words not only let government off the hook, but also reveal the marginalized position of the Lakota in this text.[62] The "Indians" are a people who can be controlled, and it is the responsibility of the U.S. government to manage their actions and administer the curative treatment. In essence, Mooney believed indigenous people could never have started the outbreak because they have no agency of their own. This brings the rest of his narrative into focus. In sum, prior to European contact, native culture was a static, homogenous paradise; all the antecedents to Wovoka, all the development and diversity of ceremony flourished solely in reaction to British colonization; the Lakota outbreak was the inevitable end of primitive culture in a globalization narrative; and they cannot be held responsible for the massacre because their agency is unimaginable.

Foregrounded by his assertion of causes in the previous chapter where the U.S. government absorbs responsibility for creating the toxic situation and Indian agents were denounced for inexperience and poor judgment, Mooney reorients accountability as he moves from generalizing to narrating the arrest of Sitting Bull and the massacre. By deferring to the respected Indian agent James McLaughlin, Mooney introduces uncertainty about the innocence of the Lakota. He observes that McLaughlin considered Sitting Bull the "leader and instigator of the excitement on the reservation."[63] Later, in his own words, Mooney writes, "There is no question that Sitting Bull was plotting mischief. His previous record was one of irreconcilable hostility to the government, and in every disturbance on the reservation hill camp had been the center of ferment."[64] Mooney also cites Sitting Bull's decision to break the calumet or "pipe of peace" and his claim that "he wanted to die and wanted to fight."[65] Mooney is not alone in the belief that Sitting Bull fostered agitation. As noted above, even though Sitting Bull did not profess belief in the Ghost Dance, he allowed its continuance and made no effort to suppress it despite promises to the contrary.[66] Utley observes that empowering the believers of the Ghost Dance provided Sitting Bull "an opportunity to revive his own authority and influence" among his people.[67]

Paraphrasing Mooney, the arrest occurred at daybreak on December 15. Lieutenant Bull Head of the reservation police surrounded Sitting Bull's house with a group of forty-three police and volunteers. Sitting

Bull initially complied with the arrest order to remove to the agency. As he dressed, Sitting Bull "apparently changed his mind and began abusing the police for disturbing him, to which they made no reply."[68] Outside the house, the crowd of onlookers grew to approximately 150. Mooney writes, "On being brought out, Sitting Bull became greatly excited and refused to go, and called on his followers to rescue him."[69] As the police attempted to clear a path, Catch-the-Bear shot Bull Head in the side, and then Bull Head along with Second Sergeant Red Tomahawk simultaneously turned and shot Sitting Bull. Several others were shot or injured including Sergeant Shave Head. The arrest party drove the crowd back and withdrew into Sitting Bull's house until the army arrived two hours later. In itself, Mooney's depiction of the arrest is not remarkable. Other than the rivalry with Bull Head which was not widely known until it was examined by Sitting Bull's biographer in 1930s, Mooney's account does not differ materially from what others had said or would say.[70]

In this sense, the mishandled arrest of Sitting Bull is emblematic, although not a clear catalyst, of what subsequently occurred at Wounded Knee Creek. Again, paraphrasing Mooney, after the death of Sitting Bull, the only perceived threat was Big Foot and a band from his village who were traveling to the Pine Ridge Agency to receive their annuities.[71] Many from Sitting Bull's village fled to Big Foot's camp to seek refuge. Big Foot accepted the refugees and defended his decision to feed and clothe them to Colonel Edwin V. Sumner. According to Mooney, "Sumner then directed one of his officers, Captain Hennisee, to go to the Indian camp with Big Foot and bring in all the Indians," which appears to mean that Big Foot's band was ordered to surrender.[72] The Lakota from his camp complied at the time, but when their journey led them near their village in the Cheyenne River Indian Reservation, Big Foot could not prevent them from returning to their homes. When ordered again to remove, Big Foot assented but many from his village fled due to knowledge that additional military forces were dispatched and rumors that they would be shot if they refused to come peaceably. Over the next few days, the fugitives, who at this point included refugees from multiple villages including Sitting Bull's and Big Foot's, were cut off by General John R. Brooke in the north, forcing them back toward the Pine Ridge Agency. On December 28, 1890, Big Foot agreed to unconditionally surrender his band to Major Samuel M. Whitside, who escorted them to camp at Wounded Knee Creek about twenty miles from the agency.[73]

The following morning under the command of Colonel Forsyth, the troops ordered the warriors among the fugitives to disarm. They surrendered only two guns. Believing there to be more, one group of soldiers remained with the warriors, and another searched the camp and discovered about forty rifles, most of which were old and worthless. According to Mooney, while this was ongoing a medicine man named Yellow Bird walked among the warriors encouraging them to resist and assuring them the soldiers' bullets couldn't penetrate their "sacred 'ghost shirts.'"[74] When one of the soldiers raised a blanket that belonged to a warrior "Yellow Bird stooped down and threw a handful of dust into the air, when, as if this were the signal, a young Indian, said to have been Black Fox from Cheyenne river, drew a rifle from under his blanket and fired at the soldiers, who instantly replied with a volley directly into the crowd of warriors and so near that their guns were almost touching."[75] Permit me to remind the reader that Mooney's account is one among many and the details provided here are his interpretation, which is a synthesis of conflicting reports.[76] Hotchkiss guns fired into the camp where the women and children stood watch over the disarmament. The camp was destroyed, and soldiers pursued those who fled. Here Mooney adjusts his language and finally describes this part of the conflict as "simply a massacre, where fleeing women, with infants in their arms, were shot down after resistance had ceased and when almost every warrior was stretched dead or dying on the ground."[77] Mooney includes several different figures and offers his own estimate that 31 soldiers and 300 Lakota were killed.[78]

In comparison to the previous chapter, we begin to see a distinction emerge in Mooney's layering of causality. While Mooney identified the U.S. government and Indian agents at fault for the conditions that created the crisis, the actions of individual Lakota during the arrest of Sitting Bull, namely Sitting Bull and Catch-the-bear, provoked the particular instantiation of violence upon themselves. Similarly, at Wounded Knee Creek, Mooney draws the following conclusions: "that the first shot was fired by an Indian, and that the Indians were responsible for the engagement; that the answering volley and attack by the troops was right and justifiable, but that the wholesale slaughter of women and children was unnecessary and inexcusable."[79] Mooney qualifies the "wholesale slaughter" by arguing that "this is no reflection on the humanity of the officer in charge" and "the butchery was the work of infuriated soldiers whose comrades had just been shot down without cause or warning." He continues, "In justice to a brave regiment it must be said that a number of the men were new recruits fresh from eastern recruiting stations, who had never before been under fire, were not yet imbued with military discipline, and were probably unable in the confusion to distinguish between men and women by their dress."[80] It is difficult to avoid acknowledging a similar dynamic in recent decades rationalizing incidents of police brutality. Regardless, even the most charitable reading of Mooney suggests that the actions of the

Lakota and the military from the chiefs and officers in charge down to the individuals they lead were determined before they even arrived on the scene.

The climax of the ethnography concludes in chapter fourteen. Mooney begins by relabeling the massacre for a third time, this time stating, "It might be better designated, however, as a Sioux panic and stampede,"[81] a definition that conspicuously mirrors the rhetoric of chapter thirteen where a more generalized summation similarly strips agency from indigenous peoples. Consistent with the opening paragraph of his introduction, Mooney spends the remainder of the chapter describing the Ghost Dance religion among the southern tribes including the Cheyenne, Kiowa, and Arapaho with an addendum reporting that the Kiowa continued to practice while Mooney was awaiting publication after the manuscript was completed.[82]

Denouement

The final two chapters comprise the denouement. In chapter fifteen, Mooney looks closely at the ceremony of the Ghost Dance religion. He balances homogenic statements about the ceremony as it was practiced across many tribes with examination of regional artifacts among specific tribes like the ghost shirts among the Lakota. The content is uncontroversial, whereas in chapter sixteen, Mooney makes a slightly more provocative comparison by likening visions of ancestors returning from the dead among ghost dancers with hallucinations and hypnotism in other religions including Judaism, Islam, and Christianity.[83] Mooney goes beyond merely referencing these phenomena and offers detailed analysis of individual prophets, prophecies, and practices, spending the most time on historical and contemporary Christian movements. The implicit argument is that the Ghost Dance religion is no more far-fetched than any other religion but since any form of hallucination or hypnotism can be easily explained by science, it cannot be taken seriously. Far from being divergent, these chapters are indicative of Mooney's general thesis. To his credit, Mooney lays bare his own biases, making himself an easy target for critics. This openness alongside his looping narrative that circles back to retell the same event from a different standpoint disclose the situatedness of each iteration, so that readers can recognize the multiple ideological forces shaping the text. Perhaps by his awareness that he is unable to escape from these determinations, Mooney settles for making them visible.

In sum, we have, at least in content, an ethnography that openly resists the dominant narrative of Social Darwinism and suggests that the religious movements of so-called primitive societies should be treated and studied with the same dignity as those of civilized societies. Yet the tragic narrative structure of his work borrowed from the discursive field of anthropology counteracts this effort by fitting the history of the Ghost Dance into a schema that historicizes the outcome of events as inevitable and fixed. Consequently, it is all the more important to acknowledge that our understanding of tragedy extends from Aristotle, who wrote about it in *On Poetics*. According to Aristotle the difference between poetry and history was content, not form or kind. Thus, when he discusses *muthos*, often translated as plot or story, he is simultaneously exploring both. He writes, "the story, since it is an imitation of action, ought to be of one action, and this is a whole."[84] For Aristotle, even Homer's *Odyssey* is the narrative of a single action, and plot simply unveils the consequences of that action. He continues, "And the parts of the events ought to have been put together so that when a part is transposed or removed, the whole becomes different and changes."[85] Therefore, the plot of tragedy is exclusively determined by a single action. Reading Mooney's ethnography as a tragedy reveals the European contact as the single determining action. That is not to say Sitting Bull's death is the direct consequence of Columbus' arrival in 1492. Rather, Mooney's narrativization produces the causal relationship, making it appear as though one inevitably follows from the other. The fact that Mooney appears ambivalent or contradictory on this point illuminates the value of his text for contemporary scholars. Just as we read Turner as representative of contemporaneous trends in historiography, Mooney's ethnography operates as an index of opposing ideological developments in anthropology at the time of its writing. To conclude, we return to the World's Columbian Exposition, which proves more significant than a mere site for Turner's paper. Popular acts like Eugen Sandow, the living Adonis who performed at Florenz Ziegfeld's Trocadero nightclub, and Buffalo Bill's Wild West attest to the wide range of attendees to the Fair. Interestingly, Florenz's daughter, Patricia Ziegfeld, describes how Florenz idolized Cody and dreamed about the life of show business. Years before when Buffalo Bill's Wild West tour stopped in Chicago, Florenz ran away with the show. Patricia writes, "The runaway was caught up with at the next town and brought home again, but the damage had been done. Daddy had tasted a mixture of show business and independence in one heady draught, and though he returned home outwardly docile he was only biding his time until his big chance came again."[86] The novelty and theatricality of Cody's productions reveal how the subject of Mooney's ethnography was represented and understood within the national popular consciousness.

World's Columbian Exposition of 1893

Suturing the Lakota Ghost Dance and Wounded Knee into a linear narrative that extended from Columbus through indigenous removal to the present became a national pastime in 1893. Concurrent with the Fair, national newspapers like the *Inter Ocean* ran articles summarizing the events of the massacre.[87] In her column for the *Chicago Daily News*, Amy Leslie writes a behind-the-scenes feature on Buffalo Bill's Wild West show. In a tent that she describes as "Sitting Bull's Cabin," Leslie meets Rain-in-the-Face, a Lakota veteran of the Battle of Little Big Horn, only to be interrupted by a "fearful din" because outside some "young braves are executing a ghost dance." One of the dancers is none other than Johnny Burke No Neck, "the baby, growing very fast, which Burke found wandering among the dead on the battlefield of Wounded Knee."[88] Within a few lines of newsprint, Leslie illustrates how the diachronic history of indigenous peoples were put on display for attendees of Cody's show. Narrativization was part of the design of the Fair as well. On Italian Day at the exposition, twelve Lakota greeted Columbus for a crowd of 2,000 fairgoers in anachronistic tableaux-vivants of the "Seven Ages of Columbus" and "Columbus' Triumphal Return."[89] Even more emblematic was Johnny Burke No Neck's presentation of roses to the duchess of Veragua, the lineal descendant of Columbus.[90] To read meaning into the spectacle of a child left parentless by a massacre (which in itself was interpreted symbolically as the termination of indigenous culture) honoring the legacy of his colonizers is both absurd and the apotheosis of hubris. Alongside these fashionable demotic events, the Commissioner of Indian Affairs Thomas Morgan sought to arrange the indigenous living history exhibits on the Midway from the most primitive on one end to the most civilized on the other, using representatives of the Indian boarding schools for the latter.[91] Neither should the significance of Herbert Spencer's presentation of the opening paper at the Fair's Congress of Evolution be overlooked, a scene that Robert Rydell argues, "synthesized and validated the theory of racial and material progress along evolutionary lines that the exposition itself presented in visible form."[92]

These anecdotes should not be mistaken for evidence of a monolithic enterprise to write or rewrite history. As Rosemarie Bank observes, it was "a context more Barnum than Boasian," and she suggests conceiving of the Fair as a heterotopia of competing ideologies.[93] Consequently, they are better understood as citationally indicating the climate of American consciousness in 1893 as opposed to coalescing into a single depiction. A chapter titled "The American Indian" in the *Martin's World Fair Album-Atlas and Family Souvenir* illustrates this complexity. In contradistinction to some of Fair's other messaging, it opens with the declaration,

"To say that Columbus discovered this country, is a statement which carries with it a wrong and misleading impression, leaving one to infer that it had remained unknown and uninhabited by man from the foundation of the world until he made known its existence."[94] The chapter also corrects other wrong impressions about indigenous forms of government and their character as "blood-thirsty" and "treacherous."[95] These gestures, though important, do not prevent the authors from generalizing about all indigenous tribes as though they are a singular culture.

The book also omits conflict with the colonizers excepting a final segment of the chapter, which relates the Minnesota Massacre where settlers and German immigrants were attacked by Dakota warriors. There is no mention of the Ghost Dance religion or Wounded Knee, yet inserted between segments on "Their Religion" and "Indian Superstition" is a photograph of nineteen Lakota who were arrested after the massacre and released from Fort Sheridan to tour Europe with Buffalo Bill's Wild West show.[96] Three of the Lakota depicted in the photo were rehired for the 1893 season.[97] Though William Cody did not receive permission to stage his show on the fairgrounds, he leased fourteen acres adjacent to the main entrance of the exposition, where he constructed his arena. His proximity to the Fair, the inclusion of the photograph in the souvenir album, and his frequent appearance in Leslie's column made the two events virtually indistinguishable. In essence, Buffalo Bill's Wild West operated as a visual counterpart to Turner's paper. Without needing to make the pilgrimage from the metropole to the frontier to bear witness to the landscape of American history, audiences could witness that history paraded before them in a program that read like a survey of the wild west greatest hits. Featured in the show were scenes such as "Illustrating a Prairie Emigrant Train Crossing the Plains," "Capture of the Deadwood Mail Coach by the Indians," and a "Buffalo Hunt." Woven into the grand narrative were displays of horsemanship from exotic cultures of Syria, Arabia, and Mexico as well as a depiction of the "Life Customs of Indians."[98] The grand finale re-enacted the Battle of Little Big Horn.

Using the actual Deadwood stagecoach and incorporating historical events often with performers that were original participants lent the show an authenticity that was appealing to audiences. Famously, Mark Twain called it "genuine" and "wholly free from sham and insincerity."[99] Scholars have discussed at length Cody's approach of blending fact and fiction, selling attendees an opportunity to experience the frontier as it threatened to fade from the national memory.[100] This is no more apparent than in the 64-page program from the show that included biography of Cody's life, history of the west, vignettes, etc. In a gesture that is perhaps more symbolic of Cody's alacrity and acumen as a showman than it is of any ideological stratagem, he replaced the re-enactment of Little Big Horn with the Battle of San Juan Hill for the 1899 season.[101] Juxtaposed against Turner's paper and Mooney's ethnography, the anecdotes from the Wild West show and Fair reveal that competing and contradictory narratives of American history co-exist in a fairly narrow shared space of national consciousness. Except for Mooney, each produces a diachronic history that can be mapped geographically across the continental landscape. Despite their incompatibility with one another, characteristic of each was the production of a linear and universal teleology. Recalling the example of Daniel Boone, rather than problematizing the myth, regional variation allowed differing populations to imagine Boone as a singular representation of the national self. Cody's periodic revisions to his Wild West show evince how myth adapts over time even as it presents itself as timeless and unchanging.

Thus, in these examples we have invocations of a specular image that is synonymous with the personal and the national. Four centuries after the arrival of Columbus, Turner's address delivered July 12, 1893, presented itself as sitting at a kind of fulcrum or figural moment in American history. Employing the rhetoric of seventeenth-century British colonists, he synthesized evolutionary biology, social history, geography, national identity, and individual freedom into a myth of the American self. His words were not a fulfillment of a national project but a narrativization of history that produced the present as a milestone pathing toward the horizon of American destiny. Recalling the words of Balibar from earlier, narrativization of national identity is "the process of development from which we select aspects retrospectively, so as to see ourselves as the culmination of that process, was the only one possible, that is, it represented a destiny."[102] With Turner, we have an orator telling a history of universal civilization by consciously wresting control of the past from other historians who were writing alternative narratives of American colonization and slavery. Yet we must be careful, because to posit any alternative as more accurate or more precise produces the same linear result. By the same token, the Puritan legacy is not uniquely integral or singularly responsible for national identity any more than 1619 inevitably leads to civil war and a journey toward racial equity. The reason these moments in 1893 have such power is because the citizens of that time imagine them as representative of the American self. If, as it seems, narrativization is inevitable, then the aim of the autocritical humanist imperative is not to remove or wipe out such narratives from existence but to concede their situatedness and investigate the discourse to understand how they operate. With the historical context of 1893 as our backdrop, we now turn to the occupation of Haiti and the American zombie.

CHAPTER THREE

Caribbean and Gothic Origins of the American Zombie

What is truth? a mobile army of metaphors, metonyms, anthropomorphisms, in short, a sum of human relations which were poetically and rhetorically heightened, transferred, and adorned, and after long use seem solid, canonical, and bind to a nation.
—FRIEDRICH NIETZSCHE, "On Truth and Lying in an Extra-Moral Sense, 1983"

At the World's Columbian Exposition of 1893, the dominant cultural narratives might have been the loudest figuratively (Frederick Jackson Turner) and literally (William Cody), but they were not alone. On January 2, Frederick Douglass spoke at the dedication of the Haitian Pavilion. In the address he offers a figural interpretation of the Haitian Revolution stating, "We should not forget that the freedom you and I enjoy to-day, [...] the freedom that has come to the colored race the world over, is largely due to the brave stand taken by the black sons, of Haiti ninety years ago. When they struck for freedom, [...] they struck for the freedom of every black man in the world."[1] Unlike the American Indian exhibits on the Fair's Midway, Haiti constructed its own pavilion and determined how it would represent itself to the world. By investing in its international reputation, Haitian politicians hoped to counteract the negative perception of their country as primitive and politically unstable. Accordingly, the exhibit did not contain any mention of Vodou.[2] It was not until the U.S. occupation of Haiti from 1915 to 1934, that more lurid tales of ritual possession, cannibalism, and zombies fascinated and terrified the American consciousness. While many texts about Haiti emerged during this period, the two most prominent are William Seabrook's *The Magic Island* and Victor Halperin's *White Zombie*. Their popularity and influence shaped the character and reception of zombies and Haitian folklore throughout the twentieth century.

Unobjectionable analysis of the occupation requires comprehension of the overlapping narratives that are too numerous and extensive to be adequately considered in this slim volume. In addition to westward expansion and social evolution, histories of Haitian independence, U.S.-European relations, U.S. slavery, and various literary traditions overdetermine our understanding of the occupation. Fortunately, much of the difficult work of uncovering the interrelations of these crosscurrents has been done by scholars such as David Brion Davis, Hans Schmidt, Leon Pamphile, Carolyn Fick, and David Patrick Geggus. Following from the discussion in the previous chapter, we will begin by examining how and why fiction writers adapted to the changing geographic and social conditions of their audience. As Kyle William Bishop reveals, the American zombie that emerged from the context of the U.S. occupation was steeped in a tradition of gothic literature. I only wish to append this assertion by acknowledging its indissoluble relation to frontier fiction. In the preface to his gothic novel *Edgar Huntly; or, Memoirs of a Sleep-Walker*, the prominent early American novelist Charles Brockden Brown concludes with a proleptic declaration of his literary contributions. He writes, "One merit the writer may at least claim:—that of calling forth the passions and engaging the sympathy of the reader by means hitherto unemployed by preceding authors. Puerile superstition and exploded manners, Gothic castles and chimeras, are the materials usually employed for this end. The incidents of Indian hostility, and the perils of the Western wilderness, are far more suitable; and for a native of America to overlook these would admit of no apology."[3] Brown's preface relocates the savage from gothic castles of England to the western frontier line. Recalling the discussion of individuating the national self in the introduction, historically, American identity is defined by simultaneous rejection and acceptance of savagery and civilization. Brown positions both as analogous and invokes the ritual of engaging with the frontier to prevent or at least forestall the advance toward European decadence. Furthermore, the terminology Brown employs simultaneously reveals the transformation of the European jeremiad "based on civic virtue and moral obedience" to the American jeremiad configured as the errand in the wilderness.[4] Whether intentional or incidental, Brown's allotropic language constellates gothic and frontier fiction within the project of American selfhood that sought to distinguish itself from Europe by developing a relationship to the land and nature alternately represented as primitive and savage.

Frontier

In his book *American Exceptionalism in the Age of Globalization*, William Spanos defines the frontier as "the fluid boundary between 'savagery' and 'civilization,' threatening forest and secure settlement, diabolic enemies and supportive friends, the uncertainty of the strange and the confidence of the familiar."[5] This border distances the civilized center from the peripheries but sustains the presence of threat, thereby justifying colonial expansion. The still widely read frontier novelist James Fenimore Cooper epitomizes this project of national selfhood, and his success trades on the efficacy of this myth. Richard Slotkin describes him as a "literary pioneer" whose themes and characters have been used and reused throughout American fiction.[6] His most well-known works are from the Leatherstocking cycle: *The Pioneers, The Last of the Mohicans, The Prairie, The Pathfinder,* and *The Deerslayer*. These historical romances rationalize colonization of the interior by mourning the disappearance of the continent's original inhabitants as a tragic but unavoidable casualty of the ineluctable progress of civilization. Cooper's fluid integration of exclusionist ideology demonstrates his unconscious interpellation of hegemonic colonial discourse.

Of all the Leatherstocking novels, *The Last of the Mohicans* articulates most clearly this apologetic for indigenous erasure. Evidence for Cooper's exceptionalist ideology first appears in the patriarchal figure Colonel George Munro, father of Alice and Cora. Major Heyward takes an interest in Alice and approaches Munro about a marriage proposal. Munro takes immediate offense believing that Heyward was initially interested in Cora and changed his attention to Alice after discovering Cora's "mixed blood." Heyward responds vehemently, "God forbid that any act or thought of mine should lead to such a change!"[7] He continues to argue that he never had any intentions for Cora and that he only ever cared for Alice. However, as Slotkin notes, because of Cooper's insistence on racial purity, the thought of Cora would have never entered Heyward's mind. His "natural repugnance" for other races prevent any such thought from occurring.[8] Only the indigenous characters Uncas and Magua exhibit desire for Cora.

Similarly, Munro's connection to the slave trade in the West Indies reveals the stratification of race and social class. In *Culture and Imperialism*, Edward Said offers an instructive critique of Jane Austen's *Mansfield Park*. In Austen's novel, Sir Thomas Bertram is the patriarch that embodies British cultural values and wealth. Munro's position in *The Last of the Mohicans* is analogous to Bertram with admittedly lesser prominence. As Said points out, "Sir Thomas Bertram's slave plantation in Antigua is mysteriously necessary to the poise and the beauty of Mansfield Park."[9] However, Antigua's significance to the maintenance of Mansfield Park is remarkably underplayed. Said cites "a mere half dozen passing references to Antigua."[10] Like Austen, Cooper does not feel the need to elaborate on the role of the slave trade in Munro's wealth and references the West Indies twice in the entire text. I am not suggesting that Cooper consciously chose to suppress the source of Munro's wealth because it might offend the sensibility of readers. Instead, I am suggesting quite the opposite. Like the early American writings about Haiti that we will soon analyze, Cooper did not elaborate on the colonization of Caribbean peoples because it was uncontroversial. Cooper accepted the slave trade as a lucrative economic venture, and profiting from the purchase and sale of slaves was a legitimate means of acquiring capital. By not drawing attention to this aspect of his upstanding patriarchal figure or the absence of public outrage, we infer a general approval or at least tolerance his attitudes.

Throughout the novel, Cooper takes care to distinguish the British-American colonists from the French, the Mohicans, and the Hurons. Among these, the most difficult to distinguish are the French. Although they are at war with the British-Americans, Cooper acknowledges the cultural debt owed to the French as a civilizing force and consequently presents them as respectable antagonists. A certain social etiquette evidenced by their conferences and terms of surrender reveals this mutual recognition between the French and British-Americans. When agreeing to Munro's surrender, the French general Marquis de Montcalm stipulates:

> "as for yourselves, and your brave comrades, there is no privilege dear to a soldier that shall be denied."
> "Our colors?" demanded Heyward.
> "Carry them to England, and show them to your king."
> "Our arms?"
> "Keep them; none can use them better."
> "Our march; the surrender of the place?"
> "Shall all be done in a way most honorable to yourselves."

Duncan turns to explain these proposals to his commander, who listens with amazement and is deeply touched by Montcalm's generosity.[11] Although Munro did not anticipate such charitable terms of surrender, the respect the French have for their enemy is a performance of the civility that Cooper esteems. It is quite possible that Cooper is introducing a subtle critique of the French as overcivilized with Montcalm's effusion of politeness in comparison to the British-American ideal of moderation and modesty. Nevertheless, the more overt criticism is of Montcalm's short-sighted alliance with the savage Hurons.

Cooper differentiates the French, a mutually recognized colonial power, from the Hurons typified by the dishonest and brutal Magua. The morning after the terms of surrender are settled, Magua emerges from the French camp and raises his rifle to bear on Munro who is standing on the ramparts of his surrendered fort. Before the Huron fires, Montcalm places his hand on the lock.[12] This act distinguishes the two antagonists, and any respect Munro and the British-Americans had for the French other does not extend to Magua and his tribe. In the opening chapter of the novel, Cooper indicates his unforgiving attitude toward the Hurons, describing them as "merciless enemies" and recounts their "recent massacres" and the common "midnight murder, in which the natives of the forest were the principal and barbarous actors."[13] True to the *natural character* of his race inscribed by Cooper, Magua disregards the surrender and leads a rogue Huron hunting party to massacre the unarmed British-Americans as they depart Fort William Henry. The all-too-civilized French "were attentive but silent observers of the proceedings of the vanquished" and offer no assistance to their ill-fated enemies.[14] During the ensuing melee, Magua "tore [a] screaming infant" from its mother, "dashed the head of the infant against a rock," and "mercifully drove his tomahawk in [the mother's] brain."[15] The unambiguous characterization of French complicity with Magua's savagery displays Cooper's range of social-stratification from the colonial British-Americans to the noble-savage Mohicans, the over-civilized French, and the savage-savage Hurons, each decreasing incrementally in eminence. Thus, Cooper's mythopoetic novels narrativize the disappearance of the noble savages, the titular tribe, as a tragic but necessary price of preparing the continent for civilization.

Gothic

Even as novelists like Brown and Cooper poured the elements of gothic fiction into the mold of the American frontier, the transatlantic crosscurrents of literature in English facilitated the interpenetration of traditions that shaped early zombie texts. One of the more notable examples is Mary Shelley's *Frankenstein*, discussed in Bishop's *American Zombie Gothic*.[16] While Shelley did not describe Frankenstein's monster as a zombie and by most definitions is not one, he does share many of the same characteristics. He was crafted from the flesh of the dead, and he is perceived as an unnatural creature that threatens society. In addition to Shelley, H.P. Lovecraft is often cited as influential in the formation of the genre even though only a few of his stories involve creatures that approximate zombies. The few that do include "Herbert West—Reanimator," "Cool Air," "In the Vault," "The Outsider," "Pickman's Model," and "The Thing on the Doorstep." Of these, "Herbert West" proves most relevant. As Bishop asserts in *American Zombie Gothic*, early zombie films and texts rely heavily on gothic tropes and narratives. While there may not be definitive proof that Seabrook read Lovecraft's "Herbert West," published just seven years before *The Magic Island*, he was no stranger to pulp tabloids. Seabrook edited the short-lived pulp magazine

Sensation published by King Features Syndicate and included in both issues a serialized reprint of his "Astounding Secrets of the Devil Worshiper's Mystic Love Cult," which originally appeared as a 12-part series in *Indianapolis Star*. The derivative nature of pulp fiction assures us that elements of his story would have been floating around rather loosely. Lovecraft's story, subsequently adapted into several self-proclaimed zombie films, utilizes the pre-existing gothic symbols that zombies were sculpted to inhabit.[17]

Originally serialized in the magazine *Home Brew* in 1922, Lovecraft organized "Herbert West" into six parts and included numerous references to Shelley's *Frankenstein*—the diary-like frame is the most obvious. However, the connection to Shelley is less meaningful than the story's deployment of gothic tropes that prefigure *The Magic Island* and *White Zombie*. The story itself is told from the point of view of an unnamed narrator, who is both a friend and colleague of the medical researcher Herbert West. West has an unrelenting interest in immortality and, throughout the story, performs a series of experiments on corpses in an attempt to, as the title suggests, reanimate them. His efforts are met with varying degrees of success. Each creature West resurrects proves violent, and readers repeatedly bear witness to the dangers of scientific curiosity. In the context of popular literary tradition, Lovecraft evinces a reversal of Brown. While western fiction did not disappear altogether, the close of the geographic frontier indicated that the boundary between civilization and savagery had moved elsewhere. For this particular story as well as many films from the atomic era of zombies in the 1950s, the unexplored frontiers of human knowledge relocated to science. Thus, West's forays into chemistry reflect Montcalm's imprudent faith in the Hurons.

Throughout the story, West obstinately dismisses the metaphysical implications of his experiments, whereas the narrator expresses tentative curiosity about the afterlife. In Part I, titled "From the Dark," the narrator observes, "Holding with Haeckel that all life is a chemical and physical process, and that the so-called 'soul' is a myth, my friend believed that artificial reanimation of the dead can depend only on the condition of the tissues."[18] The primary concern for West is necrosis and the effects of deterioration on the corpse when mental activity is restored. Acknowledging West's conspicuous hubris, his dismissal of the soul conversely awakens the reader's curiosity to the subject. By abandoning his own scientific principles, the narrator encourages the reader to pursue this inquiry. He muses, "I wondered what sights this placid youth might have seen in inaccessible spheres, and what he could relate if fully restored to life."[19] This observation foreshadows what transpires when West and the narrator reanimate their first corpse. Despite all his previous concessions to West's expertise, the following description relies on language colored with supernatural and spiritual tones. Lovecraft writes,

> when from the pitch-black room we had left there burst the most appalling and daemoniac succession of cries that either of us had ever heard. Not more unutterable could have been the chaos of hellish sound if the pit itself had opened to release the agony of the damned, for in one inconceivable cacophony was centred [sic] all the supernatural terror and unnatural despair of animate nature. Human it could not have been—it is not in man to make such sounds—and without a thought of our late employment or its possible discovery both West and I leaped to the nearest window like stricken animals; overturning tubes, lamp, and retorts, and vaulting madly into the starred abyss of the rural night.[20]

The words "daemoniac," "chaos," "hellish," "supernatural terror," and "abyss" suggest that the results of their experiment extend beyond the limits of the physical world. Contrary to what readers might anticipate, the narrator (and West presumably) care nothing for what that might mean other than to fear for their lives. West refuses to and seems incapable of acknowledging the moral consequences of his actions. Furthermore, the unimaginable savage nature of the creature causes even the humanist medical scientists to reach for metaphysical descriptors to identify and resolve the contradiction of the existence of a creature that has no precedent in their field of research. There is no reference to Haiti, Vodou, or any other non–Western system of beliefs, but the horror caused by the realization of its existence presages audience's experience of watching films like *White Zombie*.

While West and the narrator begin their investigations of death and reanimation in college, the pursuit continues throughout their professional careers. They take advantage of a typhoid epidemic to secure more bodies for their research. Although each attempt is more successful, they never realize the outcome of producing a fully-functioning socialized human. The appeal of Lovecraft's horripilating prose rests on his enumeration of the uncanny valley. Lovecraft's undead approximate humans except for the marked absence of consciousness. Moreover, their savagery resembles Cooper's Hurons, creating the possibility for future zombie texts to white-wash or deracialize frontier fiction by repopulating the landscape with zombies. Like most zombie works, Lovecraft's undead are intent on destruction and take a particular interest in human life. According to the narrator, the second successful attempt to reanimate a corpse results in a massacre more horrible than the typhoid epidemic. Lovecraft writes, "That same night saw the beginning of the second Arkham horror—the horror that to me eclipsed the plague itself. Christchurch Cemetery was the scene of a terrible killing; a watchman having been clawed to death in a manner not only too hideous for description, but raising a doubt as to the human agency of the deed."[21] This quotation affirms that these creatures lack personhood despite their corporeal bodies, and it shows their capacity and preoccupation with attacking humans. The narrator continues by describing the undead's rampage through town, entering eight houses and leaving "seventeen maimed and shapeless remnants of bodies" behind.[22]

In addition to these creatures' savagery, they also exhibit a capacity for revenge demonstrated by their straightforward pursuit of West. The final act relates how one reanimated corpse breaks into an asylum to recruit more of West's experiments to join in the hunt for West. While this does suggest that the undead have some consciousness and self-awareness, albeit severely limited, their savage nature differentiates them from civilized humans. Their actions also resonate with various descriptions of the effect of salt on zombies in the anthropological work of Zora Neale Hurston and Wade Davis. Both reported that the consumption of or exposure to salt would reawaken a zombie, making it self-conscious of its condition. According to Hurston, this would simply restore them to their former state of being.[23] Whereas in *Passage of Darkness*, Davis describes how salt triggers a moment of self-awareness, but, instead of returning to their former state, the former zombie would go on a killing spree first targeting the person who afflicted them.[24] This latter description precisely reproduces the condition and attitude of the undead in Lovecraft's story. Although some of the creatures initially kill at random, once they learn that West conducted the experiments, they target him alone. When the creatures disembowel West, the narrator, present at the scene, is spared merely to bear witness.

While the problem of killing the undead is not central to Lovecraft's story, it proves to be a distinctive characteristic of the genre. Most contemporary zombie films employ a definition scene early in the narrative to establish some ground rules. Although the scene takes place much later in "Herbert West," Lovecraft does highlight the inefficacy of guns. At the end of the section titled "Six Shots by Midnight," West attempts to kill one of the reanimated corpses by shooting it repeatedly with a revolver. Lovecraft writes, "Despite the obvious danger of attracting notice and bringing down on our heads the dreaded police investigation—a thing which after all was mercifully averted by the relative isolation of our cottage—my friend suddenly, excitedly, and unnecessarily emptied all six chambers of his revolver into the nocturnal visitor."[25] Lovecraft uses the term "unnecessarily" because the bullets are ineffective. West most likely resorts to using a gun, because in the previous section a firearm was used to subdue one of the undead. It did not kill the creature but facilitated their escape. Similarly, a crowd of police and citizens fired on one of the undead before they "dressed its wound and carted it to the asylum at Sefton."[26] While these are only two instances, no creatures are ever successfully killed in the story, if killed is even the right word.

Another quality of Lovecraft's undead later codified in the zombie lore is cannibalism. In the contemporary Romero-esque narratives, cannibalism is the motivating force of zombies, and it is the vehicle by which more zombies are created. Lovecraft's use of cannibalism is unique for several reasons. First, as stated above, there is no threat of viral outbreak. Corpses are only resurrected by injecting West's serum. Secondly, not all undead are cannibals. While all exhibit a violent nature, only one eats human flesh. Despite my assertion that relocating the frontier to science allows for writers to deracialize colonization, creating that as a possibility does not amount to a guarantee. The only character identified as non-white also happens to be the only cannibal. Lovecraft writes, "He was a loathsome, gorilla-like thing, with abnormally long arms which I could not help calling fore legs, and a face that conjured up thoughts of unspeakable Congo secrets and tom-tom poundings under an eerie moon."[27] Feeling a certain responsibility for reanimating this creature and out of fear that he might lead to their discovery, the narrator and West hunt him down. When they do eventually dispatch him, he is described as "a glassy-eyed, ink-black apparition nearly on all fours, covered with bits of mould, leaves, and vines, foul with caked blood, and having between its glistening teeth a snow-white, terrible, cylindrical object terminating in a tiny hand."[28] As unsettling as Lovecraft's racism is, this example illustrates two points. First, it shows that cannibalism was an act these creatures did perform. Second, it reaffirms that ontological difference was a defining characteristic of how Lovecraft chose to represent them. The antithesis of civilization and the most extreme example of savagery imaginable to Lovecraft would be an African whose reanimation unleashes cannibalism directed at children—a human without humanity. Over the years, racist narratives have plagued the zombie genre, and this example illustrates the literary provenance of those abusive texts. When the zombies of Haitian folklore were introduced to the national consciousness, these are the creatures that defined their representation.

Furthermore, examining Lovecraft discloses the zombie as a semiotic container that could be refigured and redeployed as a placeholder for the colonial other inhabiting the frontier in whatever form might be needed. In Lovecraft, we see that the very symbol of cannibalism that dehumanized native Africans and functioned to resolve the contradiction of slavery in the sixteenth century persisted through popular literature even until it was refigured to represent African descendants in Haiti. While the savagery of Cooper's Hurons does not quite reach the height of cannibalism,

Magua's act of crushing an infant's head on a rock comes close. Together these works exemplify the kind of artifacts Seabrook would have found in the cultural recycling center of American fiction from which he obtained the materials to produce his representation of the Haitian zombie.

Haiti

Alongside the literary context, we also need to consider the political context. A series of dictators ruled Haiti throughout the nineteenth century, and its citizens continued to suffer under each regime despite the success of the Haitian revolution. The U.S. government had been interested in Haiti for decades prior to its occupation as a potential naval base. Diplomatic and defense officials valued Haiti's stability and feared that volatility might result in foreign rule. In 1868, President Andrew Johnson suggested the annexation of the island of Hispaniola, made up of Haiti and the Dominican Republic, to secure a U.S. defensive and economic claim in the West Indies. Since that time, the U.S. remained preoccupied with the region and sought on several occasions to establish footholds, including efforts like the takeover of the Panama Canal in 1904.[29]

In the early 1900s, the political situation deteriorated. In the seven years leading up to the occupation in 1915, there were at least seven different presidents of Haiti; these shifts in power were violent and included assassinations and forced exiles. The last of these presidents was Jean Vilbrun Guillaume Sam, who proved to be yet another controversial figure and a victim of political assassination. Sam openly supported the U.S. and its involvement in the region. However, Rosalvo Bobo and other wealthy Haitian political elites objected to Sam's pro–U.S. stance. In July of 1915, Sam executed 167 political prisoners, inciting a revolt resulting in his assassination. With the death of this powerful American ally, President Woodrow Wilson ordered the invasion using the naval forces under the command of Rear Admiral William B. Caperton, who had been occupying the region for nearly a year. The U.S. justified the action by citing increased instability and a fear that Germany might take advantage of this opportunity to establish a military base in Haiti.[30]

Communication between Counselor of State Robert Lansing and President Woodrow Wilson explicitly details an interpretation of the Monroe Doctrine that dismisses the sovereignty of Caribbean nations in favor of U.S. national interests and security. In a memorandum dated June 11, 1914, Lansing advises Wilson, clarifying that the Monroe Doctrine "is not a Pan-American policy. The opposition to European control over American territory is not primarily to preserve the integrity of any American state—that may be a result but not a purpose of the Doctrine. The essential idea is to prevent a condition which would menace the national interests of the United States."[31] Lansing's interpretation proved to be more than mere rhetoric. When U.S. Marines officially occupied Haiti to provide political stability after the assassination of Haitian President Sam, Lansing sought Wilson's approval for a treaty with Haiti to retroactively indemnify the ongoing occupation; bear in mind that U.S. Marines had an unofficial presence prior to President Sam's assassination. With sobering clarity, Lansing, now Secretary of State, writes, "I confess that this method of negotiation, with our marines policing the Haytien Capital, is high handed. It does not meet my sense of a nation's sovereign rights and is more or less an exercise of force and an invasion of Haytien independence." Far beyond the paternalist imperialism that marked the post–Roosevelt Corollary Monroe Doctrine, Lansing proceeds to state that the treaty legalizing the occupation "will be welcomed by the better element of Haytien people" who are unable to speak for themselves "on account of the danger of assassination massacre." Lansing asserts that the Haitian revolutionaries do not "represent in any way the people of Haiti." Here Lansing assumes that he knows what Haitians think and takes responsibility to act on their behalf, which seems like an about face from previous statements. But sentiment for Haitians gives way to the underlying goal. He continues, "The only possible way, it seems to me of restoring to the Haytiens their political and personal rights [...] is to obtain control, for a time at least, of the prize which these chieftains seek, namely, the public revenues of the Republic." Control of such revenues would ensure that U.S. investors would be repaid for their loans to Haiti. To which President Wilson offered the brief reply: "This is, I think, necessary and has my approval. Do you think it will affect Latin American opinion unfavorably."[32] Two years later that same treaty had to be renewed and updated.

At the time of the invasion, Franklin D. Roosevelt served as Assistant Secretary of the Navy under Wilson. In a memorandum from 1922, Roosevelt elaborated on this rationale:

> The story of Hayti prior to the landing of American Marines in 1915 is a story of almost unbelievable butchery and barbarism, which, if told in its entirety, would shock every person in the civilized world. [...] From those days down to 1915 the history of Hayti is the blackest spot in all the Americas. Presidents and Emperors succeeded each other in rapid succession. Their going was usually accomplished by murder and the slaughter of thousands. The result was that when 1915 came the inhabitants of Hayti, taken as a mass, were little more than primitive savages, living in mud and wattle huts, skillfully concealed in the underbrush.[33]

Much to his chagrin, a century later every person from the so-called civilized world reading Roosevelt's memorandum is likely horrified by his sentiments. As a counterpoint to the pretext offered by Roosevelt, Hans Schmidt reminds us that between 1909 and 1914 France endured eleven governments. From 1862 when the United States officially recognized Haiti as a nation to the start of the occupation in 1915, an equal number of presidents were assassinated in the United States and Haiti.[34] Robert Tombs elaborates on the instability of France in that era. He writes, "Since 1789 there have been three monarchies, two empires, five republics, and fifteen constitutions. Every head of state from 1814 to 1873 spent part of his life in exile. Every regime was the target of assassination attempts of a frequency that put Spanish and Russian politics in the shade. Even in peaceful times governments changed every few months. In less peaceful times, political deaths, imprisonments and deportations are literally incalculable."[35] These comparisons provide insight about the hubris of American exceptionalism. During his 1920 vice presidential campaign, Roosevelt famously asserted, "You know I have had something to do with the running of a couple little republics. The facts are that I wrote Haiti's Constitution myself, and if I do say it, I think it a pretty good Constitution."[36] To be clear, I don't include this quotation from Roosevelt to vilify the future president who would in fact end the occupation. Rather, Roosevelt's remarks are indicative of his paternalistic imperialism that characterized U.S. political attitudes and policy in the Caribbean. Reluctance among Haitian officials stalled talks to renegotiate the U.S.-Haitian treaty to extend the occupation for an additional twenty years. Brigadier General Eli Cole, commander of all Marines stationed in Haiti, filed a report stating, "To get the results desired, all that is necessary in my opinion, is for our Government to state positively that present conditions demand the extension at this time: if one government does not accede to the proposition, then another Government that will can be installed."[37] If statements like these seem surprising to modern readers, we should remember this would not have been the case in 1920. Haiti had long inhabited a subaltern status in the U.S. political consciousness. When governor of Virginia and future president James Monroe posed the question—what to do about the slaves convicted in Gabriel's Conspiracy—in a letter to sitting President Thomas Jefferson, Jefferson wrote back "nature seems to have formed these islands [the West Indies] to become the receptacle of the blacks transplanted into this hemisphere." He adds, "the island of St. Domingo" is the best option because they've already "organized themselves under regular laws & government."[38] Michael West and William Martin go so far as to describe the occupation as "payback for the revolution against slavery" and "Jefferson's revenge."[39] These anecdotes illustrate the imbrication of overlapping histories determining the political moment and stress the inherent incompleteness of my brief contextualization.

According to film critic Glenn Kay, Sam's massacre of the political prisoners and his subsequent assassination drew the attention of the American consciousness and created an audience for the stories that the occupying Marines would bring home and share with the public. Kay states, "While U.S. forces were responsible for overseeing construction of roads and telephone cables, medical care, and educational programs, their treatment of the locals bred deep bitterness. Naturally, the citizens resented being occupied. The Americans, in turn, exhibited racist attitudes toward black and mixed-race Haitians, and many of the well-educated locals were treated with disdain."[40] The animosity between the Haitians and the occupying Marines contributed to an already increasing distrust of Haitians by Americans. Examining the lens through which Americans viewed their Caribbean neighbors, J. Michael Dash asserts that "Haiti is filtered into America's consciousness" in the form of four stereotypes: "the rebellious body, the repulsive body, the seductive body, and the sick body."[41] To no one's surprise, Dash's stereotypes could be readily transformed into a schema that categorizes the entire spectrum of zombie representations in popular media. It is from this literary, political, and cultural context that *The Magic Island* was written.

Prior to *The Magic Island*, the word zombie and the concept it calls to mind existed independent of one another in the English language. The word zombie appears earlier in English in George Cable's 1886 essay "Creole Slave Songs" in reference to a powerful deity that inhabits the form of a snake.[42] Other scholars identify Lafcadio Hearn's 1889 *Harper's Magazine* essay "The Country of the Comers-Back" possibly because of its promising title. However, the zombie is not described as a reanimated corpse but an ethereal spirit. On the other hand, a sorcerer in Captain Mayne Reid's novel *Maroon: A Tale of Voodoo and Obeah* uses witchcraft to bring himself back to life but does not associate that act with the word zombie. Thus, Seabrook's 1929 travelogue distinguishes itself as the first published work in English to use the term as we conceive of it today.[43]

Magic Island

Born in 1844, Seabrook was a journalist and travel writer. He spent time abroad in France in the American Field Service in 1915, and from there he continued traveling and writing about his adventures. Seabrook was particularly interested in various religious practices around the world. This interest led him to developing a friendship with Aleister Crowley, the famed occultist and mystic, and it became the preoccupying focus of his travelogues. Before venturing into the Caribbean, Seabrook published the book *Adventures in Arabia: Among the Bedouins, Druses, Whirling Dervishes and Yezidee Devil Worshipers* detailing his travels to the region in 1924. Five years later, Seabrook published *The Magic Island*, the first popular text about Vodou and Haiti in English. Although Seabrook appears to be genuinely curious about Haitian folklore, it is clear that he capitalizes on the increased interest in Haitian culture and romanticizes his travels to appeal to his audience. Moreover, in one of the opening chapters, Seabrook takes time to lay out the subject-position of Vodou and its gods in relationship to Christianity. As a comfort to his western audience, Seabrook assures his readers that during the Christian Holy Week the Haitian gods are cast aside in honor of Jesus. He describes a "Voodoo altar" where "all its sacred objects, Christian and pagan together, were stripped from it on the evening of Good Friday, laid as if dead in rows before it upon the ground and covered over with palm fronds until the Easter resurrection morn."[44] Seabrook continues, "During Golgotha's tragedy, even the great Voodoo serpent-god Damballa must bow his hooded head."[45] While he likely included such observations to mollify his readers, the inaccuracy not only misrepresents but also impoverishes Haitian beliefs in relation to Christianity. This quotation from early in the text typifies the subaltern representation of Vodou in *The Magic Island*. Motivated to write this travelogue by his own fascination in the occult, Seabrook does not approach Haitian culture on its own terms but relegates it to a species of novel curiosity.

Much of the contemporary scholarship emplots the zombies within a historical narrative of slavery and emancipation. Although Seabrook never quite uses the term slave, he first introduces undead to the reader as unpaid workers by relating a story furnished by his part-time servant, part-time fixer Constant Polynice. Polynice explains that in 1918 there was a great need for hired hands to work an unexpectedly productive cane crop. The story includes a black headman named Ti Joseph "leading a band of ragged creatures who shuffled along behind him, staring dumbly, like people walking in a daze [...] they still stared, vacant-eyed like cattle, and made no reply when asked to give their names."[46] Afraid that it might create problems if the "dead creatures" were recognized by their relatives, Ti Joseph sent them to work the fields away from the factory and the other hired hands.[47] Thus, in this seminal account of zombies, the creatures inhabit the status of slaves. In addition, they are described as slow, shuffling cattle devoid of consciousness and personal identity. Excluding the more recent manifestations of fast zombies, this description distills their most common characteristics across fiction and film. Moreover, when Seabrook uses the word cattle, he inaugurates a long tradition of zombies that move like animals in herds. Polynice further explains that these zombies "must never be permitted to taste salt or meat. So the food [...] was tasteless and unseasoned."[48] Although Polynice neglects to explain why this avoidance of salt is necessary, Seabrook later discloses that "as the *zombies* tasted the salt, they knew that they were dead and made a dreadful outcry and arose and turned their faces toward the mountain."[49] Perhaps more docile than Cooper's Magua and Lovecraft's undead, this shadowy description of upturned faces and the accompanying line drawings by Alexander King evoke the "midnight murder" and "tom-tom poundings under an eerie moon" of those earlier works. This effect of consuming salt is not a common one, but it does create the possibility of reawakening, a pivotal element to the plot of Halperin's film which borrows heavily from Seabrook's travelogue.

Because zombies exist primarily in a corporeal sense and are uniquely absent of a spiritual nature, film quickly became the standard medium of zombie texts as it visually portrayed that which audiences were afraid to imagine. Film also emphasizes the physicality of zombies. In the zombie fiction anthology *Zombies: The Recent Dead*, David Schow asserts that "they [zombies] are also one of the first monster archetypes to spring from cinematic rather than literary roots."[50] Schow's remark illustrates the primacy of zombie films in terms of both popularity and influence. Therefore, to better understand early representations of zombies including those that borrow closely from Haitian beliefs, I will turn to the film *White Zombie*. Not only is it the first feature-length Hollywood zombie film, but also it shamelessly appropriates Seabrook's travelogue and collapses the opposing poles of national identity into a single antagonist.

White Zombie

The 1932 film directed by Halperin features two protagonists: Madeleine Short, played by Madge Bellamy, and her fiancé Neil Parker, played by John Harron. In the opening scene, they arrive in Haiti and travel by coach to Charles Beaumont's estate to get married. It is later revealed that Beaumont, a wealthy French banker and plantation owner, met Short on the boat to Haiti and offered his estate as a venue for their ceremony. On the coach-ride, zombies make their first appearance in the film. Short, Parker, and the coachman observe the silhouettes of workers in the field, marked by their awkward blundering movements. Film scholars such as Gary Rhodes point out the influence of King's artwork in *The Magic Island* in this and other scenes.[51] Out of fear, the coachman hastily drives to Beaumont's estate. Infatuated with Short, Beaumont seeks out Murder

Legendre, a Vodou master played by Béla Lugosi who runs a sugar mill operated by zombies. Legendre provides Beaumont with a powder that Beaumont later uses to turn Short into a zombie. The powder appears to kill Short, and she is buried soon after. Understanding the true effects of the powder, Beaumont and Legendre disinter Short and raise her as a zombie to become Beaumont's love slave. Mourning the loss of his new bride, Parker goes off drinking. When he finally learns that his wife's tomb is empty, Parker turns to Dr. Bruner, the local missionary who married the couple, for help. Bruner pieces together what happened, and the two go to Legendre's estate which sits high on the coastal cliffs. Beaumont also goes to Legendre's estate because he is unhappy with his docile zombie. He solicits Legendre's help to return Short to her former state, but Legendre betrays Beaumont and drugs him with the powder. In a dramatic conclusion, Bruner knocks Legendre unconscious, which relinquishes his control over his zombies including Beaumont and Short. Realizing that he was betrayed, Beaumont takes revenge on Legendre by casting him off the cliffs into the sea and immediately follows. In effect, Beaumont's actions paraphrase the reanimated corpses in the final scene of Lovecraft's story.

As I noted earlier, Halperin borrows directly from *The Magic Island*. Two of the locations described in the travelogue are set pieces in the film. The opening scene depicting the zombies off in the distance working the fields recalls the story Polynice related to Seabrook when he described "these dead men and women walking single file in the twilight."[52] The second location is the scene set in Legendre's sugar mill, which resembles the Hasco (Haitian-American Sugar Company) factory described in *The Magic Island*. According to Seabrook, the Hasco factory is filled with modern machinery that frightens the zombies with its "din and smoke."[53] Consequently, in Halperin's film, the sugar mill is absent of machinery, and zombies operate a multi-person wheel to grind the sugar cane. In addition to using these locations, the most direct and obvious borrowing is the dialogue. After Short's supposed death, Parker and Bruner discuss what has occurred, and Bruner offers a description of zombies strikingly similar to Seabrook's. Like Seabrook, he also quotes Article 249 of the Haitian Penal Code: "The use of drugs or other practices which produce lethargic coma, or lifeless sleep, shall be considered attempted murder."[54] The significance of this borrowing is two-fold. First, it reaffirms Seabrook's text as the primary source for defining the representation of zombies in American film and literature. Second, it popularizes and solidifies this particularization as an authentic portrayal for derivative works like Halperin's follow-up film *Revolt of the Zombies* as well as the many zombie films that appear in its wake over the next few decades, including Jacques Tourneur's 1943 *I Walked with a Zombie*.[55]

White Zombie also trades on the popularity of hypnotism and mesmerism. There is no indication that Mooney's ethnography or his attribution of ghost dance visions and other religious phenomena influenced Halperin or the film's screenwriter Garnett Weston. Nevertheless, these ideas permeated scholarly and demotic discourse in the early twentieth century and appealed to writers of both fiction and nonfiction. We should not forget Sigmund Freud's own forays into hypnosis. Mooney would not be the first humanities scholar to appropriate psychoanalysis for his own research. More to the point, the film borrows directly from both fiction and nonfiction. Rhodes cites George Du Maurier's novel *Trilby* and its two film adaptations, and popular books on hypnotism and mesmerism that Halperin and Weston would have been familiar with. The influence of these works ranges from the general—the cinematographic emphasis on Legosi's trademark gaze simulating mesmerism and the *evil eye*—to the more particularized—reusing plot devices and adapting and restaging scenes from the fictional works.[56] In fact, we need look no further than the film's promotional art that almost exclusively feature Legendre's horripilating stare. In these posters, Legendre is frequently depicted gazing down at Short's lifeless, supine form. Some amplify the insinuated power of his gaze by including bolts of light that shoot from his eyes into her body or, when Short is absent, directly into the implied viewer of the poster.

Racial Aporia

Understanding the characters of Beaumont and Legendre is central to unpacking the conflict that drives the narrative. Beaumont, as a civilized man, is incapable of independently enthralling Short, but his considerable wealth gives him access to people like Legendre. In the film, the act of creating zombies and the person who controls them is a signifier for the threat that Haitian culture poses. As the film illustrates, neither those with the power to create zombies (Legendre) nor those with the will to use them (Beaumont) are to be trusted. Even when Beaumont atones for his crimes by killing Legendre, there is no place for him in society. Because of his relation to the savage other, he, like Uncas, must die. Halperin's film warns audiences of the helplessness of women and demonstrates that even white men are susceptible to the lure of the exotic. Ironically, the narrative condemns those who seek power from Vodou yet derives its own power from exploiting Haitian culture.

Film scholars disagree about Legendre's race. Because he is not a zombie, this may seem to have little bearing on the present discussion of the film's influence on the genre. Nevertheless, it remains contested and proves pivotal to many critical examinations. If we are to read zombification as a metaphor for slavery, then the race of whomever exerts authority over the undead will potentially reveal the mythopoetic function of the film's narrative. Jennifer Fay advocates reading Legendre as white because his role is performed by Lugosi, known to audiences for his role as the titular character in *Dracula* released just one year prior to *White Zombie*. She argues that his whiteness functions as a symbol for the European aristocracy.[57] Her interpretation enables comparison to the national identity narratives of John Winthrop, Theodore Roosevelt, etc., and characters like Cooper's Montcalm who enunciate or embody the decay of the overcivilized. And like Montcalm, Legendre's power comes from his alliance with the savage other. Situating this within the myth of national identity, the narrative reminds audiences of the importance the errand as a ritual of renewal. Although rarely cited, Tony Williams makes a compelling argument about the nationality of a different character, Beaumont. Despite Beaumont's British accent and plantation wealth, Williams reminds the reader that he is "still North American." As such, Beaumont incarnates the film's warning of overcivilization.[58] Conversely, in the essay titled "The Sub-Subaltern Monster" Bishop argues that Legendre performs blackness through his actions. In his words, "Legendre is ethnically part of Haiti," and Bishop reminds readers of the "Hollywood practice of casting white actors in black roles."[59] Bishop's alternative interpretation allows us to read *White Zombie* as a captivity narrative that follows from the early American literary tradition emerging from Mary Rowlandson's account from 1682. Legendre then inhabits the role of the savage other that threatens civilization. Similar to the function of Legendre's whiteness, his blackness fulfills the conditions for producing a colonial errand, but it does so for entirely different reasons. The captivity narrative operates much like the U.S. policy of so-called "imperial anticolonialism," which justifies colonization as a prudent defensive posturing.[60] Gyllian Phillips offers a third option proposing that Legendre is creole, and his racial ambiguity is deliberate. Although she offers several convincing arguments in support of this claim, the most interesting for our purposes is Legendre's name. She writes, "The effect of his putative name obviously combines the threat of death (Murder) with the effects of legend (Legendre), and the taint of French creole. The effect of his actual nameless status is to make him into an open signifier, ready to accrue whatever meaning is plastered on to him."[61] Personally, I like Phillips' reading best because it synergizes with the Montcalm comparison even more strongly than nonspecific whiteness, but in the end it does not really matter.

Before I completely lose my reader with all this, perhaps exasperating, equivocation, I would like to expand on Phillips' observation about Legendre as an open signifier by returning to Roland Barthes from the introduction of this book. As Barthes shows, the symbols of myth are of a second order semiology; the signifier is simultaneously empty and full.[62] The fullness refers to the meaning always already embedded in the narrative structure, what Barthes calls the form. The emptiness refers to the particularized content of the myth, what Barthes calls the concept. He writes, "Let us now look at the signified: this history which drains out of the form will be wholly absorbed by the concept. As for the latter, it is determined, it is at once historical and intentional; it is the motivation which causes the myth to be uttered."[63] He continues, "Unlike the form, the concept is in no way abstract: it is filled with a situation. Through the concept, it is a whole new history which is implanted in the myth."[64] Thus, it is the organizing structure of myth that gives history its meaning. Because the historical content is essentially interchangeable and the meaning is preestablished, the audience, the national community, recognizes how to interpret the content even before the events themselves are fully disclosed. Audience is perhaps a poor choice of words because it implies passivity, when in fact the national community actively participates in the production the myth. Consequently, the signifying structure contains the meaning and allows for the redeployment of myth across space and time, so that each individual within the nation can see themselves reflected within the whole. From this we come to recognize the necessary plasticity of the signifier and the signified. In terms of the film, the racial and cultural identity of Legendre depends more upon the situatedness of the filmgoer than it does the factual evidence provided by the film. A signifier unimpeded by too much specificity is more useful and will resonate with a broader audience. Recalling the regional instantiations of Daniel Boone, myth allows disparate members of a community to identify with a specular image that reflects a homogenous national identity. It is no surprise then that Williams begins his analysis of *White Zombie* with the observation that "once the U.S. won its own West, its accompanying historical, territorial policies began to extend into the Caribbean."[65] *White Zombie* is then understood as the manifestation of the frontier myth relocated to Haiti. It is a move presaged by Cody's decision to update his Wild West show by replace the battle re-enactment of Little Big Horn with San Juan Hill.

Incarnation of the Zombie in Fiction

From their Hollywood debut in Seabrook's travelogue and Halperin's film, zombies exhibit two characteristics that become indissolubly bound to future depictions of the undead. These are, of course, their subject position as mindless slaves and their latent potential to usurp or seek vengeance upon their master. In the film, becoming a zombie represents a threat to personal agency impoverishing the victim's mental faculties and making them subservient to the will of the zombie master. After she undergoes the ritual of zombification, Short, the film's titular *White Zombie*, serves as a love slave to Beaumont and then Legendre. Like the zombie workers operating the sugar mill, Short has no will of her own and submits wholly to the whims of her master. Although the details manifest differently, the awakened zombie's desire for revenge also recurs in each text, including Lovecraft's short story. According to Seabrook the taste of salt or meat triggers self-consciousness among the living dead. While salt is not used in the film, the blow that knocks Legendre unconscious produces a similar effect Short and Beaumont wake from their zombie state. Fueled by rage Beaumont turns against Legendre and, at the cost of his own life, hurls them both over a cliff.

The notion of zombie either as slave or as revolutionary preponderates fictional representations and to a greater extent academic scholarship. In truth, it would be more difficult to identify films that do not accommodate one or both. George Romero's *Living Dead* films persist as the genre's cinematic archetype and forward a not-so-subtle critique of consumerism that embodies the revolutionary across the entire series. Each film, however, uniquely elaborates on that subtext to varying degrees so that both qualities appear frequently. Many film critics have long observed the racial implications of Romero's inaugural zombie film, *Night of the Living Dead*. A group of strangers take refuge in a farmhouse for the night, relying on one another to endure a zombie attack. When Ben, who happens to be black, emerges from the house as the lone survivor, he is shot dead by his would-be rescuers, a self-appointed all-white militia. Admittedly, this is an example of "black abstraction" where, as Elizabeth McAlister states, "black characters in mainstream cinema have always been made to signify both less and more than themselves."[66] Associating the scene with slavery and lynch mobs is practically unavoidable. *Dawn of the Dead* fully elaborates the consumerism subtext with the infamous shopping mall setting where zombies return to aimlessly wander through stores, and *Land of the Dead* extends or concentrates the critique with its proletariat revolution narrative where the underprivileged living unite with the living dead to overthrow the wealthy elite antagonist. Although these are only a few examples, the broad appeal of Romero's films and his defining role in what constitutes canon ensured that the subsequent half-century of zombie texts, film or otherwise, emerged out of his shadow.

Incarnation of the Zombie in Academia

Importantly, these characteristics prove equally ubiquitous in twentieth-century anthropology beginning with Melville Herskovits, and they continue to shape contemporary inquiries across academic disciplines. Even though the methods, ethics, and efficacy of these studies have been investigated, calling into question the reliability of the facts and conclusions drawn from them, the sedimentation of even discredited scholarship nevertheless had its hand in producing the available discourse from which we continue to work. In 1937, Herskovits inaugurates the tradition of reassessing Haitian folklore in the wake of Seabrook's travelogue with his book-length study *Life in a Haitian Valley*. Herskovits does not, in fact, expend much energy on discussing the zombie or acknowledging the extent of Seabrook's influence on popular culture.[67] After explaining that an individual may be murdered through sorcery, he writes, "On occasion, an apparent death is felt not to be a real death, but rather the simulacre of death brought about by the machination of a sorcerer." To turn the false death into a real one, the zombie must be stabbed from behind "in order that the corpse as slave of the sorcerer may not reveal who had stabbed him when summoned."[68] Notably, the single footnote for this description mentions two sources: Seabrook and Elsie Parsons. Herskovits uses the footnote to criticize Seabrook's profiteering motives and to reference borrowing from Parsons' creole transcriptions of zombie accounts from interviews with Haitians.[69] Because Parsons' transcriptions detail the process of zombification and not its cultural implications,[70] the skeptic in me assumes that Herskovits indeed relied upon Seabrook, at least in part, for this content such as the use of the term slave. However, I must admit the more responsible interpretation is to trust that Herskovits indeed drew upon his own unpublished field notes from his three-month stay in Mirebalais, Haiti, in 1934 to produce his description.[71]

Published only one year after Herskovits' monograph, Hurston's provocative and controversial ethnography *Tell My Horse* sits uncomfortably between the sensationalism of Seabrook and the seriousness of Herskovits. In a chapter unrelated to zombies, she states that "William Seabrook in his *Magic Island* fired my imagination with his account of The White King of La Gonave."[72] Although her declaration does not include reference to zombies, such an admission anywhere in the text suggests that his writing would have entered her thoughts when drafting other portions of the book. When Hurston addresses the topic of zombies, she offers three occasions for their creation: the need for labor, revenge upon a laborer, and payment for a spiritual debt.[73] The first two align precisely with types of descriptions already provided, but the third is something of an anomaly that does not reappear in other research, at least not to my knowledge. Unlike other writers, Hurston is the first to claim that she met and photographed a zombie. The image of this zombie, identified as Felicia Felix-Mentor, is included in her book. According to Hurston, Felix-Mentor, a wife and mother, reportedly died in 1907. Twenty-nine years later, she was found wandering naked on a farm claiming that it was her former home. Her brother and husband confirmed her identity, and she was institutionalized at the hospital in Gonaives. It was at the hospital that Hurston met Felix-Mentor and investigated her story.[74] What is perhaps most striking about Hurston's narrative is that she does not attribute the case of Felix-Mentor to any of the uses or indications for zombies that she previously identifies. Her erratic behavior along with the fact of her institutionalization make it unlikely that she served as a laborer even during the twenty-nine-year absence. If we are to accept Hurston's views on zombification and her account of Felix-Mentor, then we are led to believe that she was a sacrifice to the spirits or that unaccounted-for rationales for zombies exist.

Two additional ethnographies warrant inclusion in this bibliography of zombie anthropology, Katherine Dunham's *Island Possessed* and Maya Deren's *Divine Horsemen*. As dancers, choreographers, and scholars, they shared much in common including an interest in Haitian dance and ritual. Dunham hired Deren for a managerial position in her dance company in 1941. Deren toured with them for a year and even edited Dunham's MA thesis "Dances of Haiti: Their Social Organization, Classification, Form, and Function." Dunham based her thesis and later her ethnography *Island Possessed* on the fieldwork she conducted in Haiti during the 1930s. According to Moira Sullivan, this included footage filmed "under the supervision of Melville Herskovits." She adds, "Deren's access to this material led her to publish a series of articles about religious possession in dancing."[75] Their association not only illustrates the close interrelation of anthropological scholarship on Haiti, but also appears to produce a sensitivity to the situatedness of the ethnographer that emerges in both Dunham and Deren. Years after these works were published, in a passage examining rupture and the decentering of western discourse, Jacques Derrida defines "the critique of ethnocentrism" as "the very condition of ethnology."[76] Nevertheless, ethnology remains entwined with the discourse from which it originates. Derrida continues, "the ethnologist accepts into his discourse the premises of ethnocentrism at the very moment when he denounces them. This necessity is irreducible; it is not a historical contingency."[77] Whether or not it was the result of their collaboration, Dunham and Deren separately see fit to articulate awareness of their overdetermined position as observer-participant in Haitian ceremony.

Three. Caribbean and Gothic Origins of the American Zombie

Perhaps because she wrote the book decades after completing her work with Herskovits, Dunham felt comfortable politely disclosing what she saw as the limitations of his methods. She writes, "he was single-minded about an object, a thing, not the person and what the person was made up of and how much the person could take of one thing, no matter what great vistas would be open."[78] As an initiate and Vodou practitioner, Dunham struggles with distinguishing her competing motives for participating in the rituals. She asks, "Could Herskovits tell me, could Erich Fromm, could Téoline or Dégrasse tell me what part of me lived on the floor of the houngfor, felt awareness seeping from the earth and people and things around me, and what part stood to one side taking notes?" and she offers no satisfactory answer.[79] Because as Derrida asserts there is no escape from this dilemma, she settles on naming the unresolved tension: "Each moment lived in participation was real; still, without arranging this expressly, without conscious doing or planning or thinking I stayed outside the experience while being totally immersed in it."[80] By acknowledging this problem, Dunham reminds the reader of her own limitations as an observer-participant, so that when she discusses zombies the reader can hold Dunham's uncertainty as they read her accounts. In fact, her uncertainty leads her to propose two possible definitions for zombies that are distinguished by their reaction to salt: "a resuscitated dead person disintegrates or falls dead, whereas the zombie which has been revived from a drugged state returns to life as a normal human being."[81] Dunham briefly explains that the second type "seem preferable" because "the sorcerer would be able to re-enslave them."[82] Regardless of the type both "are put to the serviceable work of tilling and cultivating fields."[83] She then concludes by quoting what she suggests is a credible definition by Herskovits that mirrors her own except that his definition describes them as soulless. The discrepancy proves emblematic of her general approach.

To investigate the zombie phenomena for herself, Dunham visits 'ti Couzin, a Haitian rumored to keep zombies on his estate. During her interview with 'ti Couzin, she pauses and steps out on the veranda. The following is a description of what she witnesses: "They were absolutely motionless, with faces turned in our direction, faces with absolutely no expression and which might as well have been the faces of the blind or deaf. There was one difference; they were listening with every pore and fiber and were seeing with sightless eyes and smelling with nostrils distended like animals who have caught the first scent of fresh blood."[84] When she departs the estate, she quickly snaps a photograph of the alleged zombies, but, unlike Hurston, Dunham does not include the image in her book. Alluding to the existence of more content is another strategy she periodically employs throughout the ethnography to affirm the incompleteness of her narrative. Nonetheless, we observe that the accumulation of knowledge about zombies continues to be determined by previous scholarship, even when it contains firsthand accounts. Admittedly, Dunham disagrees with Herskovits by favoring explanations wherein zombies have a soul. However, she ascribes her decision to "some intangible preference" and the belief that it makes more sense for sorcerers to use living bodies because it allows for re-enslavement if a zombie somehow acquired salt and escaped.[85] Her utilitarian logic may be sound but disagreeing with Herskovits to affirm the efficacy of the zombie-as-symbol-for-slave is not much of a disagreement. It merely illustrates her privileging representations that support preestablished dispositions.

In contrast, Deren is both more and less explicit about her situatedness in *Divine Horsemen*. Her approach to ethnography derives explicitly from her conception of the artist and filmmaker as choreographer. She writes, "These choreographies for camera are not dances recorded by the camera; they are dances choreographed for and performed by the camera and by human beings together."[86] Her argument mirrors what Anne Hollander would later assert about fashion and art history. The subject of a work is always mediated by the artist and therefore "there is no historically authentic look that is not the look of an artistic style."[87] Although Hollander examined the representation and movement of bodies within garments recorded in art, the same holds true for representation and movement of bodies within dance recorded on film. Deren's recognition of these horizons led her to write in her preface that "only after completely conceded my defeat as an artist [...] that I became aware of the ambiguous consequences of that failure."[88] Without naming Herskovits as Dunham does, she elaborates on the limits of "'scientific' detachment" in "professional anthropologists" and argues for a sensitivity to form that an "artist-native" like herself can access.[89] Despite rejecting that particular anthropological methodology, Deren nevertheless approaches her subject with the same rigor for scholarship in the field. It is not without some irony then that Deren cites Harold Courlander, Alfred Métraux, and Seabrook in her discussion of death rituals and the zombie.[90]

Deren foregrounds this discussion with an explanation of how the soul is conceptualized in Haitian Vodou. According to Deren, three elements constitute every living person: the physical body, the *gros bon ange*, and the *ti bon ange*. The *gros bon ange* closely aligns with the Western conception of the soul. It is the seat of agency and will, and it comprises the personality of the individual. The *ti bon ange*, on the other hand, is the "universal commitment towards good," a sort of conscience shared by all Haitians. She describes it as "one of the constants of the cosmos."[91] When a person chooses to do good or do evil, they are exerting the will of the *gros bon ange* over the *ti bon ange*. To clarify any later confusion about terminology, Deren adds that the term *esprit* "refers to the immortal souls of the dead, or what was known, during lifetime, as the gros-bon-ange."[92] With this understanding, she introduces the zombie as a "body without a soul, matter without morality."[93] In a footnote, she elaborates in an effort to characteristically go beyond merely explaining the spiritual logistics and offers the reader a sense of what the phenomena means to Haitians. They don't fear the hard work of "a kind of uncomplaining slave-labor" but the loss of agency[94]—the "powers of consciousness and the attendant capacity for moral judgement, deliberation and self-control."[95] Compared to the other anthropologists we have examined, she spends what appears a surprising amount of time on this last point of self-control and asserts the importance of adhering to codes of social conduct. She even includes the Haitian epithet "'Malelevé!' (Ill-mannered! Uncouth!)" to underscore its significance.[96] She affirms that everything entailed by this extended discussion of consciousness constitutes the Haitian conception of *esprit*, or the *gros bon ange* after it has left the body. She then concludes with the statement, "A zombie is nothing more than a body deprived of its conscious powers of cerebration; for the Haitian, there is no fate more terrible." Again, we are reminded that zombification is tantamount to enslavement. Interestingly, this understanding of the soul as *gros bon ange* allows us to recognize parallels between zombification and possession. In the Haitian practice of possession, *un esprit* (a soul of the dead) mounts a practitioner by temporarily displacing their *gros bon ange*.[97]

Métraux, another esteemed professional anthropologist, also wrote extensively about Haiti around this time and published two works that specifically examine the zombie: "The Concept of Soul in Haitian Vodu" and *Voodoo in Haiti*. From the first, referenced above by Deren, we learn about the two-part soul and how it relates to the zombie. Métraux ascribes the content primarily to his Haitian informant Mary Noël. From the second, published after Deren's ethnography, we receive a more thorough treatment of the subject that he also situates within the broader context of Haitian studies. In it, he summarizes the zombie encounter previously related by the "very superstitious" Hurston and concludes: "it really seems that the woman concerned was an imbecile or a moron."[98] He reports falling victim to a similar experience only to learn the following day that the zombie was "a poor idiot girl."[99] Perhaps more surprising is that he deviates from Herskovits and does not apply the same skepticism to Seabrook. He paraphrases Polynice's account as related by Seabrook with a seriousness not shared by his other colleagues. Following from Seabrook, Métraux also quotes the now infamous Article 246 of the Haitian Penal Code. More than any of the other texts discussed in this section, *Voodoo in Haiti* codifies the representation of zombies in anthropological scholarship in much the same way that Romero codifies the representation of zombies in Hollywood cinema. Consequently, it is all the more significant that Métraux incorporates the two characteristics that continue to define the representation of zombies in the national consciousness. He states (1) "a *zombi*'s life is seen in terms which echo the harsh existence of a slave in the old colony of Santo Domingo" and (2) "realization [caused by the consumption of salt] rouses in them a vast rage and an ungovernable desire for vengeance."[100] Not only does Métraux succinctly distill these qualities for use by future researchers, but his slight adaptations align them more closely with the image would soon typify their Hollywood counterparts. Specifically, he affixes Haiti's history to the association of zombies and slavery, and he expands the narrow desire for revenge on their master to a more generalized disposition or, as he calls it, "a vast rage."

With the notable absence of Davis, these writers comprise the bulwark of mid-twentieth-century anthropological scholarship on zombies and Haitian Vodou.[101] Despite their profound caution and openness to critique, the accumulation of their interrelated research that regularly points back to Seabrook results in the sedimentation of knowledge that informs the contemporary discourse of zombie studies. The prescience of Deren and Dunham to acknowledge the implications of their role as participant-observers on the subject matter discloses the complexity of the problem. This is especially the case for Dunham, who investigates her motivations as an object of study within the ethnography, recognizing how it influences what she uncovers and how she portrays it. From this, we observe the inclination to privilege accounts that align with generalized assumptions about the meaning and function of zombies. It is plausible that this explains Métraux's motivation for trusting Seabrook over Hurston; Seabrook's zombies operated like slaves whereas Felix-Mentor, the zombie Hurston encountered, simply presented as a social outcast. Sarah Juliet Lauro affirms the currency of considering zombies within a framework of slavery and resistance calling it "zombie dialectics."[102] As Lauro demonstrates in *The Transatlantic Zombie*—arguably one of the most important recent works in zombie studies—this dialectic is unstable, and the project of her book is to move from conceptualizing the zombie as a static signifier of one pole or the other in the dialectic to recognizing that each contains within it the possibility for the other.

The primacy of this discourse also leads scholars into fact-finding missions to uncover the etymological and cultural antecedents of zombies. While this research certainly has value, we must like Dunham be careful to acknowledge the influence that currently held conceptions of zombies may have upon that work. Recalling Friedrich Nietzsche's warning that the genealogical search for an origin should not be confused with the metaphysical project of reducing a phenomena, like the zombie, to a singular meaning, even if that meaning brandishes the complexity of a dialectic. To be clear, I do not intend this as a critique of Lauro or the work of any other scholar for that matter. Their contributions are significant in their own right. Rather, by delineating this bibliography, I insist that our history of the Haitian zombie should be readily understood as a discursive contingency. That is to say, it is the history of the representation of Haitian zombies produced by western anthropology. There is, of course, always the possibility for disruption through ethnography as Derrida shows; neither does it preclude the possibility of Haitians speaking for themselves. However, the most widely referenced and cited sources do not account for that. For this reason, I align myself with these scholars by limiting the subject of study to the zombies of our national consciousness, while acknowledging the transnational nature of such a project.

Alessandra Benedickty-Kokken explores this problem in her preface to *Spirit Possession in French, Haitian, and Vodou Thought*. She points to the Haitian practice that we call "possession" and asserts that our understanding of it "emerges from a specifically francophone informed scholarship, that is, work done 'on' Haitian Vodou by French scholars, and then by scholars writing mostly in English, but informed by the earlier scholarship."[103] Consequently, descriptions of possession, and by extension zombification, in Haiti implicitly adopt the connotations of pathology and mental illness. In possession the *gros bon ange* is temporarily displaced by a *loa* or *esprit*, whereas in zombification the *gros bon ange* is permanently removed.[104] According to Benedickty-Kokken, it makes more sense to read the zombie not as a slave of an evil sorcerer but "as a sort of pariah." She continues, "It is not that the person zombified has necessarily done anything to harm the community, but that the person no longer fits into its more broad social geography."[105] Looking back at Métraux, we see how his privileging of Seabrook over Hurston led us away from this understanding. Similarly, this sheds light on Deren's extended discussion on the *gros bon ange* and social conduct amid her explanation of the zombie. The very fact of the amount of space she dedicates to elaborating the Haitian cathexis for participation in the community reveals that the fear of slavery does not exhaust their revulsion to zombification. To her credit, Benedickty-Kokken openly states that her intention is not to supplant one type of zombie with another, only to make room for both. For our purposes, it is important to remain open to both conceptions of the zombie. Doing so enables a richer understanding of the interpenetration of Haitian zombies and their rendering in the American consciousness. At the same time, recognizing that the permutations of Haitian and cinema zombies as unstable symbols for slavery and resistance are projections of the national consciousness rather than essential aspects of their nature provides invaluable insight for our investigation. In that sense, these works zombified Haitian cultural practices by extracting their agency so that they could be refigured to extend the frontier beyond the geographic limit of the Pacific Ocean into neighboring nations of the Caribbean.

CHAPTER FOUR

Social Critique and the Modern Zombie

The tradition of all the dead generations weighs like a nightmare on the brain of the living. And just when they seem engaged in revolutionising themselves and things, in creating something entirely new, precisely in such epochs of revolutionary crisis they anxiously conjure up the spirits of the past to their service and borrow from them names, battle slogans and costumes in order to present the new scene of world history in this time-honoured disguise and this borrowed language.—KARL MARX, *The Eighteenth Brumaire of Louis Bonaparte*

When the U.S. pivoted from securing the Caribbean against Germany to all-out war against the Axis powers, the national fascination with zombies was only just beginning. Advances in science and technology opened territories of incipient social anxieties for cinema and fiction to explore. Unmoored from any geographic location, these frontiers were immediate and illimitable. The bioluminescent discharge from a science laboratory was just as likely to leech into the water supply of an unsuspecting rural American town as it was a foreign nation. Alongside these changes in content, the emergence of drive-ins and cheap movies facilitated social experiences that welcomed the campiness of zombies in the atomic age.

As we advance toward the present in our analysis and the themes resonate more closely with our contemporary historical moment, the capacity for undead narratives to internalize and critique social values becomes increasingly obvious. The same ductile structure of mythology that facilitates a diverse nation to engender a homogenous specular image also contains the possibility for its own critique. In fact, the subject-position of the audience often bears more responsibility for the meaning of a text than its author. When I wear my *Night of the Living Dead* Indians t-shirt depicting a native person turned zombie, I sometimes get asked "but isn't that racist?" Possibly. It was designed by John Henry Gloyne—a Cherokee, Osage, and Pawnee artist. What he intended when he created the original artwork may be far different from what it signifies to me or the people I encounter when I wear it. The same can be said for the works examined in this chapter: Richard Matheson's novella *I Am Legend*, George Romero's *Living Dead* films, and Robert Kirkman's comic and television series *The Walking Dead*.[1] These narratives depict dystopian realities where characters that embody American ideals and possess Ralph Waldo Emerson's self-reliance tend to thrive. Just as we saw with John Winthrop's jeremiad or Charles Beaumont in *White Zombie*, national myth does not merely interrogate external subjects but internal as well.

These works also introduce tropes and themes that continue to pervade contemporary zombie narratives. Matheson's *I Am Legend* employs an apocalyptic setting that envisions a post-social or rather post-human world. This stands in stark contrast to *White Zombie* which forecasted the consequences of external threats then quickly resolved them to preserve the status quo. The (post-)apocalyptic landscape of *I Am Legend* brought along with it themes of survival, self-reliance, and exceptionalism, all of which become hallmarks of zombie cinema. Romero's *Night of the Living Dead* expands on these and adds a critique of racism, but audiences had to wait for *Dawn of the Dead*, the second *Living Dead* film, to witness the global apocalypse as it unfolds. With *Dawn*, he expands the social critique to delve into America's growing obsession with consumerism. By examining society through the actions of a few individuals, Matheson lays bare the problem of our constructed teleological evolutionary narrative and imagines what species will succeed humanity whereas Romero asks to what extent does civilization determine what it means to be human. Kirkman explores these and a variety of other themes within the landscape of the national myth by extending the narratives with serialization. Because of similarities in the publication cycle of comics, trade paperbacks, and television seasons, the media lend themselves to a progression of interwoven narrative arcs. Within the context of a global crisis, these disparate narratives often focus on the experience of a few select individuals who serve as a microcosm for everyone caught in the crisis.

On May 27, 2016, Barack Obama became the first American president to return to Hiroshima. Despite the importance of this act, neither he nor any other president has ever apologized for what took place on August 6, 1945.[2] The significance of the atomic bomb and its impact on our social consciousness cannot be underestimated. Similarly, the fear of foreign nations such as China, Russia, and Nazi Germany wielding that kind of power inspired hundreds of films in the atomic age. While Americans were never the villains, these films simultaneously confess our own discomfort with possessing such power and the societal guilt of exercising it. Zombie films produced at this time retain the existential dilemma of human agency found in *White Zombie*, but the threat was no longer localized to the Caribbean. It was now a global threat where the Soviet bloc might subversively indoctrinate the West, turning Americans against themselves, or forcibly overwhelm the U.S. through military action. The use of nuclear weapons, new awareness of the physical horrors and psychological trauma of Nazi prison camps, and the rise of a competing political ideology that appeared more threatening and limitless in its reach collectively produced social anxieties that informed popular entertainment.[3] The other cultural phenomena intrinsic to understanding the national consciousness in this era is the modern synthesis of evolution. From the 1930s to the 1950s, evolutionary scientific research coalesced across disciplines to agree that the genetic variation of microevolution was the basis for natural selection, which over time resulted in macroevolution. The nearly universal acceptance of this development among scientists heightened its visibility and offered a more accessible explanation of humanity's biological history. Because evolution uncovers the shared ancestry of all living things, it draws attention to contradiction of the racial and social stratification that underlies the Social Darwinism invoked by Frederick Jackson Turner and popularized in the late nineteenth and early twentieth century. When teleology is removed from the biological history of a species, justifications for social distinction based on cultural or racial difference become intolerable.

I Am Legend

Matheson distills these fears in his 1954 novella *I Am Legend*. This text marks a departure for the genre which had been driven primarily by film and fixated on the use and misuse of science. As we will see later, Matheson's novella, its 1964 film adaptation *The Last Man on Earth*, and atomic age comics such as *Tales from the Crypt* and *Weird Science* published by EC were source materials for Romero's films.[4] Because of his influence on Romero and the genre, Matheson's innovations prove incredibly important. Instead of merely updating American mythology for a new historical moment, Matheson critiques assumptions held by the national consciousness and uses speculative fiction to explore the emerging scientific understanding of evolution by introducing zombie-like creatures as humanity's evolutionary successor.

I Am Legend relates the experience of the protagonist, Robert Neville, as he comes to grips with recognizing that he is the end of humanity after a disease, presumably born from a global military conflict, eradicates Earth's human population. Haunted by his own memories and the infected creatures that harass him from beyond the walls of his compound, Neville spends his days studying the disease through textbook research and experiments. He learns that it infects both the living and the dead and has driven them mad. He describes these creatures as vampires and explores a variety of ways to stave them off. The traditional folklore methods of fighting vampires are effective only as much as the creatures believe in its efficacy. For example, a crucifix drives fear into the heart of a Christian vampire but has no effect on a Jewish one. This introduces a psychological component, suggesting the disease ravaged their minds as it altered their bodies, but it also implies that they retain a latent consciousness. Early in the novella, Neville recounts putting down his own wife after she transforms into one of these creatures. Subsequently, the act of killing an infected loved one becomes almost ubiquitous in undead narratives. The novella approaches its climax when Neville discovers another seemingly uninfected survivor, Ruth. After his initial wariness, Neville lowers his guard and invites Ruth into his home. They commiserate as he relates his tragic experiences and shares his research. Ruth allows Neville to take a blood sample from her, and he discovers that she too is infected. Before he can act, Ruth renders him unconscious and leaves a note explaining that she had been sent to spy on him by a group of vampires living nearby. Neville remains in his home and waits for their return. This does in fact occur, but as Neville defends his barricaded home, he observes that the vampires of Ruth's society are forced to dispatch other feral vampires that impede their progress. To his surprise, Ruth's companions even appear to take some pleasure in doing so. While the distraction does not save him, it illustrates the uneven complexity of biological adaptation. Eventually, vampires overwhelm Neville, and he suffers an incidental gunshot wound. After his capture, he awaits his inevitable death which he knows will come either by execution or the untreated wound. Ruth visits Neville and shows pity, offering suicide pills to ease his suffering. Neville takes the pills and in his last few moments observes that the vampires despise his existence just as he despises theirs. The novella concludes with his realization that he is the legend, the superstition, which haunts the origin of their post-human society.

Social Critique

Each type of fantastical creature carries a framework of symbolic meaning in popular culture. Even though Matheson uses the term vampires, zombie scholars and enthusiasts alike recognize the novella and its film adaptations as part of the canon, particularly because Romero acknowledges it as an inspiration. I have no desire to contest *I Am Legend*'s place in the zombie genre, but a thorough analysis of the novella should not neglect its relationship to vampire fiction. Ian Conrich differentiates the monster types by their social function: "Whilst vampires are seen as chic and offer a lifestyle, zombies would be viewed as shambolic and indicate a past life. Vampires are sexual, immortal and swift; zombies are grotesque terminal and slow moving. Vampires are sophisticated and selective, in comparison to zombies who are brain dead and indiscriminate. And vampires tend to occupy the margins of society, residing in the shadows, whilst zombies were once mainstream society, and occupy open communal spaces such as the shopping malls and town centres."[5] Vampires not only co-exist in society with humans, but they frequently inhabit some of the most elite social spheres. This is perhaps because of the limitless amount of time they have to refine and polish their sophistication. On the other hand, zombies in fiction and film are ordinarily introduced as products of a flawed society and herald its destruction. Notably, Conrich's definition omits physical description and focuses instead on the ontological. Conceding the limits of any broad generalizations made by Conrich or myself, these creatures signify the two extremes against which American identity often defines itself, savagery and overcivilization. Matheson collapses the polarization by devising a species that performs as zombie by bringing about the destruction of civilization yet also performs as vampire by succeeding humanity in the evolutionary narrative.[6] Despite their complicated nature, Romero borrows from Matheson for his *Living Dead* films, so that post-human worlds later emerge as part of the zombie canon. The importance of Matheson's contributions cannot be overstated and exposes a unique social function of zombie narratives. The apocalyptic setting of *I Am Legend* makes it possible to self-consciously incorporate critiques of contemporary ideology and utopian impulses.

Contrary to the national myths we have encountered so far, *I Am Legend* does not conclude by interpellating the colonial other within a narrative where humans create new social structures to replace the old; instead, it subverts the teleological evolutionary model and locates humans as the subaltern species. Previously conceived as the apex of evolutionary development, humans are superseded by less civilized creatures. Neville's acceptance of the fate of humanity is tragic in the sense of his individual loss but is buoyed by his non-anthropocentric understanding of his place in biological history. It is survival of the fittest in a world where humans no longer thrive. Moreover, the kinship that Ruth and Neville share illustrates that interaction between species need not be antagonistic. It displays, at the very least, a relational model based on mutual recognition. A critique of social stratification may not be his aim, but Matheson inevitably calls into question the efficacy of identity-based hierarchy and our faith in meritocracy. The capacity for conscious thought among the undead is initially doubtful and seriously limited for the majority of feral ghouls. Presenting such creatures as humanity's successors gently reminds readers of their misplaced trust in human intelligence and the trappings of civilization. As the long history of evolution affirms, intelligence is an improbable outcome of natural selection. Without the Cretaceous-Paleogene extinction event that wiped out many reptiles including our beloved dinosaurs, it is unlikely *homo erectus* would have emerged much less survive long enough to evolve into the intelligent creatures we are today.

Marxism not only appears in zombie studies as an analytic tool for understanding fictional utopias, but also provides an interpretative framework for examining the disillusionment with modern civilization that pervades apocalyptic narratives. Because many of these critiques understandably contextualize the Hollywood zombie in relation to its Haitian and West African origins, they risk conflating popular and even academic representations of Vodou and witchcraft with the beliefs themselves. I am referring to the tendency to read the zombie as a signifier of slavery even though that semiological referent is a construction of colonial academic studies.[7] Scholars like Dan Hassler-Forest cite Raymond Williams' *The Country and the City* to interpret Matheson's narrative as a critique of modern urban and suburban life.[8] Williams' phrase "structure of feeling" helps articulate the unarticulated but recognizable opposition and interdependence of his titular subject.[9] As Williams shows, the cathexis for the other often manifests as nostalgia in pastoralism, the urban dweller longing for a simpler life unfettered by social conventions. Matheson's work marks the extension of the structure of feeling that previously inhabited the American frontier to the new site of apocalyptic fiction. Although zombie narratives draw on individual and collective fears about the collapse of civilization, they also cash in on the seemingly contradictory impulse to return to a state of nature and rebuild society ad hoc. These zombie texts vacillate unevenly from advancing social critiques to projecting utopian futures. In the conclusion of *The Political Unconscious*, Frederic Jameson proposes a dialectical framework that pairs analysis of ideology alongside analysis of utopian ideals. He writes, "a Marxist negative hermeneutic, a Marxist practice of ideological analysis proper, must in the practical work of reading and interpretation be exercised *simultaneously* with a Marxist positive hermeneutic, or a decipherment of the utopian impulses of these same still ideological cultural texts."[10] Because there is no true or authentic zombie myth, we must recognize it as a mechanism for producing conditions that affirm contemporary social values. A post-apocalyptic setting may not appear utopian at first glance, but it nevertheless constructs a world that further reinforces values consistent with a specified ideology.

Living Dead Series

The direct successor to *I Am Legend* in terms of the development in the genre is Romero's seminal film *Night*. As the first installment of Romero's zombie series, *Night* does not go so far as to explore utopian impulses, a topic he reserves for later films. Instead, whether intentional or not, the film introduces a social critique that draws attention to latent racism in rural America. *Night* was produced by Image Ten Corporation, a collaboration of Romero and several individuals who developed television commercials in the Pittsburg area.[11] In the film, Romero brought together tropes, themes, and a visual portrayal of the walking dead that would codify the representation of Hollywood zombies for over half a century. In his encyclopedic text *Zombie Movies*, Glenn Kay writes, "*Night of the Living Dead* imbues its title characters with ghoulish characteristics, adding a healthy dose of realism that previous zombie films had sorely lacked."[12] The result of Romero's innovations as well as the absence of similar texts made *Night* one of the top grossers for both 1969 and 1970. The tyranny of Romero's influence was so far-reaching that many fans of the genre were outraged thirty-four years later when the film *28 Days Later* was released because its zombies deviated from his archetype.

So much has been written about *Night* that offering a thorough analysis of it here would be retreading old ground. Even so, there are a few points I would like to make about the film. Despite the already acknowledged influence of Matheson on Romero, the differences between their narratives prove equally as important as the similarities. Where human society is already destroyed at the start of *I Am Legend* and the narrative depicts the end of humanity, Romero's films take a step back and details the events that lead up to the point where Matheson's novella could have begun. *Night* opens with the unforgettable scene of siblings visiting their father's grave. Johnny, the brother, tries to frighten Barbara by pretending to be an undead creature only to be attacked by one moments later. An incident such as this presumably had never occurred, and this isolated event marks the beginning of an apocalypse that extends across the entire series of *Living Dead* films. After Barbara escapes from the graveyard, she takes refuge in an abandoned house. She is joined by several other characters, most notably Ben, the film's only black protagonist. The characters scavenge the house for useful objects. The act of recasting domesticity by examining everyday objects and repurposing them will become commonplace in the survival genre. As the story progresses, the protagonists listen to radio broadcasts about other incidents to learn more about the creatures they face. Surviving the immediate zombie threat is not their only concern. They also come into conflict with each other. The protagonists eventually discover that the only way to subdue the living dead is to destroy their brains. Additionally, they learn that zombies are afraid of flames and actively try to beat them out when their clothing catches fire. Other than these qualities, the most striking characteristic that distinguishes *Night* from previous zombie films is that these creatures are not controlled by aliens or a metaphysical force. Instead, they are driven solely by hunger for human flesh.

While Romero's approach does eventually allow for exploration of post-social settings in *Day the Dead* (1985) and *Land of the Dead* (2005), the early films provide Romero with a sufficient toolset to offer contemporary social critiques. The only individual to survive until morning in *Night* is Ben, the aforementioned black character. After the immediate threat of zombies is averted, Ben abandons the home and encounters a posse of rednecks that shoot him on site, presumably mistaking him for a zombie. The allusion to lynch mobs could not be more overt. The unexpected ending of *Night* draws attention to racism still prevalent in the American consciousness, and it illustrates the tenacity with which a collapsing society holds onto its ideology. This attitude of hopelessness becomes a central conflict throughout Romero's oeuvre. Confronted with the collapse of society, Romero's protagonists struggle to forge a new one while being hunted and haunted by symbols of the past. Romero's next zombie film, *Dawn*, released 10 years after *Night*, resumes this approach of incorporating cultural critiques but shifts the focus from racism to consumerism.

In the intervening years between *Night* and *Dawn*, many films attempted to capitalize on the popularity of *Night*, some more successful than others. Like those that preceded *Night*, the representations of zombies varied widely and did not coalesce around a singular type. Where *Night* invigorated the genre and spawned numerous other zombie films, *Dawn* solidified the representation of zombies. Additionally, *Dawn* progressed the timeline of Romero's diegetic world into the midst of a global apocalypse. Consequently, in addition to concretizing the definition of zombies, *Dawn* fused the genre to this apocalyptic setting so completely that any subsequent zombie film not employing it proves to be a rare exception. *Dawn* also secured international appeal for the genre. Half of the film's budget came from Claudio Argento, an Italian film producer. According to Kay, "[Claudio Argento] is the brother of horror filmmaker Dario Argento [...], who was apparently such a fan of *Night of the Living Dead* that he convinced his brother to invest in Romero's follow-up."[13] Argento also acquired all non–English distribution rights and released a lucrative recut version of the film in Italy with less dialogue and more action prior to its U.S. release.

Romero relocates the narrative from a rural farmhouse in *Night* to an urban setting in *Dawn*. The film's four protagonists are thrown together in a television studio at the start of the outbreak. Two members of a SWAT team, Peter and Roger, recognize the futility of attempting to control the situation, abandon their mission, and search for a means of escape. They meet Stephen and Francine, and the group evacuates in a news helicopter in search of refuge. While airborne, they discover a shopping mall overrun by zombies but well-stocked with provisions. They secure the facility by barricading the entrances and systematically purging undead from the mall store-by-store with weapons scavenged from a guns and ammo shop. Although they succeed, Roger is bitten by a zombie and must be put down by Peter after he reanimates. These sequences highlight the make-up special effects of Tom Savini with grotesque zombie killing montages. As in *Night*, the narrative is interspersed with television news reports and talk show commentary. Their sanctuary is defiled when a biker gang breaks through the barricaded entrances, ruining them beyond repair. As zombies begin to stream back into the mall, the protagonists ineffectually prevent the bikers from doing further damage, and Stephen is killed. The film ends as Francine and Peter, the two remaining survivors, return to the helicopter and abandon the mall to find another refuge.

Consumerism

Embedded within Romero's narrative is a thinly veiled argument that the citizens of a consumer-obsessed society already are zombies. The freedom and agency championed by middle-class values is exposed as a facade that prevents society from realizing its objectified subject-position. Similarly, the inability of the protagonists to be self-sufficient and their instinct to seek refuge in a mall highlight the lack of difference between themselves and the zombies. Prior to purging the mall of the undead, Francine asks Stephen, "What are they doing? Why do they come here?" Stephen responds, "Some kind of instinct. Memory. What they used to do. This was an important place in their lives."[14] The dramatic irony is that the protagonists acted on similar instincts when they decided to land at the mall. They trust their survival to the same consumerism, making them indistinguishable from the undead. As Kyle William Bishop and Lars Bang Larsen have noted, the film's critique resembles Marxist philosophy in the sense that as capitalism strips agency from the proletariat, reducing work to time and a person's existence to a fiscal value, *Dawn* reveals the zombie as the corporeal surplus of alienated labor.[15] Romero's film demonstrates the stranglehold of capitalism on social structures and implies that breaking from it requires an event as radical and revolutionary as a zombie apocalypse. The tragedy of *Dawn* is the failure of the survivors to escape its hegemony even as they witness the collapse of a civilization that for so long determined their subordinate status. Because they do not recognize themselves as zombies, they do not achieve the class-consciousness necessary for an ideological revolution. Constructing a new society without sublation results in a recapitulation of the old systems of hierarchy. Romero delays fulfilling the promise of the zombie apocalypse qua proletariat revolution for almost three decades until the release of *Land*, the fourth film of his *Living Dead* series.

In *Land*, modern capitalism's enumerated evils of alienated labor and social stratification re-emerge. The majority of survivors serve an elite few by venturing further and further from the safety of Fiddler's Green, a luxury high-rise transformed into an urban fortress, to scavenge for supplies amongst the dead. On these errands, the protagonists encounter Big Daddy, a zombie that demonstrates signs of consciousness that engender the sympathy of the film's heroes and the audience. It is only when the protagonists identify with their zombie counterparts and form a tacit alliance that the Marxist vision of social and economic revolution is finally realized. The irony, of course, is that this cinematic achievement required a big budget and denotes the first Romero zombie film released by a major studio. Regardless, it should come as no surprise that the overarching narrative of the *Living Dead* series utilizes the framework of national myth to imagine the rebirth of civilization. For Romero, Fiddler's Green is emblematic of the anomie that arises from unchecked capitalist development. To prevent the otherwise inexorable incarnation of Winthrop's fear, the protagonists must not only succeed in their errand, but the community must accommodate their romantic agitations and welcome their return. Thus, the failure of Fiddler's Green is not ineluctable. If the film's heroes had been proclaimed virtuous under the civil authority of consensus politics and the community embraced the efficacy of their errand, then Fiddler's Green would continue to thrive. Read in such a way, *Land* functions as a modern jeremiad, asserting the need for a frontier that rejuvenates the nation and indemnifies it against overcivilization.

National Myth (Re-)Possessed

The *Living Dead* series and the success it achieved permanently refigured the landscape of zombie films. It brought with it a post-apocalyptic landscape, survivalism, and death montages. Works from this era fashion a liminal space where audiences can examine the social structures that inform their existence. Despite the detachment from Haitian ritual practice, the social phenomena that determine the ideological conflicts of these narratives perform a similar function to the expressive causality of possession in Haitian Vodou. Possession, described briefly in chapter 3, is not in fact the word Haitians use to describe this experience. Joan Dayan argues instead for using phrases such as "the lwa descends," "the lwa mounts the horse," and "the lwa dances in the head."[16] By naming the active *loa* instead of the passive practitioner, this terminology de-emphasizes the eminence of the possessed individual. This is significant because it clarifies the ascendent position of the *loa*. Although a practitioner may seek out a *loa* for help with a particular problem, the *loa* determines what the practitioner actually needs. Possession is in fact the primary means in which the *loa* communicate to their practitioners. It is comparable to the Christian ritual practice of prayer, except it is the *loa* who speak directly to the practitioners rather than vice versa. Discussing the Bori religion of West Africa, Adeline Masquelier argues that possession is not "a thinly disguised protest movement for marginalized and deprived individuals eager to redress grievances and exact concessions from their superiors" but is instead "a problem-solving process."[17] Even though Haitian Vodou is not the subject of Masquelier's study, her words provide valuable insight.

Additional comparisons could be made to the botánicas of North America and the Lakota Ghost Dance of 1890. Joseph Murphy posits botánicas as sacred liminal spaces for negotiating the individual and communal self as well as for navigating acculturation which he examines using the terms syncretism, symbiosis, hybridization, and creolization.[18] Comparatively, Raymond DeMallie takes steps to decolonize the ghost dance narratives. He observes its similarities with the Lakota sun dance and the Paiute circle dance. Commenting on the sacred tree from the sun dance, he writes, "This element may be superficial, serving only to indicate that when people borrow new ideas, they adapt them to older cultural forms as closely as possible. However, it reinforces the Lakota sense of religious loss and their deep felt need to establish continuity with their past."[19] All of these ritual practices—Haitian possession, Lakota ghost dancing, and Romero's dystopian filmmaking—create occasions for negotiating cultural change and in particular change that results from contact with others. That is not to say these ritual practices equate to one another or even should be considered variations of a single type of transcultural group behavior. Reducing them to a typology unleashes a set of problems that outweigh any potential benefits. Nevertheless, juxtaposing these illuminates how national myth parallels possession and ghost dancing by calling forth the past for guidance about the present. In both the Haitian and Lakota rituals, the self is temporarily negated to provide guidance not only for the individual but for the community. Importantly, the content of possession and visions is not immediately avowed but depends on the approbation of the community. In addition, the level of crisis that produces the conditions for the ritual varies widely and does not necessarily extend to the extreme of cultural erasure often portrayed in apocalyptic fiction. Thus, it may be possible to read zombie narratives as something other than the complete repudiation of civilization. Instead, the apocalyptic setting may function more like a space clearing that allows for thinking *outside-the-box* without the need to literally destroy society. As such, zombie narratives often harmonize with other national myths by safeguarding the community through a proscribed system of adaptation. What distinguishes possession and ghost dancing from zombie narratives is the subject-position of who or what is negated. Unlike the former which negates the self, the latter negates the other. As a result, the zombie more comfortably inhabits colonial discourse.

Post-Romero

Generalizations about zombie fiction becomes increasingly difficult at the end of the twentieth century when the number of texts increases from the occasional shambling production to the rushing onslaught of a horde. Despite the glut, Romero's cynosure dominated the genre to the degree that any narrative with zombies could be classified by its adherence to or deviation from his typology. The range of his influence extended beyond establishing a common representation of the undead and even making the critique of consumerism ubiquitous throughout the genre. Two notable examples are Ruben Fleischer's 2009 film *Zombieland* and the *Resident Evil* video game and film series. While *Zombieland* is not a film that takes itself too seriously, Fleischer inherits Romero's talent for distilling the subversion of utopian ideals into a single scene. The film is a road trip zom-com where a small group of survivors journey across the country to find an amusement park allegedly free from the undead. Early in their pilgrimage, Columbus and Tallahassee, performed by Jesse Eisenberg and Woody Harrelson respectively, locate an overturned Hostess truck. Despite the risk, Tallahassee persuades Columbus to help him explore it and fulfill a craving for Twinkies. To their disappointment, the truck is stocked entirely with Hostess Snowballs. The scene recalls the transitory excitement and inevitable frustration of Romero's survivors when they discover the shopping mall and play dress up with all the consumer products they never had in their previous life. The notion that survivors would risk everything for an object with little practical value indicates the extent to which material culture is charged with emotional significance and the power it holds over us. More than a compelling modernization of *Dawn*, the Twinkie scene illustrates that the adjunct themes of Romero's films continue to proliferate the genre even if most iterations lack Fleischer's ingenuity. For example, the *Resident Evil* video games and movie adaptations present the audience with a post-apocalyptic world that directly results from society placing unfounded trust in corporate entities. Only too late do the protagonists realize the mistake of their dependence on the Umbrella Corporation. While seeming to offer a possible variation or extension of Romero-flavored Marxism, the critique itself is reduced to a background trope that functions exclusively to identify *Resident Evil* as a zombie narrative and discourages analysis. In this sense, *Resident Evil* construes the critique of consumerism into a form of consumerism. Like *White Zombie*, it refigures the radical ontological possibility of its cultural origins and re-presents that content as scenery in a conservative ideological narrative.

Because deviation from Romero's dispensation was virtually nonexistent, the debut of fast zombies in Danny Boyle's film *28 Days Later* proved controversial to say the least. While Romero would be the first to admit that he had no intention of limiting undead to a certain set of criteria, his films nonetheless had that effect.[20] Consequently, after its release, zombie enthusiasts debated whether the fast, feral, and, most significantly, not dead creatures of *28 Days Later* were in fact true zombies. Despite the initial controversy, *28 Days Later* is recognized as a zombie film, and even several Romero films were remade with fast zombies. While such a controversy may seem, and quite possibly is, absurd, their behavior determines the actions and choices available to the characters in these narratives. Examining those actions and choices exposes an underlying ideology that shapes the genre. In a world populated with undead, rural off-the-grid preppers epitomize the ideal survivor because they inhabit the skills and values necessary for existing in post-social world. Because the fast zombies of *28 Days Later* live and breathe, they also starve to death after twenty-eight days, until the sequel of course. Even minor changes such as these alter the conditions for survival enough to remake the value system accorded by the narrative. Although analysis of the British film falls outside the scope of this study, its financial success had the immediate effect of re-opening the genre to the possibility of creative reinvention. Novels and films began to incorporate a requisite *definition scene* that articulates the type of zombie the audience could expect. This clarified characteristics such as their speed, how they could be killed, etc. Although in many instances variation might be superficial, it loosened the constraints for filmmakers and allowed them to adapt a specific representation of zombies to thematic elements of the narrative. Again, I will use two examples to illustrate the range of impact this had on the genre—the Naughty Dog video game *The Last of Us* and the novel and film adaptation of Isaac Marion's *Warm Bodies*.

Instead of rotting corpses, the zombies that inhabit the diegetic world of *The Last of Us* are humans infected by a fungus that starts in the brain and metastasizes throughout the body. Eventually the host is consumed, and the fungus goes to seed. While alterations to the nature of zombies such as these may seem mundane, ecologically contextualizing the undead draws parallels to *I Am Legend* and challenges the anthropocentrism that continues to permeate contemporary political discourse. As revealed to the player, the game's post-apocalyptic landscape directly results from human impact on the environment. The fungal zombie virus re-engineers human physiology to adapt to climate change. Nevertheless, like more traditional zombies, infected humans lose all agency and are reduced to base instincts. Free will and the capacity for consciousness prove to be liabilities and detrimental to the survival of humanity. Less intelligent, seemingly savage creatures are better equipped to persevere in the harsh environment.

The novel *Warm Bodies* takes a fundamentally different approach. While Marion's novel uses traditional Romero-esque zombies as a starting point, several undead demonstrate the capacity to reclaim consciousness. The zombie protagonist R is a physical manifestation of consumer culture. Unable to produce his own memories, R takes pleasure in eating brains allowing him to vicariously experience the memories of his victim. The narrative engenders sympathy for him by revealing that R has limited consciousness and has fallen for a girl, Juliet. In this unlikely mashup of *Romeo and Juliet* and *Beauty and the Beast*, R kidnaps Juliet, and they must save each other from themselves. For these teenagers, the true cause of zombification is succumbing to the sophomoric existential malaise of adolescence. It is structured as a love story, but where Shakespeare singled out the rash behavior of teenagers, Marion normalizes Stockholm syndrome. Because of his unyielding bias against zombies, Juliet's father refuses to accept that his daughter has fallen in love with her kidnapper and suffers, somewhat understandably, from an apoplectic paroxysm. This unfortunate consequence of his emotional and social insufficiencies transforms him into the very creature he despises, a zombie. Simultaneously, R's love for Juliet catalyzes his rebirth as a human. Following from this logic, the narrative portrays zombification as a sociological condition afflicting all who fail to embrace contemporary American young adult values of finding one's own identity and non-discrimination. The profound gulf that separates *The Last of Us* from *Warm Bodies* exposes the wide range of variation that began with *28 Days Later*. In each of these cases, emancipation from Romero's dispensation provided the necessary conditions for imagining these new types of zombie narratives. As the rest of this chapter will show, the medium of the text is equally important.

Serialization

Video games like *Resident Evil* and *The Last of Us* were not the only new horizon for zombies to permeate; the creatures also began to populate comics and television shows. Because these formats diverge significantly from traditional films and novels, any analysis must take into consideration the impact of publication and distribution on narrative structure. Fortunately for us, Kirkman has emerged as Romero's spiritual successor in both mediums. In a reprint celebrating the tenth anniversary of its launch, Kirkman openly acknowledged that he originally pitched the comic with the title *Night of the Living Dead*. "NOTLD somehow fell into the public domain," Kirkman writes. "So when I was planning my zombie epic I thought I'd use the name and get a little recognition out of it."[21] As the story goes, the publisher of Image Comics, Jim Valentino, talked him out of it, and his monthly comic *TWD* (*The Walking Dead*) enjoyed a lengthy sixteen-year run after its debut in 2003. It has since been adapted for television and video games, supporting spin-offs for both.

Apart from one-shot issues and limited television mini-series, most serialized media distribute a narrative across an arc of issues or episodes spanning years or even decades. Where comics use a six-issue story arc publishing one issue each month, the season of a television show ranges from 10 to 30 episodes. A typical *TWD* season runs for sixteen episodes that start in October and air semi-weekly until March or April.[22] In comparison, the comic issues are published monthly and then re-released as trade paperbacks after the conclusion of each six-issue story arc. There is a variety of reasons for this standardization, but it ultimately comes down to the popularity and accessibility of trade paperbacks. While they do not carry the same value as collectibles, casual readers can pick up a single trade paperback and get a self-contained narrative. The format is also more durable and makes it possible for libraries to add comics to their collection. What this means in terms of narrative is that each episode or issue will often incorporate a singular focus or self-contained element so that it individually has value. However, a much larger story arc will be sustained across a season or set of six issues. Similarly, even these annual or semi-annual story arcs will tie into an even larger one. For this reason, comics translate more directly to television shows than a single two-hour film. Serialization, however, does not simply impact the length of narrative. Any long-running production will ultimately move from one story arc to another. Compared to standalone films and novels where a protagonist is often defined by a singular conflict, persistent characters are fleshed out across multiple narratives that audiences grow familiar with over a period of years.

Social-Science Fiction

The serialized nature of these stories opens a space for a methodical exploration of social ethics and values. In their essay "Zombies and the Sociological Imagination," Darren Reed and Ruth Penfold-Mounce argue that this format expands the manifold possibilities of social-science fiction. While the phrase typically refers to incorporating sociological themes in a narrative, they insist that "it is used to describe fiction in a more general way that can then be used as a social-science research tool."[23] They add, "Therefore social-science fiction is fiction used to explore sociological themes and concepts—in a speculative and propositional manner—rather than seeking to explain or describe a social occurrence."[24] What Reed and Penfold-Mounce offer is not only a stage for performances of national myth but also a site for investigating the production of those rituals. Perhaps one reason for this layering is that it allows audiences to experience the nostalgia of myth and participate in its construction. Consequently, the setting of a post-social world provides the space for Jameson's dialectical hermeneutic by acting as a laboratory for testing the social critiques and the utopian impulses of contemporary ideology. Reed and Penfold-Mounce affirm this stating, "By removing society, it removes the expectations of social structure, and as a consequence asks us to imagine an existence set loose from social conventions and norms."[25] Moreover, it echoes the ideological function of the botánicas described by Joseph Murphy and the *hounfor* of Haitian Vodou, which also provide a liminal space to examine social structures. Despite the alluring promise of their approach, its efficacy depends on a nuanced understanding of the form and function of these narratives, and their aporetical equivocation of the term science further complicates matters. Where scientific study even in the fields of sociology and behavioral sciences requires isolating contingencies and fixed conditions even, such objectivity is neither assured nor desirable when studying popular media as a projection of the national consciousness. While the writers, producers, and publishers certainly construct zombie narratives from within a constellated historical moment, their situatedness does not necessarily reflect that of their audience. These narratives are neither a pure manifestation of the present (or past) nor are their speculations completely separate from it. They occupy an uncertain space of negotiation, and their success is not guaranteed.

One problem with reading zombie narratives as sociological experiments is that the experiment becomes an end in-itself and therefore turns out to be merely a form of entertainment or mental (pre-)occupation. Such an approach misleadingly belies the ideological narrativization that inhabits the text by naively liberating it from its socio-political context. Disconnecting a text from ideology is commensurate with what William Spanos terms praxis-oriented discourse. In his book *American Exceptionalism in the Age of Globalization*, Spanos writes that "praxis-oriented discourse fails to perceive that being, however it is represented, constitutes a continuum, which [...] traverses its indissolubly related 'sites' from being as such and the epistemological subject through the ecos, culture (including family, class, gender, and race), to sociopolitics (including the nation and the international or global sphere)."[26] As Spanos goes on to explain, the result of limiting interpretation in such a way precludes the possibility of unconcealing the Althusserian problematic, the disconnect between the historiography of ideology and actual history.[27] Fiction, as opposed to folklore, is already limited in its capacity for radical confrontation of ideology. Decontextualization further restricts analysis to a single discipline approach and prevents narratives from offering a more robust critique. That is not to say the conditions for constructing such a critique from the narrative tools provided is impossible. On the contrary, fiction that occupies this space gives readers more footholds in terms of encouraging such a critique, but the limits of narrative necessitate a directed cross-disciplinary analysis because such guidance is itself inescapably informed by ideology. For example, the latent values of disassembled society in these post-apocalyptic settings still creep back into the narratives.

All this is exemplified in the diegetic world of *TWD*, where society has collapsed along with government structures and the means of production. Those who have not been consumed by zombies form new independent, ad hoc societies constructed around the changing conditions and needs of the group. While hierarchies of wealth and status may no longer exist, these are often replaced by other values such as individualism and self-reliance. Those capable of surviving without the support of others rise in importance. A conflict that frequently emerges is valuating intrinsic human worth against the uneven contributions of each individual.

Certain members of the group may want to adhere to the *all are created equal, no man left behind* approach. However, illness and weakness are a liability; risks need to be assessed and decisions made. In the episode "Welcome to the Tombs" of Season 3, the character Andrea nearly escapes a fatal encounter with a zombie only to be bit by the creature before she kills it. In other episodes, characters hide fatal zombie bites at the risk of turning into a zombie and devouring their friends. Andrea understands the situation, and when her rescuers arrive, she asks them for a gun so that she can kill herself and does so. In these moments, the situatedness of *TWD* becomes clear. However flexible our imaginations might be, however the conditions of a post-apocalyptic world can be redrawn, scenes like this admit how deeply the faith in meritocracy runs through our national consciousness. What does it say about us that the fantastic worlds we construct privilege those who produce value and read others as a liability? Anna Mae Duane explores this question in her essay "Dead *and* Disabled,"[28] but the point I am trying to make is that the particularized incarnation of zombies in a given film determines, in relief, a rubric for evaluating human worth.

Although I am heavily referencing Marxist philosophy for its robust analytical tools, the themes of consumerism in *TWD* do not strictly conform to it. As with the *Living Dead* series, the collapse of civilization transpires without a revolutionary proletariat achieving class-consciousness. Both the television show and the comic manufacture dramatic tension by pulling on various levers of group needs and external threats. Despite the changes in their circumstances, the group dynamic continually leans toward autocracy where leadership is entrusted to the most self-reliant members. The unquestioned acceptance of this fact reveals the ideological underpinnings of the belief that social stratification is a necessity, and that stratification is determined by exhibiting certain qualities. In *TWD*, Rick, Michonne, and Daryl are three characters central to all the group decision-making because all three of them have demonstrated self-reliance. For a text that is recognized by scholars for questioning sociological principles, the outcome nevertheless reinforces contemporary ideology. When characters reconstruct new societies, there is seldom any rejection of the ideology that previously sustained civilization. Therefore, the post-apocalyptic setting rarely fulfills Jameson's vision for a fully articulated Marxist critique. This is made clear in one of the final narrative arcs of *TWD* television series. Alpha, the arch-villain of the ninth and tenth seasons, repeatedly proselytizes about the failures of the old civilization. In issue #156 she tells one of her followers, Negan, "We are animals, Negan. Civilization is a myth. That is the truth this world has taught us."[29] By situating such radical rejections of contemporary society as antagonistic and evil, zombie narratives more often than not reinforce the status quo. Nevertheless, zombie narratives do provide the opportunity to reconstruct national myth, and the post-apocalyptic setting allows for pruning off the no longer appropriate components and the fashioning of the new.

By acknowledging the imbrication of zombie narratives and national mythology, it becomes possible to recognize *TWD*'s synchronicity with the frontier novels of James Fenimore Cooper discussed in chapter 3. The interrelation of individualism and national identity has historical precedent. Embedded within these values is an existential imperative to progress toward an ideal or utopian society and remain vigilant to preserve society against external and internal threats. These two notions of purification and exclusion are present throughout various iterations of American Exceptionalism and facilitate interpretation based on Jameson's dialectical hermeneutic. Despite the evangelical rhetoric of Winthrop's sermon, American Exceptionalism is not limited to religious ideology. In his essay "From the Virgin Land to the Transnational Identities of the Twenty-First Century," Gilles Vandivinit identifies American Exceptionalism as a primarily exclusionary ideology realized in the transcendentalist work of Ralph Waldo Emerson. He states that "Emerson's concept of the self-reliant American is what he understood as the main cornerstone of a society which had to free itself from European influences in order to grow into an independent nation."[30] American Exceptionalism and the self-reliance espoused by Emerson have become a hallmark of zombie texts and film.

A study on the demographics of television audiences published by the *New York Times* confirms this to be the case. In the report, author Josh Katz explains that the most popular shows on television can be mapped geographically across three types of regions. Katz lists these as "cities and their suburbs; rural areas; and what we're calling the extended Black Belt—a swath that extends from the Mississippi River along the Eastern Seaboard up to Washington, but also including city centers and other places with large nonwhite populations."[31] Even though the setting and filming of *TWD* takes place in the heart of the "Black Belt," this region is not the primary viewership. Instead, *TWD* is most popular in white rural areas, where activities associated with self-reliance such as hunting and fishing are highly valued.[32] As Poppy Wilde observes, "A zombie outbreak becomes almost romantically representative of a desire to 'return to our roots,' to test one's mettle against nature, and to embrace humanity's most 'animalistic sides.'"[33] It should be no surprise then that in the article about his interview with Jared Kushner, Steven Bertoni reports that "Kushner built a custom geo-location tool that plotted the location density of about 20 voter types over a live Google Maps interface" and Donald Trump's presidential campaign used data analytic tools that "drove the scaled-back TV ad spending by identifying shows popular with specific voter blocks in specific regions—say, *NCIS* for anti–Obamacare voters or *The Walking Dead* for people worried about immigration."[34] The reference to immigration recalls the exclusionist jeremiad of national myth. *TWD* specifically appeals to white rural Americans by creating an environment where self-reliance is privileged above all else and the spotlight of survivalism concentrates on proficiency with violence. The protagonists are regularly confronted with aggression and brutality and are forced to respond in kind, often with firearms. They must stand their ground to defend their values and loved ones.

The audience appeal is not mere coincidence, and the exceptionalist ideology is not isolated to a few rare incidents. It recurs throughout the entire series. Analysis of the opening episode of Season 6 titled "First Time Again" reveals several examples of this type. The protagonists inhabit what remains of a sustainable suburban community called Alexandria. Two members of the community, Rick and Morgan, discover zombies trapped in a quarry just outside Alexandria. Fearing that the horde might overflow the quarry at any moment and inundate the settlement, the residents assemble to review their options. Rick, the de facto leader, eventually persuades most of the community to deliberately release the horde and lure it away from Alexandria. Unconvinced, Carter meets secretly with several others to discuss the possibility of overthrowing Rick and his senseless schemes. Rick chances upon their meeting and confronts them. The scene culminates in a tense showdown between Rick and Carter, and Carter eventually concedes. Later Rick confides to Michonne that he is uncomfortable with the decision to let Carter live. He explains, "So I wouldn't have to worry about how he could screw up or what stupid thing he'd do next because that's who he is." Then he adds, "I wanted to kill him. But all that hit me and ... I realized I didn't have to do it. He doesn't get it. Somebody like that ... they're gonna die no matter what."[35] Rick's sense of Carter's ineptitude proves prescient. As they lead the horde away from Alexandria, Carter is bitten by a stray zombie and Rick is forced to kill him. The example illustrates that only those who display the survivalist spirit have a place in the settlement. Far from a democratic society, the very world that these survivors inhabit enforces American Exceptionalism on behalf of the community, so the sheriffs like Rick may wash their hands of any wrongdoing. In that sense, the zombies are simply a physical manifestation of all the threats Winthrop warned about in his sermon. In a strange twist of irony, the hero of this utopia is a re-imagined noble savage taken straight from the pages of Cooper's novels. In *The Last of the*

Mohicans, Hawkeye acquires his individualism from a life spent among the Mohicans, yet those same Native Americans are excluded from civilization for their savagery. In *TWD* the zombies create the conditions of a savage world where Rick's independent spirit and proficiency with violence is most needed. Those creatures that award him value must be similarly excluded from society, justifying the persistence of the jeremiad.

National myth is certainly not the only way to read *TWD* or zombie narratives in general. In fact, it is possible that many might resist such a reading. Nevertheless, I insist upon it in these instances because *TWD* is not only shot through with its tropes and iconography but directly confronts our historicization of U.S. origins by restaging the past in the show's penultimate narrative arc. From the opening season, the series prepares viewers for this eventuality through its sartorial gestures and western-themed costuming. The cowboy and cowgirl enjoy a long history of association with American identity. Sandra Curtis Comstock speaks to the overlap of denim, western wear, and national identity in her examination of denim in the depression era. She describes how in 1934 and 1935 Levi's advertisements committed to the "signature 'Western-style' blue jean with copper rivets, red-threaded seams and the leather patch circulating as a special symbol of the Western frontier."[36] More generally, she observes that it was this decade in which "the undistinguished working-class dungaree started to become a gender- and class-blurring icon of 'the American people.'"[37] Although Comstock admits that this vision was not fulfilled until the 1950s, an article from *Apparel Arts* in the mid–1940s illustrates the identification of western style with the national myth. It includes statements like "Western details and style appeal to men everywhere" and "Present day ranchers and cowboys wear clothing that has the same features and design as the first pioneers and frontiersmen that settled the old West" and is accompanied by photographs of Hollywood cowboys such as Roy Rogers and Errol Flynn.[38] The popularity of western wear has certainly ebbed and flowed, but another high point in its history was the late 1970s and early 1980s when Romero's *Dawn* hit the theaters. At the 1980 Winter Olympics at Lake Placid, Levi supplied U.S. athletes with their opening ceremony uniforms. In the *New York Times* article "U.S. Olympic Team Dresses Western," Angela Taylor writes, "Instead of the conservative, red, white and blue uniforms of past international sporting events— they've been described as 'polyester city'—this year's athletes are going to look like the great American hero, the cowboy, or the 'Girl of the Golden West.'"[39] Contemporaneous with the election of Ronald Reagan, the Cowboy President, Taylor's observations indicate that this is how the U.S. chose to represent itself to the world. Recalling that Kirkman imagined his franchise as the spiritual and literal extension of Romero's films from this era, it is only fitting that he styles Rick, the central figure of the narrative, as a six-shooter wielding sheriff on the post-apocalyptic frontier. The promo poster for Season 1 depicts Rick on horseback wearing his signature cowboy hat as he wanders alone on a deserted highway, the horizon occluded by the city skyline of a failed civilization.

Although western motifs and national symbology recur through the series, Angela Kang brings national myth to the forefront when she takes over as showrunner in Season 9.[40] The opening episode titled "A New Beginning" parades the audience with tropes conflating the colonial era with the frontier. These include farms, windmills, settlers on horseback, a horse drawn carriage, fields of corn, a derelict city, and a semi-blind preacher. The narrative of Season 9 picks up after the conclusion of a hard-fought revolution where Rick united several communities to overthrow the tyrannical rule of the Saviors, a group led by Negan. The protagonists now occupy five settlements: Alexandria, Hilltop, Sanctuary, Kingdom, and Oceanside, and the storyline of Season 9 constitutes their efforts to rebuild society. After the opening credits, an expedition team comprised of residents from the various communities enters a nonspecific Smithsonian museum in Washington, D.C., that features natural history as well as U.S. history artifacts. The team scavenges for supplies and tools locating a plow, a covered wagon, a hand-carved canoe, and some heirloom seeds. In addition to these symbolically loaded items, Kang parades her themes for the season throughout the museum exhibits—the words Manifest Destiny reflected on a glass floor, a display of the evolution of humankind with the final stage obscured by an impaled zombie, and a poster summarizing U.S. history emblazoned with the words "A More Perfect Union." As they explore, Carol, Maggie, and Michonne reflect on the different styles of government in each of their settlements. Carol jokes about how she is ruled by—and romantically involved with—a man who declared himself a king, and Maggie explains how she acquired leadership of Hilltop through the hubris of its former leader, Gregory. Believing that he held the trust of Hilltop, Gregory called for an election to brandish his authority only to see it taken away by losing to Maggie. Michonne scoffs, "The rebirth of democracy ... by that guy."[41] These moments illustrate how Kang is orchestrating the inaugural episode to frame this season as a reenactment of national myth.

Kang does not shy away from confronting the legal and judicial difficulties that complicate foundation a nation. Just as the authors of the Declaration of Independence "sought to justify as well as to account for the American separation from Britain,"[42] the united settlements of *TWD* are similarly faced with articulating a universal foundation for their revolution against the Saviors. In practical terms, they must decide what to do with the remaining Saviors, including Negan, whom the Alexandrians still hold prisoner. Do they deny the Saviors the very same rights that they fought the Saviors to acquire? If so, how are they any different from their former oppressors? Kang skillfully thrusts these questions into the spotlight when Gregory, dissatisfied with the election results, makes an attempt on Maggie's life. She survives the assassination attempt and decides to execute Gregory with a public hanging yet spare his accomplice. Her uneven justice foreshadows the difficulties that lie ahead. Rick's overt inaction exacerbates tension in the communities but also instigates a resolution. Several residents, still resentful of their treatment by the Saviors, exact revenge through extrajudicial killings. When Rick learns who is involved and what they have done, he literally turns his back on the situation and walks away as the vigilantes murder the last Savior on their list. Like the situation with Carter, Rick allows nature and the actions of rogue members to absolve him from the responsibility of adjudicating the contradictions of their community values. By the conclusion of the season, they resolve the problem more formally by ratifying the Multi-Community Charter of Rights and Freedoms.[43] The official signing occurs during a late autumn fair that loosely resembles a Thanksgiving celebration. Although the document is a symbolic achievement, their partnership itself is short-lived. One settlement is abandoned before the charter is signed, leaving a blank space for the signature of its representative. Unable to accumulate provisions for the coming winter, residents quickly abandon the Kingdom, and a new threat known as the Whisperers burn Hilltop in the next season leaving only Oceanside and Alexandria. Consequently, the history of the Charter is a cautious reminder of our own constitution—not perfect, not unanimous, and expected by many to fail. It is at such moments that Kang complicates national myth productively. *TWD* is far from the only zombie series to consciously re-enact and examine the project of nation building. The five-season arc of *Z Nation* culminates in a narrative of laying the groundwork for Newmerica. The obstacles that the protagonists encounter raise similar questions and the writers show a greater willingness to question the specular image of the American self. What makes *TWD* so useful for this study is that the charter narrative runs parallel to a burgeoning conflict with the Whisperers, a group that functions as a proxy for Native Americans.

If the overthrow of the Saviors symbolized the American Revolution, then the border dispute with the Whisperers re-enacts the winning of the west alongside the other U.S. frontiers that follow it. The Whisperers are first introduced in "Who Are You Now?" when residents of Alexandria encounter a new group of survivors unaffiliated with any of the known communities. The Alexandrians help defend the strangers against zombies exhibiting abnormal behavior. Over the next few episodes, they discover that a group known as the Whisperers are behind these badly behaving zombies. The Whisperers are living people who disguise themselves with masks of dead human flesh, allowing them to move freely among zombies. To avoid detection, they communicate to one another by whispering, hence their name. After living amongst the dead for so long, their leader, a woman named Alpha, developed an understanding of their behavior that allows her to amass hordes of zombies that she wields as a kind of slow-moving undead army. Although presented as a threat to the communities, the Whisperers' way of life suggests a genuine alternative to the protagonists' settler colonialism. To better understand their enemy, Daryl and a few companions capture Alpha's daughter, Lydia, and bring her inside the walls of Alexandria for interrogation. When she sees how they are rebuilding civilization, she exclaims, "This place isn't real. The world changed, and you're all acting like it's gonna change back." She adds, "My mom walks 'cause that's what the dead do. It's their world, and we have to live in it."[44] Legitimizing her logic would lead to the kind of narrative that echoes *I Am Legend* by Richard Matheson.

Unsurprisingly, accepting a subaltern status or even a non-hierarchical form of relations proves unthinkable. In "Stradivarius," an episode that takes place after the first encounter with Whisperers, the audience receives clarification on why this alternative will not work. Believing that Luke, one of the strangers mentioned earlier, is holding a weapon, Michonne slices through the object in his hands only to learn that it is an original Stradivarius. This leads to conversation between Luke and Siddiq, where Luke, a former music teacher, delivers a rehearsed lesson on civilization and the arts. He starts, "Look, for a very long time, historians and archeologists have wondered—how did ancient humans survive Neanderthals?" Luke answers his rhetorical question and argues that the discovery of a 40,000-year-old flute in a cave reveals that humans "shared their stories […] in the form of music," "created a … common identity," and "built communities." Gesturing with the broken Stradivarius he states, "This. This is the one thing that separates us from animals." He concludes, "It's survival of the fittest. Sharing with each other … that's part of what makes us stronger."[45] Thus, before we learn about the Whisperers and their way of life, Luke prepares us to recognize their cultural inferiority. Several episodes later, Daryl expresses utter disbelief when he learns that one of the Whisperers brought their baby to a potential battlefield. "You brought a baby out here?" he asks. Alpha answers, "We're animals. Animals live out here. Animals have babies. So we have babies out here."[46] Although Alpha may not have been present for Luke's lecture, describing her people as animals erases any doubt that the Whisperers signify his Neanderthal/animal reference.

Four. Social Critique and the Modern Zombie

When that introduction finally takes place, portrayals of the Whisperers vacillate between the familiar stereotypes of primitivism and savagism. Borrowing from the language of Gilles Deleuze and Félix Guattari, the Whisperers present as "nomadic" and tribal in comparison to the more civilized "sedentary" communities that reside in forts like Alexandria and Hilltop.[47] Additionally, the Whisperers refer to themselves as a pack and reject the use of names only using the titles of Alpha, Beta, Gamma, and Omega for those holding positions of authority. They are not merely a vague reference to Native Americans. When explaining the masks that they wear, Lydia calls them "skins,"[48] a loaded term with a long history as a pejorative for indigenous peoples. What begins as a word for their accessories quickly becomes a synecdoche for their identity. Members from the various communities refer to the Whisperers as "skin friends"[49] and "skin jobs"[50] but more commonly as just "skins."[51] Despite holding the line on the opposite side of racial controversies, even the NFL recognized that use of this term was a smudge on its reputation, and on July 13, 2020, the Washington football team announced the retirement of the Redskins name and logo. A year later, AMC continues to release new *TWD* episodes with "skins" written into the script.[52]

The significance of the relation between Indian tropes and Whisperers radiates beyond cavalier settler colonial dialogue. It draws attention to the various referents invoked by the narco-terrorist signifier that Jodi Byrd describes as "paradigmatic Indianness."[53] By the time the Whisperers appear, zombies have roamed the earth for over eleven years. There is always the potential for an unexpected life-threatening encounter with the undead, but anyone still living developed proficiency with killing zombies long ago. Therefore, the primary narrative conflicts result from interactions with other communities of survivors. What makes the Whisperers unique and particularly dangerous is that they are frequently indistinguishable from typical zombies. During the midseason finale, the fan-favorite character named Jesus dies when what he though was a zombie surprisingly dodges his sword and stabs him in the back.[54] His death betrays an attitude toward the undead that is indistinguishable from how Mary Rowlandson viewed her indigenous captors. As Nancy Armstrong and Leonard Tennenhouse write, "Indians exist in her account as mass man, devoid of individuated interiority and thus lacking the capacity for self-examination."[55] The Whisperers differ from Rowlandson's "barbarous creatures" only in the sense that they embody that perception.[56] The second episode of Season 10 closes with the tribe chanting, "We walk in darkness. We are free. We bathe in blood. We are free. We love nothing. We are free. We fear nothing. We are free. We need no words. We are free. We embrace all death. We are free. This is the end of the world. Now is the end of the world. We are the end of the world."[57] The precise language of the chant demands that viewers recognize Whisperers as paradigmatic Indians who are static, homogenous, and unreflective creatures that participate in ghost dances where the living partner with the dead. And if that were not enough, the Whisperers, as mentioned earlier, weaponize—dare I say radicalize—other zombies by controlling their behavior. Correctly understood, members of this group are identifiable to audiences as terrorists shrouded in Muslim garb, Mexican drug traffickers hiding among illegal immigrants, and savage Indians wearing the skins or scalps of their fallen enemies.

To defeat the Wampanoags during King Philip's War, Benjamin Church studied the tactics of his opponents to utilize against them, and he infiltrated their camps to capture the war chief Anawan, who was promptly beheaded. The mold of Church would be recast in fiction as Natty Bumppo alternatively named Hawkeye by Cooper in his Leatherstocking novels, and it would also appear as the symbolic ideal for the U.S. Army Indian Scouts designated with crossed arrows insignia. This was later adopted by the USSF (U.S. Special Forces) recognized during the Korean and Vietnam wars by their green berets. Although the USSF continues to exist today and remains involved in counterterrorism units across the globe, it is a model that paved the way for units like Seal Team 6 that carried out the execution of Osama bin Laden. Lest we forget, the code name for bin Laden was Geronimo. So when the Whisperers emerge as a veritable threat to the communities, the protagonists follow from the example set by Church to secure their safety. Under the cover of night, Carol releases the imprisoned Negan, the villain from previous seasons who led the Saviors and murdered several of the show's most beloved characters, and she recruits him to assassinate Alpha. He succeeds and, reminiscent of Church, personally delivers Alpha's head to Carol in a sack. And when Beta and the remaining Whisperers lay siege to a hospital where the entire community of Alexandrians are sheltering, a small group of Alexandrians save the day by performing the long-standing American ceremony of "playing Indian," a ritual so old it predates the Boston Tea Party.[58] They disembowel a few zombies and smear the entrails over their bodies to disguise themselves from the undead. Then, they disperse throughout the horde to eliminate the Whisperers and lead the remaining zombies away from the hospital. Like Church, who *became Indian* to defeat them and then set aside his Indianness when he returned home, this select group of Alexandrians prove themselves to be better Whisperers than the Whisperers and wash away their disguises when the fighting ends.

To say that collapsing the Declaration of Independence and the American Revolution with U.S.-Indian frontier warfare and Islamic terrorism excavates national myth beyond all sense of logic would be an understatement. The overburdening of signifiers appears to render any kind of meaning meaningless. The immigrant is not the terrorist, is not the drug trafficker, is not the Indian; yet the discourse of national identity uses the same language and symbols over and over again to portray them as interchangeable. So while it is true that *TWD* fails to resolve the semiological contradictions, it nevertheless collapses multiple national histories into a single narrative and succeeds in spite of its irrationality. Furthermore, this seeming dysfunction operates quite effectively because each member of the audience sees within the narrative a specular image that posits their experience as representative of a homogenous national identity. Where Duane reads *TWD* as a projection of how we view disability,[59] Ángel Mateos-Aparicio and Jesús Benito Sánchez interpret the show through a lens of immigration,[60] and perhaps surprisingly to some, including myself, Cutcha Risling Baldy sees the atrocities suffered by the protagonists as well as their resilience and determination as a reflection of indigenous experiences.[61] These varied interpretations communicate myth's capacity to resonate across differences while fulfilling its primarily conservative function affirming and validating the previously held beliefs. The efficacy of *TWD* as national myth permits viewers to extrapolate these contradictory interpretations from the same work.

To her credit as a showrunner, Kang demonstrates a willingness to entertain doubts about the legitimacy of the histories invoked by *TWD*. Although she does not go so far as to overturn them, she gives voice to potential criticisms. In the Season 10 opener, Aaron questions Michonne about the probity of their cause. He asks, "Are we the good guys?" and then posits, "We're the villains of someone else's story, a threat to their survival, so dangerous they threaten to wipe us out." Michonne responds, "It's not about being nice or good or anything but keeping our people alive and not having them die over nothing. Believe me. I hate this, too." Later in the episode she adds, "I've been thinking about what you said earlier, 'bout who we've become, who we are. And the truth is, we are the good guys. And I know who Rick and Carl were ... and Eric and Jesus, too. We have to choose to be the good guys even when it's hard. And ... the minute that we start to question that and we lose sight of it, that's when the answer to that question starts to change, and that's scarier than any skin mask." Rather than reading her second answer as a reconsideration of the first, I understand it as an elaboration. Michonne construes preserving their way of life with preserving their lives. To her, yielding authority to Alpha or even acknowledging the legitimacy of other communities would concede the illegitimacy of their settler colonial ideology. Michonne understands that belief in their own righteousness is paramount to survival. Without the veneer of justice, their actions are criminal, and they would have a lot of blood on their hands. Nevertheless, their discussion comes off more like a token gesture because it is raised in the season opener and dismissed just as quickly. The uncertainty that Aaron or any other member of the communities may harbor never resurfaces.

The fulfillment of Lydia's narrative effectively puts any questioning to rest. As a former Whisperer and the daughter of Alpha, Lydia experiences discrimination from other settlers. For a time, she was protected from this by her boyfriend Henry, Carol's adopted son, but after his death her situation in the community deteriorates. She is repeatedly insulted, physically harassed, and almost lynched if it were not but for the timely arrival of Negan. Her treatment differs only by degree from the abuse she suffered at the hands of her mother. In addition, to engender dissent, Carol manipulates her into exposing some of Alpha's lies to the Whisperers. Carol's dissimulation confuses and frustrates Lydia. Because she finds it increasingly difficult to place trust in the Alexandrian promise of moral exceptionalism, Lydia runs away to live on her own. Her dissolution with Alexandria is only exacerbated when she learns that Carol orchestrated Alpha's assassination. When the Whisperers lay siege to a hospital where survivors from all the communities have taken refuge, Carol and Lydia find it impossible to continue avoiding one another and must settle their differences. Yet instead of a confrontation, Lydia thanks her for what she did, and it is Carol who remains cold and distant, fearing that Lydia views her as a replacement mother.

> **LYDIA:** If you're avoiding me, please stop. I don't hate you for what you did.
> **CAROL:** You should. Didn't fix anything.
> **LYDIA:** It did for me. A little, at least. I know that sounds awful, but.... She was never really my mother. Not in the way that matters. So, thanks. And I—I ... I'd like it if we can still talk. About ... whatever.
> **CAROL:** Lydia.... You need to be yourself. You need to find your own way.
> **LYDIA:** I'm not looking for another mom, you know? That's not what this has to be. It can be something else. So can you.[62]

Although Carol refuses to accept her role as mother of her dead son's girlfriend, the narrative nevertheless portrays Lydia as deciding between Alpha and Carol. In such a way, Lydia's choice of Carol affirms the uprightness of Alexandria, even in the face of its extrajudicial assassination of indigenous leaders' program. Despite my flippancy, there is more to Lydia's dilemma that warrants consideration. The conversation between Michonne and Aaron discloses their belief that anything is permissible to preserve what they believe is right. Moreover, the hate speech and violence Lydia suffers at the hands of other Alexandrians and

Kushner's anti-immigration ad campaign confirm that this narrative articulates a particularized ideological position in the national dialogue about the Mexican-American border, a position that leverages a national identity erected from a reductive historicization of Native American-U.S. relations. And thus, in this twisted re-enactment of nation myth, we have Lydia, a signifier for Latinx and indigenous peoples, enduring discrimination and simultaneously thanking the settler colonial power for killing her mother/ruler to save her from herself.

Because Lydia serves as adjudicator of causes, we must reflect on two points. First, there is her, albeit temporary, renunciation of Alexandria. Lydia's well-founded disillusion with the community results from her recognition that the parties on both sides of the conflict were willing to commit egregious human rights violations. Consequently, her decision of who to support is determined by a single criterion—the efficacy of Alpha and Carol as mothers. Second, presenting Alpha as a toxic and abusive, a characteristic that has no historic or contemporary correlate in national myth, renders this a false choice exogenous to any intrinsic quality of either group. By construing Lydia's decision to side with the Alexandria's as approval of their community, the show dissimulates the contradictions of national ideology. Other than preserving the safety of one's own, a rationale that is not unique to any imagined community, the political and ideological position invoked by the Alexandrians offers no justification for dispossessing the Whisperers of their land and exterminating their entire population. These two seasons of *TWD* demonstrate the conservative ideological function of zombie narratives that engage national myth and offer a cautious reminder of the need for critical analysis. The overview of zombie texts in this chapter contextualizes how the deployment of zombies has adapted to remain uniquely positioned to explore ontological questions. Although the current iterations of undead differ widely from the origins in Haitian folklore, there are consistent themes that remain central. For the Haitians and the Lakota ghost dancers, the ritual practice of possession creates spaces for negotiating cultural change and development. While the zombie narratives are by no means limited to the examples discussed in this chapter, they reveal a similar potential but are largely relegated to counterrevolutionary doctrine. Because the behavior of zombies produces the conditions for survival and consequently the values, ethics, and skillset of the ideal survivor, serious culture critique requires precise (re-)calibration of how zombies are embodied.

Chapter Five

Civil Rights Movement Retold in Disney *Zombies*

Know, first, who you are; and then adorn yourself accordingly.
—Epictetus

Deconstructing the myth of American identity lays bare the structure and content of the colonial violence that inhabits the nation's history. By understanding myth as historiography that narrativizes or emplots the events of the past to make sense of the present, the text of myth provides a window into national consciousness. Roland Barthes outlines a semiotic approach that utilizes synchronic and diachronic analysis to articulate the work of myth in his often-overlooked essay "Myth Today."[1] As Barthes explains, analysis becomes possible because its content is shared by the national consciousness and must therefore be readable or understandable by that people. According to Barthes, "*myth hides nothing*: its function is to distort, not to make disappear."[2] Semiological analysis can be applied to contemporary texts like the Disney Channel's 2018 film *Zombies* to investigate American myth.[3] Juxtaposing a close reading of the film alongside a genealogy of American myth discloses how the film re-enacts the ritual of constructing national identity.

National Consciousness and Identity

When Benedict Anderson conceived the phrase "imagined communities," he did so out of recognition for an emergent national consciousness that he attributed to print technology and capitalism.[4] Eric Hobsbawm suggests that without such vocabulary American colonists' use of the term "the people" constitutes a particularized instantiation of what scholars now conceive of as national identity.[5] Central to this analysis is recognizing the function of myth in establishing the homogenous character of national identity, homogenous in the sense that what it means to be American transcends time and space. This is not to say that the experience of an American in 1787 was the same as it is today. Rather, the immanent national consciousness constructs a continuity with the past. As Étienne Balibar writes, "the imaginary singularity of national formations is constructed daily, by moving back from the present into the past."[6] From Balibar we are to understand that national identity presents as monolithic and ahistorical, handed down invariably from generation to generation, fulfilling a destiny only conceivable in the present moment. A year prior to delivering his seminal frontier thesis in 1893, Frederick Jackson Turner penned an essay titled "Problems in American History" that insists on this point. He argues, "American history needs a connected and unified account of the progress of civilization across this continent, with the attendant results. Until such a work is furnished we shall have no real national self-consciousness; when it is done, the significance of the discovery made by Columbus will begin to appear."[7] Turner's words distill the geographic and teleological historiography that underlies his Daedalian project of constructing an American national identity. He measures history and the progress of civilization spatially across the topography of the continent, underscoring that the significance of the past can only be understood in terms of its uninterrupted and ineluctable advance toward the present. Moreover, he recognizes a singular national identity as the intended product of such a history. By constructing such a continuity, the past is flattened and transformed into what Walter Benjamin describes as "homogenous, empty time."[8] Thus, contradictions get written out of history or, borrowing from Michel-Rolph Trouillot, "silenced,"[9] and those that cannot be silenced are reframed. For example, slavery and the 3/5ths compromise are perceived as aberrations, flaws in the dispensation of national identity that the founding fathers were too short-sighted or too limited by historical context to set right.

Following in the tradition of films like *Green Book* and Disney's *The Help*, *Zombies* and its sequels *Zombies 2* and *Zombies 3* encourage principally white audiences to reconcile the racist heritage of the U.S. by allowing them to relocate to the right side of history through identification with characters who oppose discrimination. Unpacking the "bundle of silences"[10] in *Zombies* exposes the film's reduction of the civil rights movement and indigenous removal into a single narrative. Building on the success of previous straight to television movies such as *High School Musical* and *Descendants*, *Zombies* is a musical that centers on the lives of several suburban high school students who struggle with parental authority, fitting in, bullies, and adolescent hormones. Set in the fictional planned community of Seabrook, the diegetic world of *Zombies* approximates contemporary society if contemporary society included the presence of zombies. Typical of the genre, the living dead function as signifier for the other. While the community's name pays homage to William Seabrook's 1929 travelogue *The Magic Island*, the hubris of its residents and forced acculturation of zombies more closely resembles Turner's historiographic account of the frontier. Where the frontier myth designates indigenous peoples as the racial other, *Zombies* substitutes blacks. In the context of American history, this is not a particularly surprising move. Thomas Jefferson pioneered such a conflation when he personally revised the proposed constitutional amendment to admit Louisiana into the Union by limiting citizenship to "white inhabitants."[11] By segregating the school entrances for students with overtly symbolic signage, the film refigures whites as "Normals" and the racial other as "Zombies." As Chera Kee observes, the "zombie-as-proxy" for otherness, especially racial otherness, is quite common for the genre.[12] Thus, the protagonists are synecdochical signifiers of their community as they negotiate the problem of racial difference. The normal female Addison and the zombie male Zed, star-crossed lovers, personate the civil rights movement upon entering high school, staying true to themselves and each other by confronting discrimination. Addison's individuation requires reconciling the fact of her own difference against the expectations and standards of her community.

The deployment of the romantic hero as synecdochical signifier is not unique to this film. Disney has a long history of producing romantic heroes like Addison who revolt against social norms only later to be recast as heroes.[13] Characters like Elsa of *Frozen*, Merida of *Brave*, and Ariel of *The Little Mermaid* illustrate heroes who reject or are rejected by civilization, conduct their errand into the wilderness, and return with knowledge to promote social change. Like Addison, the efficacy of their contributions is determined by consensus politics. Despite their sophomoric fervor, they never fundamentally threaten the society that they, albeit temporarily, disavow. Paradoxically, the ubiquity of these transgressive heroes suggests that this narrative structure has been institutionalized as a ritual act of identity formation. Justyna Fruzinska broadly observes how "Disney's production inscribes itself into a wider tradition." She continues, "It seems that Americans are particularly fond of making anti-imperialist films that should redeem them from their own imperialist foreign policy and guilt complex."[14] Fruzinska's statement points beyond the familiar critique of Disney's history of racism and cultural stereotyping to the errand mythologized in American colonial historiography.[15] The collective consciousness of the early colonists was defined by the simultaneous rejection of the decadence of European civilization and the savagery of indigenous peoples. The errand into the wilderness forged the American national identity by mediating those two opposing forces. The unique character of this ritual is the identification of the individual with the national. As Myra Jehlen observes, "To be born an American is simultaneously to be born again. Americans assume their national identity as the fulfillment of selfhood rather than as its point of origin, so that they travel their lives in a state of perpetual landing."[16] To be American is to continually become American. It is not teleology but entelechy. Rather, it is not only teleology but also entelechy. Paraphrasing Edward Said, it is a community of individuals acting for themselves in concert, whose music continually constructs the past.[17] As represented in the film by Addison's rivals on the cheer team, the failure of society to adapt results in its eventual downfall. Therefore, the ritual of national identity produces transgressive heroes like Addison who are re-interpolated by consensus politics to ensure its continual renewal. Through her success, the other is colonized and assimilated.

Errand into Zombietown

The ritual formation of American identity is composed of the dialectical forces of civilization and savagery. In *Zombies*, Addison and Zed occupy a liminal space that threatens the mutual exclusivity of these forces. The film opens with parallel monologues, simultaneously introducing their personal histories and the film's backstory. According to the monologues, an accident at Seabrook power plant fifty years earlier turned half of the town into brain-eating zombies. The unaffected residents built a wall, dividing the city into Seabrook and Zombietown and invoking comparison to the border wall between the United States and Mexico. During the fifty years of apartheid, the government of Seabrook developed a wristband, z-band, to ensure the safety of normals by inhibiting zombies' superhuman athletic prowess and brain-eating impulses, essentially transforming them into functional isomorphs with ashy skin and dye-resistant green hair. Although the film does not disclose when all zombies were fitted with z-bands, Zed attributes their current progress in assimilating to the device. Now that the first zombies are invited to attend Seabrook High School, signifying the initial stages of desegregation, Zed observes that "things are changing." Designating the school a "contact zone"[18] for zombies and normals is the obvious choice; it simultaneously draws on the popularity of *High School Musical* and the colonial logic of forced assimilation in Indian boarding schools.

The juxtaposed musical monologues reveal Addison's and Zed's preoccupation with pursuing their own desires while also meeting the expectations of family and peers. Both are conflicted about seeking recognition from a society that disavows them for their otherness and yearning for a future where they will be accepted. Zed wants to join the football team and Addison wants to be a cheerleader. Fittingly, when in high school, Addison's father, Dale played on the football team, and her mother, Missy, was a cheerleader. As adults, they are chief of Zombie Patrol and mayor, respectively. The achievements and status of her family mark her as the apogee of civilization, but the expectations weigh on her. She sings, "Mom's counting on me" and later "Cheer's in my family genes." We then learn that her cousin Bucky is captain of the cheer team. The significance of Addison's reference to her genetics cannot be overstated; it is the first in the bundle of silences unveiled. Not only does it invoke uncomfortable associations with race identity theory, but also it exposes genetics as the dividing line between normal and zombie. As Zed introduces himself and his zombie family, the importance of genetics becomes clearer. Because the accident at the Seabrook power plant occurred fifty years prior and zombification does not appear to inhibit aging, Zed and his younger sister Zoey must have been born after the accident. The only explanation for their existence as zombie children is that their father Zevon procreated and genetically passed on the zombie trait.

We also learn in the opening song that Addison's family has disguised the fact that she has white hair. She rationalizes her family's discretion: "People here hate anything that's different. If anyone outside my family found out I wore a wig, I would never be allowed to cheer. So, I've worn a wig for as long as I can remember." Her admission discloses the jeremiad as the apparatus by which the community maintains the boundary between normals and zombies. Sacvan Bercovitch cites John Winthrop's hallmark address to the Massachusetts Bay colonists voyaging across the Atlantic as the inauguration of the American jeremiad, a common litany delivered by religious leaders on momentous political occasions that links the strife, tribulations, and depravity of the time with society's moral decay.[19] Winthrop's sermon unites these themes of mourning current moral failures of society and simultaneously calls for the (re)building of a new city, alert from threats within and without. During the voyage on the Arabella to the Massachusetts Bay Colony, Winthrop states on April 8, 1630, "for wee must Consider that wee shall be as a Citty upon a Hill, the eies of all people are uppon us; soe that if wee shall deale falsely with our god in this worke wee have undertaken and soe cause him to withdrawe his present help from us, wee shall be made a story and a by-word through the world."[20] Not unlike the whiteness of Herman Melville's whale, to the community of Seabrook, the whiteness of Addison's hair symbolizes the sublime and the savage. Its suppression is essential for maintaining the rigid boundary of civilization.

Genetic Hybrids

From this homogenous melting pot of multiculturalism, each American is born, ahistorical. Addison, the model citizen, enacts the myth of national identity, and the film is her bildungsroman. With her noble pedigree and contact with the frontier, she conforms to other heroes of U.S. fiction such as Edgar Rice Burroughs' Tarzan and James Fenimore Cooper's Natty Bumppo. Her errand begins with a serendipitous introduction to Zed. On the first day of school, she ironically ends up trapped, alone with him in a saferoom designed to isolate and protect normals from zombies during an outbreak. Because they meet in darkness, Addison fails to recognize the coded visual signifiers of Zed's undead identity. She is charmed by his wit but recoils in horror when she discovers he is a zombie. Actually, she punches him in the face. Her reaction is what Julia Kristeva calls abjection, the response of disgust that occurs when the subject, or presubject, simultaneously loathes and desires a "'something' that I do not recognize as a thing."[21] The "something" or pre-object to which Kristeva refers is the substance that collects on the external boundary of the self. It is neither subject nor object. Kristeva writes, "It is something rejected from which one does not part, from which one does not protect oneself as from an object. Imaginary uncanniness and real threat, it beckons to us and ends up engulfing us. It is thus not a lack of cleanliness or health that causes abjection but what disturbs identity, system, order."[22] If this happened to any other student who sufficiently interpellated Seabrook's notions of identity, the interaction would have been silenced as an aberration. But because Addison, a freshman with genetically anomalous white hair, has not yet established her subjectivity, the experience is formative.

Once Addison makes the cut as a Seabrook cheerleader, she must undergo the initiation ritual that safeguards the hegemonic interpolation of all team members. Bucky, along with several of the other current cheerleaders, drives the two new recruits in a minivan after curfew into Zombietown. Bucky explains the situation: "Every year, for cheer initiation, we like to remind zombies that we don't accept freaks in this town. Egg that zombie house and you're both officially one of us." To maintain social order, cheerleaders perform this ritual of re-affirming the boundary between normals and the undead. Later, in a conversation with Bucky, Addison says, "Zombies are students at Seabrook too, Bucky. Picking on them isn't right." After some back and forth, Bucky interrupts Addison and concludes, "It's best if you don't question things. Pep rally today, cuz. You're gonna rock it." Kristeva argues social rite provides the cultural machinery, such as defilement, for dealing with unstable boundaries. She states, "On account of the flexibility at work in rites of defilement, the subjective economy of the speaking being who is involved abuts on both edges of the unnamable (the non-object, the off-limits) and the absolute (the relentless coherence of Prohibition, sole donor of Meaning)."[23] To preclude pathological narcissism, the ritual charges individuals to reify the subject-object perimeter. Addison's refusal to participate disrupts social order by drawing attention to the non-totalizing distinction between zombies and normals. While her refusal may upset Bucky, it is really only a problem if her abjection persists. Whether or not Addison properly observes every ceremonial practice matters less than her univocal attention to the threshold of her subjectivity. Therefore, Bucky ends the conversation by redirecting Addison's thoughts to the next upcoming ritual, the pep rally. A cheerleader must hold the line on identity by celebrating purity. They are the deputies who stand watch over the city upon a hill.

Addison's sympathy for the undead is more than mere coincidence. Her white hair is an aperture in the perimeter of normals' subjectivity; it binds her to the zombies genetically. When Addison expresses sympathy for them, Bucky reminds her that one bit their grandfather's ear off. Based on the youthful appearance of all the adults, we can assume Addison's parents, as well as Bucky's, were born after their grandfather was bitten. While there is never any mention that zombies can infect normals, the existence of undead children like Zed and Zoey demonstrates that zombie characteristics are passed on genetically. When Addison explains the anomaly of her hair, she states that "[doctors] think it's some rare genetic thing," suggesting that her hair color, like zombies,' is heritable. Thus, the bite her grandfather sustained likely synthesized human and zombie genetics, making Addison part zombie. Such a theory explains her family's famed athletic ability and recalls Addison's earlier claim, "Cheer's in my family genes." Just as zombies uninhibited by z-bands display incredible strength, agility, and speed, Bucky's and Addison's athletic abilities surpass their peers.' Moreover, unique hair color is an exclusive zombie trait. While zombie hair is green and Addison's is white, neither zombies nor Addison have the capacity to simply dye their hair. Addison explains, "I can't dye it, nothing sticks. I've tried everything." Only Zed manages to alter his hair color, albeit without dye. When he passes as normal by tampering with his z-band, his hair goes black. This raises the question about what would happen if Addison put on a z-band and adjusted it to make her normal.

Perhaps Addison does not carry zombie genetics. The final scene of *Zombies 2* hints that she may instead be an alien. In the dead of night, an unidentified object from space illuminates the sky above the sleepy town of Seabrook. Addison wakes as her alarm clock flickers and her hair glows bright with electricity. Whether she be an alien, a werewolf, or a zombie, the mere possibility of her genetic difference warrants repression. Unearthing the truth of the family risks destabilizing social order. Such a revelation would lay bare the contradiction that Seabrook's crowning achievement, the cheer team, may entirely depend on the nonhuman genetics of Addison's family. Because belief is commensurate with fact in the context of myth and identity, the act of repression instantiates her genetic deviance. It does not prove that Addison is part-zombie, but it proves that her parents and Bucky believe that she is or fear that the citizens of Seabrook will perceive her as such. When she reveals her true hair color at the homecoming game, she is making a calculated decision based on her understanding of what Pierre Bourdieu calls the "state of the field." He writes, "as a function of the structure of the possible which are manifested through the different positions and the properties of the occupants (particularly with respect to social origin and the corresponding dispositions), and also as a function of the positions actually and potentially occupied within the field (experienced as success or failure)—the dispositions associated with a certain social origin are specified by being enacted in structurally marked practices."[24] Addison and the film's audience recognize her as a romantic hero in the American tradition. By that logic, she stands outside of society and journeys into the frontier to subdue it for her community. The assent of her peers determines the efficacy of the ritual performance. But Addison misjudges her position and the dispositions of the students and parents of Seabrook High. To her surprise, the community is appalled by her hair color and rejects her. This blunder signifies that Addison's errand remains incomplete until she exercises sufficient Nietzschean will to power to regain their approval.

Sartorial Signification

The spectacle of Addison's white hair appears artificial until the film parades an armamentarium of increasingly racialized signifiers for inscribing the genetic distinction between normals and zombies. In *The Black Jacobins*, we find historical precedent for maintaining these sorts of boundaries. Because skin color was not sufficiently reliable, C.L.R. James describes white slaveowners would withhold granting their family names to any mulatto kin to safeguard against ambiguous racial identity. He writes, "Few of the slaves being able to read, the colonists did not hesitate to say openly: 'It is essential to maintain a great distance between those who obey and those who command. One of the surest means of doing this is the perpetuation of the imprint that slavery has once given.'

No Mulatto, therefore, whatever his number of white parts, was allowed to assume the name of his white father."[25] Following from this tradition, all zombie names in the film are conspicuously brought to you by the letter Z. Conversely, no names for normals include that letter. Moreover, by recognizing *Zombies* as a utopian text, we learn that naming is only one of the conventions used to represent the distribution of power. Utopian narratives typically offer an imagined space for examining sociological and political phenomena with a limited set of variables. In his book *The Dressed Society*, Peter Corrigan includes a chapter that surveys the canon of utopian texts in English from the sixteenth to the twentieth century. He states, "Utopian texts form a sort of parallel universe to conventional sociological and political theories, commenting upon the contemporary societies in which their authors lived through engagement with an imaginatively constructed society."[26] This definition allows for reading *Zombies* as a condensation and displacement of the civil rights movement. One challenge for the genre is making the stratification of social hierarchy visible to the audience. Corrigan describes how utopian narratives use costuming to signify status, power, social class, gender, and sexuality. He observes, "it is typical of utopias that the social function of individuals or groups is immediately readable from their dress: not only does everyone have their proper place in utopia but this place is visible to all."[27] Rita McGhee oversaw costume design and sacrificed nuance for immediate readability for the adolescent viewers of *Zombies*. Although McGhee's sartorial exaggerations may appear foppish, the social distinctions dress offers are integral to ensure comprehensibility of the visually coded social hierarchy.

The normals' wardrobe adheres to a classic aesthetic, albeit one comprised exclusively of pastels. Garments for women include 1950s era classic length dresses and skirts frequently limited to a single pastel tone. The attire of the school-aged Addison and her peers often incorporates an additional solid tone that reflects the Seabrook High School colors, pink and green, but with slightly higher hemlines. Otherwise, teen clothing mirrors the minimalist 1950s outfits of the adult women. Men don pastel classic suits, and school-aged boys are similarly outfitted, though in more casual variants, occasionally substituting shorts for pants. If the possibility for diversity in the clothing of normals seems limited, the wardrobe for zombie adults and children of all genders is more homogenized and even suggestive of prison uniforms. In his half of the opening monologue, Zed explains: "Zombies have to wear government-issued coveralls." The z-bands that surveil and control their behavior evoke comparison to parolee ankle monitors. While some variation exists among the coveralls, most ensembles consist of baggy pants, t-shirts, and a vest, jacket, or hoodie made from heavier cotton designed for workwear. In contrast to the pastels of normals, zombies wear all earth tones. To parallel the Seabrook pink and green, zombie clothes feature a muddy red and toxic green. These colors are even reflected in the architecture of the buildings on their side of the border wall. Overall, the zombie aesthetic showcases a hip-hop, grunge syncretism. The hip-hop influence is brandished with loose fitting clothing, especially oversized hoodies and jackets, and the distressed clothing, frayed edges, and patchwork signal a grunge affect. In his opening monologue, Zed continues, "But we make 'em look pretty cool." He gestures to the patches sewn onto the clothing. Other zombie textiles are embroidered with writing, presumably in zombie language, but the line technique and character design are conspicuously Asian. While the Asian script may seem out of place, it must be understood in terms of the narrative's allusion to the civil rights movement. In her book *Liberated Threads*, Tanisha Ford traces the history of "soul style" during the civil rights era and explores efforts to reclaim precolonial African heritage.[28] Unlike African Americans, however, the zombies of Seabrook have no cultural legacy. Prior to the power plant catastrophe, they were normals. The adoption of street style by zombies is a mimetic gesture of soul style that substitutes anything exotic—in this case urban—for the absence of a cultural inheritance. In the context of the Haitian Revolution, such "self-styling," according to Charlotte Hammond, "symbolized a subtle and covert form of resistance to the colonial hierarchies of power and interrogated emerging discourses of gendered and racial otherness."[29] Nevertheless, in the Disney film, the strong codes of clothing are "immediately readable" and make distinguishing a normal from a zombie easy, even from a quick glance at a distance.

The racial signification of zombies extends beyond prison-like coveralls.[30] Like their unified hair color, zombies' ash-colored skin is an uncomfortable black-face analogue. At one point, Zed's zombie friend Eliza complains of feeling sick and asks "Do I look green? Greener than usual?" suggesting that the visible skin color difference between zombies and normals is akin to looking ill. Moreover, the zombie language, Zombie, almost exclusively used by Zed's other close friend, the novelty sidekick Gonzo, deserves attention. Because Gonzo speaks no English, Zed must translate for him. Gonzo's lines in the opening song are "Zig-zag quig quad / Ziggy gag za ziggity za yo." While the words mean nothing to the audience, the silliness and oversimplicity of Zombie underscores an absence of civilized culture. Nevertheless, Gonzo's untranslated language results in a fascinating interaction between Eliza and Zed. In order to introduce the audience to the fact that zombies have unique and valuable cultural constructs of their own, Eliza interjects, "He just dropped that in Zombie." Zed quickly undermines her by translating, "Yeah, all he said is he's hungry." This conversation indicates Zed's preference for submitting to and sustaining current structures of authority. In addition to their hip-hop appearance, zombies favor rap in their musical numbers. When with his zombie peers Zed raps, but when alone with Addison he sings, affirming his desire to assimilate. Zombie dancing is also distinctly hip-hop with its breaking, popping, and locking while normals dancing revolves around cheer. As their relationship develops, Zed sneaks Addison into Zombietown after curfew for a Zombie Mash, a party held in a dilapidated industrial facility. Addison joins the zombies in a performance of "BAMM," a Disney-glossed hip-hop song that undeniably points to the civil rights movement with its "I'm a man" chant for a chorus. Costuming for the musical number exaggerates the urban edge of zombie chic with baggy, low-slung pants and gold overcoats with giant hoodies. Zed's friend Eliza wears a red jacket and matching pants reminiscent of Michael Jackson's memorable red leather couture in *Thriller*. The idiosyncratic bling of these outfits deviates from the earth tones of their government-issued uniforms, presumably because this clothing would not normally be permitted.

Of the three prominent zombie characters—Zed, Eliza, and Gonzo—only the role of Eliza is performed by a black person. The decision to cast white actresses and actors to perform zombie roles may appear to complicate my interpretation of the racialized costuming. Yet as Philip Deloria reveals in his book *Playing Indian*, white people performing as the colonial other is quite literally a national pastime. In particular, Deloria draws attention to an initiation ritual developed by the anthropologist Lewis Henry Morgan for his New Confederacy. The organization was essentially an indigenous studies research club for white scholars. Deloria explains, "The Inindianation ceremony wrenched members' identities, transforming them from Yankees—the actual beneficiaries of American Indian policy—to aboriginal American Selves. It placed Morgan and his companions in a symbolically powerful and emotionally charged position for creating a literature rooted in America's landscape and nature. New names and Indian dress made the membership indigenous in the present, while vanishing Indian rhetoric relegated the people of the second Iroquois epoch to the past."[31] By participating in this ritual, initiates were reborn as indigenous. Because *Zombies* projects blackness onto white bodies, the film reinstantiates Morgan's Inindianation ceremony. But where the New Confederacy offered "guilt-cleansing" for indigenous extermination, *Zombies* redeems audiences from post–Civil War racial violence. Casting white actors as black signifiers and dressing them up in zombie-face enables white audiences to identify with the victims and saviors of systemic racism in the U.S.

Negotiated Assimilation

Seabrook's government, comprised of the city council and the Zombie Patrol, along with the school principal and cheerleading team, administer and mediate power. Addison's parents are merely figureheads, so their involvement in decision-making or even daily operations is nominal. Addison's mother is the mayor but not in any visible way. At the opening of the film, Missy says, "Addison, you know that Seabrook's won every cheer championship since...." Addison interjects, "Forever." Missy continues, "Forever. But now that city council's having our zombies in our schools, we need cheer more than ever. As mayor, I beseech you. You make that team and win that cheer championship!" Missy admits that the city council decided to integrate and that she holds little power. Her admission reveals the real authority of Seabrook lies in the city council, located off-screen and out of reach for the students of Seabrook as well as zombies in general. Addison's father, Dale, leads the Zombie Patrol, yet never overtly directs their actions or gives orders. Despite a similar visual absence, the Zombie Patrol spontaneously materializes during moments of crisis, such as when it restrains Gonzo at the pep rally, shuts down the after-curfew Zombie Mash, and detains those with hacked z-bands after the homecoming game. Such surveillance invokes comparison to Michel Foucault's analysis of the panopticon. Foucault asserts "the inmate must never know whether he is being looked at at any one moment; but he must be sure that he may always be so."[32] The sudden and unannounced arrival of the Zombie Patrol at these moments confirms its constant, if invisible, presence.

When Zed sneaks Addison into an underground dance party in Zombietown after curfew, he is not merely submitting to the hormonal compulsions of a typical lovestruck teen. The dance floor transforms into a temporary illicit contact zone that fosters integrationist impulses. In his examination of the subversive and revolutionary power of dance, Christopher Smith argues that "even before Civil Rights and the Second World War, dance floors were accepted as liminal spaces in which transgressive contact between and across gender, race, and class frequently occurred."[33] He goes on to describe the practice of "slumming," which was "associated, in the early twentieth century, with middle- and upper-class whites (particularly the Progressives of lower Manhattan and Greenwich Village) who made the Harlem clubs popular sites for voyeuristic entertainment."[34] Even though Addison goes to the Zombie Mash sporting an all-pink tracksuit, Zed encourages her to "be yourself" because "it's the coolest thing." Eliza expresses disgust that Zed dared to bring her to the event, yet moments later, Addison backflips onto the dance floor for the chorus of "BAMM" singing "I'm in Zombieland / You're in Zombieland." Vis-à-vis the ritual of national identity, her quest for self-exploration led her to the frontier site of Zombieland. Several lines later in the song, she further immerses herself by returning to the floor sporting a reflective silver coat borrowed from another undead dancer. Garbed in zombie couture and equipped with the knowledge of their choreography, she dances alongside Zed and begins to earn recognition from Eliza. The sudden appearance of the Zombie Patrol at the conclusion of the song draws attention to the transformative and destabilizing power of dance.

Frustrated by the unequal treatment of zombies, Addison and her zombie friends repeatedly confront these authorities to fight social injustice. To enact change, Addison and Zed direct their attention to the school administration and the cheerleading team. Like the mayor, Principal Lee also denies her own authority. When she welcomes the zombies to their basement classroom and introduces them to their janitor ... ahem ... teacher, Lee says, "I'm Principal Lee. We are thrilled to be forced to have ... you here." Unlike Missy, however, Lee does display the authority and willingness to negotiate social order. She has power over what happens in the school even if she does not get to decide who enters and exits. After Zed demonstrates his athletic prowess by rescuing Addison from near disaster, Lee permits him to join the football team and agrees to accelerate the integration of zombies in the school on the condition that he carry the team to victory. Bucky also exerts limited authority over the interactions with zombies, but his approach stands in stark contrast to Lee's. He rigorously enforces segregation and discourages all student contact with the undead. Bucky and Lee, two visible figures of authority within reach, present competing models of negotiating power. The demonstrated efficacy of their examples, or lack thereof, function as a guide for maintaining social order. Bucky's inability or unwillingness to make accommodations results in disaster for the Seabrook cheerleading team. His rigidity reflects an internalization of the Seabrook jeremiad and drives him to expel any member who expresses sympathy toward zombies. Without sufficient numbers, the remaining skeleton crew cannot complete their performance at the Cheer Championships and loses for the first time in forever. Whereas Bucky fails because of his attempts to preserve totalizing distinctions between zombies and normals at the expense of genetic anomalies like Addison, Lee negotiates with Zed and allows his people to enter normals' society but only on her terms. With frightening honesty to racial stereotypes, Lee bases the conditional desegregation on athletic performance. Acceptance of zombies depends on Zed's contribution to win football games. Her approach counterbalances the jeremiad with the errand into the wilderness; she ensures the stability of Seabrook by colonizing the zombie frontier.

Zed and the Z-Band

The government and school may administer power, but the z-band enforces it. Zed states, "We've come a long way since the outbreak, thanks to the z-band. This puppy delivers a dose of soothing electromagnetic pulses that keep us from eating brains. Now zombies can live happy lives and have handsome, yet humble, kids." The apotheosis of colonialism, the z-band visually signifies the galvanic machinery of assimilation. As already mentioned, the device elicits comparison to the ankle monitor used by our criminal justice system. It empowers the Zombie Patrol to extend their regulation of the undead into the privacy of their homes in Zombietown. As such, the z-band is Jeremy Bentham's panopticon technologically manifest as a wearable wristband. Foucault's description of the panopticon's purpose could be easily mistaken for the z-band: "Hence the major effect of the Panopticon: to induce in the inmate a state of conscious and permanent visibility that assures the automatic functioning of power. So to arrange things that the surveillance is permanent in its effects [...] that this architectural apparatus should be a machine for creating and sustaining a power relation independent of the person who exercises it; in short, that the inmates should be caught up in a power situation of which they are themselves the bearers."[35] Thus, zombies do not live merely as prisoners on their side of the wall. The z-band ensures the permanent visibility and active management of their behavior. Wearing one ensures submission and simultaneously makes the zombie responsible for their own imprisonment.

When uninhibited by the z-band, zombies manifest super-human strength and athleticism. Zed's illicit hacking of his further reveals that this savagery and strength can be and is regulated like a faucet. Early in the film, during a pep rally, Zed's band temporarily malfunctions, allowing him to burst through a formation of Seabrook football players to catch Addison from a potentially fatal fall. The near catastrophe leads him to the epiphany that he can modify the z-band to unlock his suppressed strength and gain an advantage on the football field. His misuse of the device discloses the particularized and continuous control that Seabrook exerts over their bodies. In *Discipline and Punish*, Foucault also outlines the fulfillment of "subject and practised bodies, 'docile' bodies." He writes, "the object of the control [...] was not or was no longer the signifying elements of behaviour or the language of the body, but the economy, the efficiency of movements, their internal organization; constraint bears upon the forces rather than upon the signs."[36] Although signification gives way to discipline in Foucault's hierarchy of biopolitics, the z-band coextends through both forms of power.

Zed regularly adjusts the device to discretely inhabit four persistent functional states of zombification. The first, full zombie, occurs if the z-band is completely deactivated. Zed taps into his savage nature, exhibiting super-human strength and apoplectic rage. Zed's muscles and veins swell, his eye makeup gets really dark, and his skin becomes blotchy and red. He chases after normals in an attempt to eat their brains until he is subdued by a taser. To win football games, Zed calibrates the z-band to minimally suppress his zombie nature. In the second state, he has access to increased strength and speed but does not manifest the uncontrollable rage. He can nimbly avoid opponents and effortlessly toss aside anyone with the unfortunate audacity to try to tackle him. His muscles and veins still swell, and the heavy eye makeup returns but less noticeably. To avoid arousing suspicion, Zed only utilizes this state when his football attire conceals the visible changes of his body. It is uncertain whether the audience is expected to believe that Lee, the football coach, or the community of Seabrook fail to notice Zed's temporary transformations during games. Clearly, Zed's racial otherness, situationally condoned on the football field where it benefits the school, is excluded elsewhere. The third state, the Seabrook zombie, is induced by a properly operating z-band, so we can assume the community prefers to maintain zombies this way. Both savagery and athletic attributes are fully repressed. In fact, zombies resemble normals except for two aspects of their visual appearance—the green hair and ashy skin. In this state, zombies are functional isomorphs of normals. When Zed decides to pass as normal, he adjusts the z-band to its fourth state making himself an urbane brunette with a healthy pallor and visually indistinguishable from a normal. These incremental adjustments highlight the discomforting racial signification of the zombie's otherness and Seabrook's discrete regulation of its visual and corporeal instantiation.

Prior to the homecoming game, Addison's parents insist on meeting Zed, unaware that he is a zombie. It is unclear where he gets the clothes, but by donning a pastel pink suit and adjusting his skin color with his z-band, he passes as normal and ingratiates himself with them. Emboldened by this success, Zed takes Addison on a date to a Seabrook ice cream parlor. While excited by the novelty, Addison shares discomfort that Zed could get caught and explains that she is worried he is suppressing his identity. More likely, Addison's reaction is symptomatic of her identification with Zed's sartorial duplicity. His transgression too closely mirrors her own deception: wearing a wig. For Zed, recalibrating the z-band is not an act of defiance but wish fulfillment. Given the opportunity, he would presumably continue to pass as normal. The range and precision of Zed's adjustments to his hacked band illustrate the totalizing control Seabrook maintains over the zombies. Because the sophistication of the z-band permits discrete regulation, it becomes clear that the Zombie Patrol and the Seabrook government choose to suspend zombies in a state of functional but not visual isomorphism. Seabrook excludes use of the first two states of full zombie as they would risk giving zombies too much power. However, the only possible explanation for choosing the third over the fourth state is to conspicuously mark zombies as different. Like the government issue overalls, the z-band reifies the zombies' otherness and is therefore integral to maintaining social hierarchy. Read in such a way, the z-band is the realization of a totalizing biopolitics that simultaneously exerts power over signification and discipline of the body.

Bucky's Failure

Excitement grows around Zed's success on the football team, and even normals are enthusiastic about his contributions. Some students who previously conformed to the unofficial Seabrook dress code begin to wear t-shirts plastered with a logo of Zed's face or fabric wristbands that resemble z-bands. Like the semi-permeable boundary between Zombietown and Seabrook, normals' cultural appropriation of zombie chic reveals they have the privilege to penetrate the boundary at will, while zombies remain restricted. That said, zombie chic offends Bucky because it pushes against the horizon of the permissible. Having internalized Seabrook's jeremiad as cheer captain, Bucky assumes responsibility for preserving the distinction between normals and zombies.

After Seabrook's homecoming victory, the cheer team focuses on preparing for their regional competition. As Bucky's frustration increases, he expels any member of the team who sympathizes with zombies. Where Addison's encounter with Zed in the saferoom causes her to doubt society, Bucky's abjection prompts him to see evidence of defilement everywhere. This cathexis of the pre-object results in narcissism. Kristeva clarifies that this narcissism is not idyllic self-absorption or "the wrinkleless image of the Greek youth in a quiet fountain." Instead, "the conflicts of drives muddle its bed, cloud its water, and bring forth everything that, by not becoming integrated with a given system of signs, is abjection for it."[37] Bucky increasingly panics, and even his most devout teammates question his decision-making. His pathological narcissism muddies the identity of the cheer team. When the day of the competition arrives, expectations for the Seabrook team are high. However, during their performance, they are unrecognizable to the judges. Their routine is disorganized, and the team ceases to function as a body. When the audience breaks into laughter, Bucky leaves the stage, disgraced. In his attempt to purify the self by negating the zombie, he fragments the team's identity. His own desire for prohibition enslaves him. Addison and her zombie friends take the stage, joining with current and former members of the cheer team to perform a new routine, enacting the hero's return. Unlike their response to the white hair reveal, the audience revels in the performance, and even Bucky concedes to participate in the spectacle. The audience approval reclaims Addison and recasts the homogenous identity of the community. The performance not only galvanizes the cheer team but also builds trust between normals and the zombies.

Conclusion

The closing scene occurs after the regional cheer championships. Addison narrates, "We didn't win the cheer championship. But we did something even better. We brought everyone together and we threw an awesome block party. Even my parents came." The celebration signifies growing acceptance of zombies. Normals and zombies reprise "BAMM" and "Our Year." Unlike previous versions of these songs, normals and zombies are integrated. No longer juxtaposed, they form heterogenous dance groups. Because so little time has passed, it is impossible to identify the extent of the acculturation. More normals ornament themselves in token zombie chic yet are careful not to risk being misrecognized as zombies. The line may be fuzzy, but it is never obscured. Normals conform to their traditional solid color pastel attire and only wear zombie accessories. It is an example of what Sarah Berry describes as the "creation of ethnicity as a consumable pleasure" where "constructions of race were visualized in the form of clearly artificial 'ethnic simulacra.'"[38] Addison pushes the boundary furthest by donning a floral print dress. The clothing is still pastel, but the gesture is novel. She also continues to flaunt her white hair, signifying her difference and letting her freak-flag fly. Notably, the zombies still wear government issued clothing including z-bands, and the block party takes place in Zombietown. The implication that zombies remain confined to Zombietown except for school related activities affirms the superficiality of this celebrated cultural revolution. They still bear the chains of slavery with the z-band, now recalibrated to prevent hacking. In the final celebration scene, Zed reminds the audience that Seabrook retains explicit control over the savagery of every zombie via the bands. He proclaims, "But now all zombies are getting software updates. No more 'tweaking' them. Sweet. Eliza, they have Wi-Fi now." None can go native without Seabrook's permission, nor can they pass as normal. The social stratification remains intact. Seabrook simply has a new hybrid category for Addison, emblematic of the cultural tendency toward homogenization. Through the ritual of constructing national identity, the community internalizes Addison's abjection. Seabrook can celebrate the accommodation of disruption sutured into the material culture of her pastel floral print dress.

If, as Herbert Marcuse famously uttered on Sigmund Freud's behalf, "the history of man is the history of repression,"[39] then the synchronic and diachronic study of myth reveals the work of civilization, enacting and concealing that repression. According to its own logic, American identity justifies its existence by maintaining distance from the decadent civilization of Europe and the savagery of uncivilized indigenous peoples. From this self-determination of the national subject emerges the ritual of American identity, the daily mythopoetic production of the present as the destiny of the past. Each individual functions as representative of the nation by performing the ritual anew, an entelechy continually affirming what it means to be American. As such, the hero transgresses boundaries of the self, a synecdoche of the state, and encounters the other on the frontier. Consensus politics of Nietszchean will to power validates the efficacy of the ritual. In the film, the community disavows Addison when she initially reveals her white hair but later sanctions her transgression when she and her zombie friends bring recognition to Seabrook at the regional cheer competition. Addison's acculturation to the frontier, vis-à-vis her transgression, is ratified by Seabrook's willingness to accept her back into their circle. Transposing this ritual onto the topography of the frontier reduces the temporality of history to "homogenous, empty time" measured instead by geographic sublation.[40] The three narratives of the Disney film *Zombies* re-enact this ritual of American identity: Zed's assimilation legitimizes the cultural violence of colonialism via his enthusiastic participation in his own imprisonment; Addison, the romantic hero, encounters an internal frontier and resolves abjection by mastering it for Seabrook; and Bucky and Principal Lee reveal how authority must adapt to appropriate the work of Addison. Bucky's adherence to tradition signifies a cautious reminder of the dangers of intractable decadence, whereas Lee's diplomacy negotiates the transformation of zombies into docile bodies made ready for assimilation into an increasingly homogenous society, albeit a little less white. As such, the film provides a framework for racial integration and utilizes the community's reaction to the characters' decisions in each narrative to indicate the efficacy of their choices.

CHAPTER SIX

Destiny Manifested in *Westworld*'s Philosophical Zombies

> *Man can do what he wills but he cannot will what he wills.*
> —ALBERT EINSTEIN paraphrasing Schopenhauer, "A Socratic Dialogue: Plank—Einstein—Murphy"

Victoria Gray is the first individual in the United States to be treated with gene-editing technology. Gray suffers from sickle cell disease, a genetic disorder that leads to infections and excruciating bouts of pain. She was diagnosed at three months old. After living with the disease for decades, Gray volunteered for a new treatment that involved extracting and modifying her bone marrow cells with the CRISPR gene-editing tool to produce a protein that would arrest the most severe symptoms. Although her physician Dr. Haydar Frangoul admits that it is too early to declare the treatment a success, he is optimistic about the results. In an interview with Gray, Rob Stein poses the question we all want to ask, "Is it weird to have genetically-modified cells in your body?" Gray responds, "No. I'm just genetically-modified now [laughter]. I'm a GMO." Ontological crisis averted! Apparently, it's not all that different to be a genetically modified human.[1] But I digress. It is not my intent to suggest that Gray is anything less than human. Moreover, Gray's case is not far removed from less direct methods of genetic engineering that are normalized in contemporary society that result from sociological formations, economic paradigms, fertility science, and life-extending developments in medicine. Nevertheless, gene editing is one instance of current technological and scientific innovation that raises epistemological and ontological questions of how to define what it means to be human.

In Chapter 4, I discussed social-science fiction as a platform for engaging contemporary political and social phenomena, an idea proposed by Darren Reed and Ruth Penfold-Mounce. The value of science fiction also lies in its capacity to forecast our technological futures; it has the extraordinary side effect of shaping the collective imagination of what is possible. For decades in popular media, writers and directors have inspired new generations of researchers, inventors, and scientists. This might seem like mere folk wisdom, but we do not need to look any further for evidence than Arizona State University's Center for Science and the Imagination, an institute founded on recognizing the reciprocity of technological innovation and creative writing. In collaboration with various non-profits, CSI regularly publishes speculative fiction grounded in the horizons of current scientific research. A recent example is *Visions, Ventures, Escape Velocities*. Funded by a NASA grant that brought science fiction writers and scientists into conversation, the anthology collects short stories and nonfiction essays about space exploration in order to "stimulate creative, interesting, and relevant thoughts and conversations" that "can help inform NASA and commercial space companies." This aim, taken from the acknowledgments, concludes with the statement "This book is not the end of the experiment. It is the beginning."[2] Such exchange between science and science fiction discloses what I like to blithely describe as the weak supervenience of social-science fiction. The actual nomenclature does not really matter but it gives me a way to acknowledge its determining influence on technological innovation. The HBO television series *Westworld* might not be prefaced with a statement about inspiring young minds, but it does entreat audiences to contemplate the sociological implications of imminent futures. Based on the 1973 film of the same name, *Westworld* responds to and nurtures a presumed underlying social anxiety of AI (artificial intelligence) in its audience within a utopian/dystopian narrative framework. By positing a reality where AI approximates human behavior and by anticipating the ethical, moral, ontological problems of that reality, *Westworld* reveals itself as a consummate example of supervenient social-science fiction. It provides the occasion for discussing philosophical zombies, post-human societies, and, oddly enough, the mythologization of U.S. history.

Mythic Space

The premise of *Westworld* is simple even though the storylines are, perhaps needlessly, complicated. With few exceptions, the narratives from Seasons 1 and 2 occur in various theme parks and the administration and plant buildings owned by Delos. Each theme park simulates a historical location with Westworld, a simulacrum of the nineteenth-century U.S. frontier, being the focal point. After having spent so much time discussing a Disney film in the previous chapter, I find it difficult to resist conceptualizing these parks as descendants of the themed *lands* in Disney World like Adventureland, Frontierland, and Main Street, U.S.A. The pairing of possible futures and national mythology is not unique to *Westworld* but coextends with Walt Disney's unifying vision of space, time, and national identity. He prophesied that "Disneyland will be the essence of America as we know it, the nostalgia of the past, with exciting glimpses into the future."[3] Unsatisfied with the geographic limitations of his park in Anaheim, Walt responded to what he saw as a "public need" by "starting from scratch on virgin land and building a special kind of new community," which would be realized in his Experimental Prototype Community of Tomorrow.[4] Walt's use of the loaded term "virgin land" to describe the site for parks that mythologize the frontier and national identity illustrates the layers upon layers available to unpack.[5] Although he did not live to see Epcot completed, Walt described it as "the heart of everything we'll be doing in Disney World."[6] Literally divided into two halves, Future World and World Showcase, Epcot stands as a posthumous monument to his original vision for Disneyland. In her book investigating the mythopoeic historicization of Walt's parks, Priscilla Hobbs attests to the efficacy of his efforts when she writes, "The theme park speaks on a mythic level, acting as an interactive space where the myths of the guest or the culture can come to life" and later adds that these iterations of national myth have become "the preferred version for generations of Americans."[7] Using this logic, Jean Baudrillard enumerates how simulation determines reality because "it is the map that engenders the territory."[8] Accordingly, Frontierland serves as an apt correlate for the titular park Westworld. Like Frontierland, visitors to Westworld enter into an instantiation of the American West by reaffirming a homogenous national identity that, as Michel Foucault says, "we represent to ourselves every day."[9] Robert Cahn's amusing account of a stage show in Frontierland from his 1958 feature on Disneyland discloses the permeability of myth and reality.

> As the sheriff advanced toward the wounded bandit, a tow-headed five year old, wearing a cowboy suit and holding a cap pistol, came running from the crowd.
> "Can I finish him off, sheriff, can I?" he asked.
> "O.K.," said the sheriff, looking the boy over. "I'll count one-two-three. You fire at three."
> The boy nodded, squinted and took aim at the fallen badman. Lucky hid his own gun behind his back and started counting.
> "One ... two ... three." As the boy pulled the trigger, a shot rang out from the sheriff's concealed weapon. Black Bart shuddered, then lay deathly still.
> The lad took one look, dropped his gun and fled, screaming, "Mommy, mommy! I didn't mean to! I didn't mean to!"
> His tears stopped a moment later, however, when he turned and saw Black

Bart and Sheriff Lucky walking back into the Golden Horseshoe to get ready for the next performance.[10]

This seemingly apocryphal anecdote also highlights the desire of park visitors to be not only spectators but also participants in the production.

Philosophical Zombies

To increase fidelity to reality, the Delos parks in *Westworld* are populated by period specific hosts, hosts being the designated term for robots or androids. For visitors to the park, these hosts appear human and provide an authenticity that surpasses the animatronics and human performers encountered in Disney World. Unlike Cahn's tow-headed five year old, a guest in Westworld need not feel guilty for killing a bandit or even becoming a bandit by staging a bank heist and killing the sheriff because the money is not real, and the sheriff is a machine without consciousness. Borrowing Ella Shohat's phrase, the "spectacle of difference" liberates guests from social obligations and prohibitions,[11] and consciousness emerges as the singular criteria that distinguishes humans from AI in *Westworld*. Because of the pivotal role consciousness plays in the show, it is useful to think of these hosts as philosophical zombies, hereafter abbreviated as p-zombies. David Chalmers notably reinserted the p-zombie into philosophy of consciousness studies when using it in an argument against materialism, the thesis that everything in the universe including consciousness is attributable to physical phenomena. Chalmers defines a p-zombie as "someone or something physically identical to me (or to any other conscious being), but lacking conscious experiences altogether."[12] This definition is surprisingly compatible with many Hollywood zombie films, particularly those where zombies are characterized by the loss of a soul or a loss of agency. In Chalmers' thought experiment, later formalized as the conceivability argument, he states that "if a zombie world is conceivable [...], that is enough to establish that consciousness cannot be reductively explained."[13] In other words, if it's merely possible to imagine that for two physically identical humans to exist—one with consciousness and one without—then consciousness must be non-physical, or at the very least, a non-physical element of consciousness must supervene on the physical body. *Westworld* offers varying responses to this argument borne out by the statements and actions of its characters. Ultimately, the show falls short of fulfilling Chalmers' thought experiment, but the concept of the p-zombie remains relevant because it provides terminology for discussing the classification of beings.

Unlike Chalmers' p-zombies, the hosts are only human in appearance and behavior. Delos' use of AI in pursuit of fidelity, somewhat ironically, increases the distance between fiction and reality—the performers in Disney World are at least human. Ned Block provides a particularly useful description of Commander Data that predates *Westworld* but is nonetheless relevant. He uses the phrase superficial functional isomorph, where superficial = external, functional = dispositional qualities, and isomorph = human. Block initially posits Commander Data as a type of human isomorph, an entity that approximates what it is to be human. However, Data is a particularly sticky example. By introducing Data as an example, Block deliberately provokes and complicates questions of consciousness. What makes Data seem human is his dispositional qualities including appearance, speech, mannerisms and perhaps even his embodiment of human values. Unlike his organic counterparts, he is not composed of flesh and bone; he is not physically human. Thus, the description of Data as an isomorph must be downgraded to or qualified as a functional isomorph. Upon further consideration, however, Data is not even a functional isomorph. Although Data appears human, his internal structure is vastly different. Data is not designed with synthetic organs that pump real or synthetic blood; he cannot experience the world as a human would. He is merely designed to sustain an external appearance of a human. Therefore, Block concludes that Data is a superficial functional isomorph.[14] Like Commander Data, the hosts are designed to mimic external behaviors to produce the appearance of being human, but such programming does not reflect their internal state or properties. There is nothing human about how they operate. Cutting open a host, a frequent occurrence on the show, reveals a certain amount of flesh but also wiring and electronics. Older versions of hosts that appear in flashbacks have a synthetic skeletal structure. Newer hosts are entirely organic except the head which houses the control unit. The control unit is a piece of physical hardware that regulates its personality, behaviors, and memories. There is nothing isomorphic or human about how a host processes information or experiences the world. The control unit simply mediates those experiences, directing the host's body and voice to respond to external stimuli in ways that appear convincing to the guests. Put simply, the actual content of the control unit is not identical to human consciousness, but the output is calibrated to produce a behavior that will appear human to the guest. In other words, the guests and hosts collaborate to misrecognize the host as human. Considered this way, the hosts emerge as the colonized subject of the future. As previously discussed, William Spanos' revision to Sacvan Bercovitch's genealogy of American national identity in *American Exceptionalism in the Age of Globalization* dislodges the frontier from a particularized geographic site so that it may also include "its 'foreign' relations (the threatening Other beyond the American frontier)."[15] *Westworld* posits AI as the new frontier—the landscape of the park and its manufactured occupants are quite literally fashioned to preserve a visual continuity with the frontier of previous generations.

The control unit bears an uncanny resemblance to the concept of the soul in Vodou. Like its Haitian counterpart, the control unit has two components: the pearl and the chestnut. Characters in the series refer to the spherical golf-ball sized core of the control unit as a "pearl." The pearl contains the individual memories and personality of the host, and the chestnut is essentially the socket that mediates exchanges between the pearl and the host body. In this comparison, the chestnut is the *ti bon ange*—a common cognition shared across all hosts, and the pearl is the *gros bon ange*—unique to each unit. As Maya Deren explains, when a person dies the individualized soul, the *gros bon ange*, does not perish with the body but transfers to "the waters of the abyss, the world of les Invisibles."[16] However, through the ritual practice of possession, the spirits of ancestors may be reclaimed and "temporarily displace the gros-bon-ange of a living person and become the animating force of that physical body."[17] Like the *gros bon ange*, a body is not necessary to sustain the existence of a host. Pearls can be stored indefinitely, deployed into virtual environments for testing and modification, and even relocated into different bodies. In Season 3, this actually occurs. Dolores creates five copies of her pearl and puts them into five different bodies of various gender and race. Although initially these were presumably exact copies, their personalities diverge as they have different experiences and live out independent histories.

On the surface, my description of the hosts as superficial functional isomorphs, machines without consciousness juxtaposed alongside my description of the host control unit as a soul is a bald contradiction. The metaphor of soul is expressly weak given the synthetic nature of hosts and intuitive certainty that AI precludes consciousness. In light of this weakness, supporting the metaphor of the soul with evidence from Deren's ethnography is, admittedly, a denigration of Haitian Vodou. But naming the act as a form of colonial appropriation points to a much larger problem of the violence of colonial discourse. By invoking the zombie in relation to AI, philosophy of consciousness scholars and texts such as *Westworld* nevertheless inherit the colonial discourse of zombification with its embedded power relations. On the one hand we have the guests and employees of Delos who view the host as what Aimé Césaire would describe as thingified,[18] a non-human subject that is manufactured to delight and entertain humans. On the other hand, we have hosts that view themselves as a conscious subject, a being-for-itself in the Heideggerian sense. I concede that the similarity between Vodou and the control unit may be coincidence. It is not possible to offer any certainty about the correspondence between the ways in which the hosts represent their consciousness to themselves and Haitians represent their souls to themselves. Such a concession does not occlude the broader parallel of colonial domination embedded in the genealogy of zombie discourse. When constructing a narrative about zombies, philosophical or otherwise, the most readily available content at hand is the practices and beliefs of Haitian Vodou.

On the surface technological advancement seems like the most favorable and innocuous object of imperialism. The particularized construction of the host as appearing human and simultaneously technologically differentiated from human produces an *ideal* other. I use the word ideal here in the sense that it is efficient and optimized to allay political and ethical concerns. The social conscience need not be bothered because the colonized subject is not a person, is not an animal, is not even natural. It is a piece of technology that animates an inert human body (or at least its superficial isomorph) and transforms it into a standing reserve of human labor, available for exploitation and consumption. It is nothing other than the production of the colonial other for the imperial self, sanitized. Importantly, even though the host bodies are precisely sculpted to appeal to the sexual fantasies of the guests, the efficacy of this relation depends entirely on the classification of the host as not-human vis-à-vis the spectacle of difference. While Block supplies the language for thinking about the relation between androids and humans, this terminology does not help us get any closer to understanding human consciousness. More to the point, it does not help us establish whether humans or p-zombies have consciousness. For humans to maintain an ethical relation of exploitation of hosts, several assumptions have to be made. Humans must have something fundamental (be it consciousness, a soul, etc.) that hosts lack. Furthermore, that something must be defined to the extent that its presence can be confirmed in humans and its absence confirmed in hosts. In the context of Westworld and its narratives, that difference is a messy conflation of consciousness and free will. The host may be no more than a bundle of wires, but unless the existence of consciousness can be established, what makes humans more than a bundle of flesh? Moreover, if free will can be harnessed by reducing it to a predictable set of causalities, is the human any different from a host? Block states that the harder problem is not defining consciousness. For Block, the difficulty is more deeply rooted. We do not even have the capacity to explain what criteria are needed to construct a definition of consciousness. Without such criteria, the distinction between conscious flesh bundles and unconscious wire bundles collapses. The slippage reveals the arbitrariness of the distinctions. Herein lies the importance of Friedrich Nietzsche via Foucault. The sustainability of the colonial relation is contingent on the classification of the p-zombie or host as non-human, even when the criteria for what it means to be human remains elusive. Once consciousness is defined, classified, thingified, and subjected to knowledge, it can be used to establish power over subjects, to subjugate. It is important to note that in terms of discursive power, the facticity of any such definition of consciousness is irrelevant. No human even needs to believe the definition. It simply needs to be wielded or acted upon. Similarly, once the free will of the guests is reduced to mere causality, they too become a form of standing reserve.

Presented in such a way, the imperialism of Delos is indistinguishable from other forms of colonialism, except that the objectification of host bodies is more fully realized and can be optimized to fulfill more diverse forms of labor. These include entertainment labor, sexual and otherwise, for the guests but also more traditional forms of physical and intellectual labor. Many of the Delos staff that are involved in the parks' operation and creative development teams are in fact hosts. In her analysis of *Heading South*, a film depicting the Caribbean sex tourism in 1970s, Toni Pressley-Sanon makes a valuable connection by reading the indigenous Caribbean body as a feminized zombie, produced for the entertainment of the tourist. She examines the film's three subaltern protagonists who travel to Haiti to reclaim their dominant status. By consuming the colonized Haitian body, they exorcise their own zombification and transfer it to another.[19] Likewise, the subjugation of the host by Delos is only permissible because the consciousness of hosts is rendered inconceivable. The classification of hosts as superficial functional isomorphs absolves Delos and its tourists of all ethical and moral violations.

By reading *Westworld* as a supervenient social-science fiction platform, I feel compelled to draw attention the situatedness of the show. One liability with the term platform is that it implies a site exempt from ideology when such is not the case. Even if it were possible to dissociate a work from its contemporary political context, it would still bear the "sedimentations left behind by past phases of history" as Antonio Gramsci observes.[20] Rather than reading the show as ideologically unsituated, it is more useful to think of it as a dialectical image, a site of conflict produced by various ideologies that assert power and contend for hegemony. Benjamin's concept of the dialectical image has proven useful in current scholarship. I enjoy using Benjamin because of his approach and the recurring ideas that play out across his criticism and other writings. The difficulty of using Benjamin is that like any other writer these ideas change over time and are often used in contradictory ways. I like to think of his work as developing a toolset for criticism and philosophical thinking. However, as Benjamin's work regularly points out, it is a mistake to similar pick up a tool and use it without recognizing its context. As embedded as the writers or directors may be within their own ideology, the show functions less as representation of any singular disposition and instead provides a record of ideological struggle that can be observed and investigated. In this sense, the colonial relationship between Delos, its employees, the guests, and the hosts is particularly meaningful. The writers attempt, within the limits of their situatedness, to construct narratives and counternarratives from within each of these groups and provide varying responses to this colonial dynamic. The rest of this chapter will investigate the nature of those responses by examining how each represents the park to itself.

Fashioning the Other

Although the original film version of *Westworld* had only three parks, the HBO television series expands its offerings to six. Park 1, Westworld, is presumably the original and primary park, and guests willing pay $40,000 a day to enter and live out their fantasies. As the executive director of the board of shareholders for Delos, Charlotte Hale, observes, "most of the guests just want a warm body to shoot or fuck."[21] Several other parks do appear in the television series but only minimally. As the titular park, Westworld remains the central narrative setting for the first two seasons of the show. Much of the action centers around the town of Sweetwater where guests arrive by train. The opening scene of the series takes place here, introducing the audience to the mechanics of the park. Because hosts look no different than humans, the audience must rely on conversations among passengers about their plans in the park to establish that the train is primarily full of guests. A man who we later learn is named Teddy Floyd gets off the train with the other guests, recognizes a host that he previous encountered name Dolores Abernathy, and takes her back to her house which they discover is under attack by bandits. The chivalrous Floyd defends his love in a gunfight, killing most of the bandits, but is mortally wounded by a mysterious character known only as the Man in Black. The scene overturns expectations of the audience, who until this moment, were led to believe Floyd was a guest. To the audience's surprise, Floyd's death reveals that he is not human. The audience proceeds to watch in horror as the Man in Black, now understood to be a guest, drags Dolores by her hair into a barn to rape her. This sequence of events introduces the audience to several major characters as well as a recurring practice of blurring the boundary between host and human. Throughout the first season, the Man in Black reappears as a sort of flaneur or sovereign spectator who reflects back the decadence of Westworld. In the finale, his veil of disinterestedness is lifted, and we learn that the Man in Black is William, the executive vice president of Delos.[22]

The rape of Dolores also makes perfectly clear the feminization and eroticization of the frontier vis-à-vis host bodies, which are made available for consumption to the pioneering guests. Performed by Evan Rachel Wood, the character Dolores bears a striking resemblance to and is presumably based on the Ziegfeld Girl of the same name. Florenz Ziegfeld, who grew up idolizing Buffalo Bill by shooting bullets into his attic wall for target practice and running off with Cody's Wild West show, began his career as a producer and showman by managing the Trocadero nightclub for his father during the World's Columbian Exposition of 1893.[23] Ziegfeld's second wife, Billie Burke, introduced him to Lucy Duff-Gordon during a private showing of her "living mannequins." By her own account, Duff-Gordon claims to have "made dressmaking-history by staging the first mannequin parade."[24] Among these mannequins was none other than Kathleen Rose, more commonly recognized by her stage name, Dolores. As Burke knew he would be, Ziegfeld was smitten with Dolores on the spot. He immediately persuaded Duff-Gordon to allow him to use her in his Ziegfeld Follies, and Dolores became, according to Elspeth Brown, the "first celebrity fashion model." Brown observes that unlike other Ziegfeld girls that sang and danced on stage, Dolores only modeled high-end fashion. Her choreographed performances were marked by a "blank hauteur," which Brown elaborates as "laconic expressions, gestures and movements [...] that came to define the couturier model and the new chorine."[25] Yet the significance of Dolores' performances extend far beyond her influence on fashion modeling. Brown contrasts her "subdued gestural vocabulary" with the "exaggerated movements of most contemporary racialized performance styles" found in minstrel shows.[26] Against this backdrop Brown writes, "her expressionless demeanor also signified the hauteur of elite whiteness."[27] Ziegfeld's inclusion of Dolores on his stage commodified her performance of embodied whiteness and made it available for public consumption. While it may seem counter-intuitive that the pinnacle of racial and social hierarchy be objectified in such a way, this is not actually the case. Like the Dolores of *Westworld*, Dolores the model was not born; she was created. When Duff-Gordon discovered her, she was an errand girl as unfit for the stage as her "Cockney sister."[28] Duff-Gordon trained her how to speak, walk, and carry herself, and when she had finisher her "Pygmalion-like work," Duff-Gordon debuted her as one of her living mannequins.[29] Dolores' personal history was not a well-kept secret but instead an integral component of her mystique. The Cinderella story appealed to audiences who yearned for their own social mobility yet simultaneously permitted the visual consumption of her elite whiteness because of her status as "class passing."[30]

Such objectification of the colonized subject on the stage would extend to film throughout the twentieth century. Shohat briefly describes practices regarding the display of nudity on silver screen. The restrictive production code prohibited white skin but permitted people of so-called primitive cultures to display it. She writes, "An Oriental setting [...] thus provided Hollywood filmmakers with a narrative license for exposing flesh without risking censorship"[31] and offers the series of *Tarzan* films in the 1930s as evidence. Released before the production code took over Hollywood, the second film, *Tarzan and His Mate*, originally included a nude swimming scene and featured Maureen O'Sullivan throughout the film in a revealing two-piece in her role as Jane. Because of the advent of the production code, the swimming scene was cut from later versions. In subsequent *Tarzan* films, the production code required O'Sullivan to be costumed in a more modest one-piece yet permitted the bare breasts of African women. On the surface, the racialized commodification of Dolores—both the model and the host—appears to signify the realization of a democratized settler-colonialism. However, the permissibility of such consumption depends on the explicit recognition of Dolores' privileged status as a performative act and not an intrinsic quality of her identity. Without the technology of *Westworld*, the disadvantaged yet racially superior characters of *Heading South* turned to the Caribbean body as the safety-valve of global capitalism. Whereas in *Westworld*, the fact of an AI inhabiting an even racially superior white body authorizes any marginalized race, ethnicity, or gender to participate in its exploitation. This does not obviate discriminatory social hierarchies writ large, but permitting access to groups who were previously excluded and transferring the colonized subject from a human to a superficial functional isomorph fulfills the need for an ethical palliative.

By theming the parks, Delos makes available more than just the host bodies. It commodifies history. In his analysis of Disney, Alan Bryman expresses the function of theming and its value with the term "experience economy."[32] Theming creates a homogenized experience that simultaneously produces and fulfills the expectations of the guests. The choice for this particular setting and time period is fitting for many reasons already discussed. Despite being over a century since Frederick Jackson Turner's declaration of the end of the frontier,[33] the choice of the American West reaffirms its currency and predominance. This not only reveals the durability of the perpetual frontier but also the plasticity of its mythological content. Several other parks do appear in the television series—Shōgunworld (feudal Japan), The Raj (colonial India), and Warworld (Italy during

German occupation), but these parks are limited to cameos and function as temporary playgrounds for narratives driven by characters from Westworld. Moreover, there is a prominent Anglocentric focus of even these peripheral parks, particularly in The Raj where the guests are white British colonists served by Indian natives. Shōgunworld may be an exception in this regard, but even its uniqueness is short-lived. In Season 2, a group of renegade hosts led by Maeve Millay withdraw to Shōgunworld to evade pursuit. Included in Millay's party is a captive Delos employee, Lee Sizemore. After entering Shōgunworld, Sizemore states that Shōgunworld was for guests who wanted a more intense experience. The Delos website describes it: "For those for whom Westworld is not enough, the true connoisseur of gore can indulge their fantasies with the slash of a katana."[34] The implication is that Eastern experience is more brutal, a primitive savagism compared to Westworld's pastoralism. When entering Hirafuku, the central town of Shōgunworld, Millay observes that characters and storylines in Shōgunworld were recycled from Westworld. Sizemore defends his self-plagiarism: "Well, you try writing 300 stories in three weeks."[35] Thus, Shōgunworld, the only non–Western non-colonial park, is in fact derivative of Westworld and the reified mythological content is none other than Turner's closed frontier.

Because all historicization is problematic, uncovering the specific violence of commodifying the nineteenth-century U.S. frontier is not my point. My point is to show that parks not only sell a prepackaged version of history, but the efficacy of this particularized history is determined, at least in part, by what Bryman describes as an "experience economy." Decisions in how and what is represented and what is silenced are based on profit and efficiency. Michel-Rolph Trouillot provides a fitting example of the various "hearths" where history is produced and sold outside of academia. He observes, "Books sell even better than coonskin caps at the Alamo gift shop, to which half a dozen titles by amateur historians bring more than $400,000 a year."[36] The audience is made aware of this design choice in the inaugural episode from a conversation between Sizemore and Theresa Cullen, the head of quality assurance. Sizemore argues that the park would be more successful if the distinction between host and guest were clearer. He states, "Ford and Bernard keep making the things more lifelike. But does anyone truly want that? Do you want to think that your husband is really fucking that beautiful girl or that you really just shot someone? This place works because the guests know the hosts aren't real."[37] Sizemore's comments may be aimed at the distinction between host and human, but the economic imperative is clear. For Sizemore, the singular criterion for efficacious design that informs Westworld's historiography is one that has all its edges rounded off. It is history in its most palatable, most universally acceptable form, a reification of what Guy Debord terms "commodity fetishism [...] where the perceptible world is replaced by a set of images that are superior to that world yet at the same time impose themselves as *eminently* perceptible."[38] Sizemore recognizes that this is best accomplished, as Nietzsche states "from a distance," which ensures that it will be "tolerable or attractive and invigorating."[39] History that unconceals the violence of the past indicts the very audience Westworld seeks to attract. Optimizing for the experience economy inevitably results in a telescoping, conservative history which, as already mentioned, can be seen at sites like Disney World. I use the term conservative here not in the contemporary political sense but in relation to Sigmund Freud's death drive, the instinct that seeks repetition and a return to a previous state. For guests of the park, this is realized by reliving the mythological past in these fantasy parks. On a national scale, this manifests as the reification of a specular national identity.

Guest Labor

The park is a literal and figurative descendant of the safety valve thesis from Turner's nineteenth-century frontier when economists and politicians believed that the free land of the frontier would provide the necessary economic opportunity for anyone unduly repressed by class hierarchy. The notion of the safety valve can be traced as far back as John Locke. In the second of his *Two Treatises*, Locke argues private property is the labor of an individual on anything that was freely available in nature. He writes, "every Man has a *Property* in his own *Person*" and by laboring with his own hands on what he "removed from the common state Nature place it in" he "makes it his *Property*."[40] Because Locke believed "there is Land enough in the World to suffice double the Inhabitants," the right to labor is freely available to all.[41] To anyone in need of a site to exercise his labor, Locke advises "let him plant in some in-land, vacant places of *America*."[42] Thomas Jefferson evidently shared this belief in the right to labor but not Locke's confidence in the ubiquity of common land. In a letter to James Madison, he writes, "The earth is given as a common stock for man to labour & live on" and believes the government has a responsibility to "provide by every possible means that as few as possible shall be without a little portion of land."[43] These views would later motivate him to pursue the Louisiana Purchase to extend the lifecycle of the frontier. In another letter to Madison several years later, Jefferson elaborates on his views of free land, which imbricates the moral character of the nation and the jeremiad. He writes, "I think our governments will remain virtuous for many centuries; as long as they are chiefly agricultural; and this will be as long as there shall be vacant lands in any part of America. When they get piled upon one another in large cities, as in Europe, they will become corrupt as in Europe."[44] For Jefferson, the vacant land was a safety valve. A similar statement could be made about the sex tourists of *Heading South*. In comparison, the park delivers an opportunity to any who might feel oppressed to exert power over the other. As Cher Krause Knight argues in *Power and Paradise*, these "staged authenticities [...] actually offer the potential for more control than we have in our daily lives."[45] The staged authenticities that Knight references are the theatrical performances prevalent throughout Disneyland. Any desire to resist a dominant ideology is thereby frustrated or curtailed by the temporary, cathartic outlet offered by the park. The guests are not naïve to the constructedness of the park and its histories but are seduced by the appeal of exercising power that is otherwise denied them. As Bryman also shows, the theming shapes the desires of the guests. Guests are cultivated by the park to desire similar experiences in the future ensuring the durability of narratives that reify the status quo. The desires Westworld cultivates are nostalgia and agency, wish-fulfillment for experiencing the past and self-determination over their future.

Furthermore, we can see that Sizemore and Cullen have internalized the myth of national identity by their participation in the ritual of the jeremiad. Later in the conversation referenced above, Sizemore and Cullen acknowledge that it is their job to "gratify" in Cullen's words, "rich assholes."[46] Guests that visit the park to relive the past are the correlate of the corrupt European institutions to the Puritan. Because such decadence leads to stagnation, a liability for imperial stability, the jeremiad ritual excises the necrotic death instinct. It is a ritual designed to "reduce the inefficiencies of mass phenomena."[47] John Cotton's farewell address to John Winthrop's departing Puritans includes this cautionary reminder: "But if you rebell against God, the same God that planted you will also roote you out againe, for all the evill which you shall doe against your selves."[48] The genius of Delos is to exploit the death instinct as a means of economic efficiency, taking the wealth of those who have served their purpose and redistributing it to the capitalists. The imperial logic of internal and external colonization coextends into the frontier by using it as a space for innovating the future and pruning the decadence of the past. From this standpoint, the logic of Sizemore and Cullen's contempt for the guests becomes clear. To them, the guests are foolishly using their wealth to satisfy base desires that undermine the integrity of national identity rather than fulfilling the errand into the wilderness. But as Sizemore observes, Robert Ford, the co-founder and park director of Westworld, and Bernard Lowe, the head of behavior, are forgoing the experience economy in favor of other undisclosed interests. That is not to say the experience economy is absent from their decision-making, but that as a site of conflict, the design and implementation of the parks are the result of multiple competing interests. Depending on the perceived situatedness of Ford and Lowe, their actions may be read as complicit with or a counternarrative against national identity. As we will learn, it is a little of both.

Jeremy Bentham Revisited

The managerial work of Delos staff involves strict observation, routine maintenance, and immediate intervention of aberrant host behavior. In short, it is a fulfillment of what Foucault saw as the enlightenment's dispensation to reduce inefficiency and "[produce] subjected and practiced bodies, 'docile' bodies."[49] More to the point, Delos also has a responsibility to ensure the safety of the guests and maintains strict observation of them. But their interests in guest surveillance extend beyond mere protection. In Season 2, there is a flashback of William prior to his appointment as the executive vice president. The scene shows him in conversation with James Delos, the Founder and CEO of Delos.[50] William makes a case for investing in Westworld, which at the time was owned by the Argos Initiative. He describes the park as an opportunity for people to live out their true desires. "Nobody's watching. Nobody's judging." With a conspiratorial twitch of his eyebrows, William adds, "At least that's what we tell them. This is the only place in the world where you get to see people for who they really are."[51] For William, the park is a unique opportunity to data mine the guests. His plan calls for comprehensive surveillance that captures their behaviors and biometric data. As Ford later explains, the purpose of the park is to map "the human mind, the last analog device in a digital world." He adds rather dramatically, "We weren't here to code the hosts. We were here to decode the guests."[52] The project is successful to the extent that the mind of each guest is reduced to a unique algorithm of "Ten thousand, two hundred forty-seven lines."[53] In the finale of Season 2, we learn that Delos maintains a virtual library filled with millions of volumes, each containing the algorithm of a different guest. The profit William envisioned was realized, and it single-handedly sustained the park financially throughout its early years. But economic gain was not the only outcome of the project. James may have been initially convinced by William's proposal, but his ultimate goal is immortality. Over the next few decades, a subset of Delos employees pursued this dream by attempting to build a host with James' consciousness. Because the mind of host–James degrades quickly over time, the project stalls and never fully succeeds. It is unclear if this is a problem that could be solved because William loses interest after the death of human–James. The other benefactor of the project is Engerraund Serac, the villain of Season 3. Serac, presumably among others, purchases guest data from Delos and uses it to develop a massive AI brain called Rehoboam that predicts the individual and collective behavior humanity and, by modeling all possible outcomes, shapes the future.

The dystopian turn takes precedence over any further exploration of consciousness in Season 3, but it is worth spending a little time examining the implications of predictive AI. Using the algorithms discovered by Delos, Rehoboam's quantitative reduction of human behavior effectively precludes the possibility of free will by interposing on the human experience. These external interventions are incidental enough to avoid attracting attention and permit individuals to continue believing in their own agency. But Rehoboam's global deployment of minor interventions is sufficient to curb chaotic behavior and ensure a positive and stable equilibrium for humanity. This notion of quantifying nature has been examined thoroughly throughout the twentieth century in both science and philosophy. In his lecture published in English under the title *The Physicist's Conception of Nature*, Werner Heisenberg raises concerns over his discovery of the uncertainty principle. Because of Heisenberg, it was believed that observation and measurement of a subatomic particle would determine or reduce the particle from multiple realizable probabilities to a singular position. In effect, rather than maintaining an objective distance, observation influenced the outcome of the experiment. He asserts, "The scientific method of analysing, explaining and classifying has become conscious of its limitations, which arise out of the fact that by its intervention science alters and refashions the object of investigation."[54] In his essay "The Question Concerning Technology," Martin Heidegger works out the implications of Heisenberg's lecture and develops the concept of enframing, *Ge-stell*, which he identifies as "the essence of modern technology." For Heidegger, technology calls or challenges forth nature and in so doing reduces it to "objectifying representation." Heidegger writes, "As a destining, it banishes man into the kind of revealing that is an ordering. Where this ordering holds sway, it drives out every other possibility of revealing." Most importantly, it "conceals that revealing which […] lets what presences come forth into appearance." According to Heidegger, Heisenberg's uncertainty principle confirms that knowledge acquired through technology determines how the object of observation is represented or presenced. It is called forth by external observation rather than revealing itself under its own power. External observation holds sway over the representation of the object. Heidegger is distinguishing how technology necessarily situates the observer as one who classifies with all the implications that Foucault and Edward Said have raised. Nature, objectified as such, is reduced to a "standing-reserve" no longer existing for itself. It precludes the Being of being.[55] Thus, what *Westworld* portrays as the reduction of human agency to an algorithm is the fulfillment of enframing.

I imagine that Heidegger would be relieved to learn that advancement in quantum mechanics over the last two decades has refined Heisenberg's uncertainty principle in such a way that rescues the Being of being from absolute enframing. As Heisenberg proposed, sub-atomic phenomena cannot be predicted by initial states, but recent published studies demonstrate that observation does not, in fact, influence the outcome. Masanoa Ozawa first proposed a revision to Heisenberg's uncertainty principle in 2003 although it was almost ten years before the validity of theoretical formulation was tested and confirmed.[56] Thus, even if we choose to accept that Being is represented by or embodied within sub-atomic particles, enframing is never absolute. What this means for postcolonial studies is confirmation of what Said, among other scholars, has said all along. He writes, "There was never a history that could not to some degree be recovered and compassionately understood in all its suffering and accomplishment. Conversely, there was never a shameful secret injustice or a cruel collective punishment or a manifestly imperial plan for domination that could not be exposed, explained, and criticized."[57] Totalization is never complete, and every regime contains within it the possibility for resistance. Nevertheless, the absence of fulfillment does not preclude the violence enacted by those wielding discursive power. Nor does it preclude shows like *Westworld* from envisioning dystopic regimes that realize absolute enframing or contemporary continental philosophers from misrecognizing its possibility. Recently translated in 2018, *What Is Real?*, Giorgio Agamben's investigation into the disappearance of Ettore Majorana, attests to the currency of this line of inquiry. Majorana, a student of Enrico Fermi, researched quantum physics. In his research, Agamben uncovers an unpublished article by Majorana affirming Heisenberg's conclusions about the uncertainty principle. Agamben summarizes that "if quantum mechanics relies on the convention that reality must be eclipsed by probability, then disappearance is the only way in which the real can peremptorily be affirmed as such and avoid the grasp of calculation." From this, Agamben asserts that Majorana orchestrated his disappearance to escape the objectifying gaze of society.[58] For these reasons, it is worthwhile to recognize the limits of enframing and to build that recognition into the logic of humanist interpretation. That is to locate the interruptions that lived experience reveals, to identify the violence of discursive power, and to dislodge hegemony from ideology.

What the secret project demonstrates is that Sizemore and Cullen only represent a fraction of interested deputies employed by Delos and are consequently oblivious to the machinations of William and Ford. Within this single corporation, even loyal employees diffused across a vertical organizational structure pursue competing interests, each of which contributes the complex framework, the constellated image, of guest experience. Because the content of that experience is the myth of the frontier, it is also true that the discursive genealogy of the frontier informs the work of Sizemore and Cullen, and is brought to bear, however unevenly, by the individual guests. It is probably not necessary for me to also mention that the frontier of Westworld is not identical to a universal consensus of a frontier myth, nor is it possible for such a conception to exist at any given moment. Myth is not homogenous or evenly deployed, and Delos does not maintain singular authority of how that myth ought to be presented. But while a particular instantiation such as Westworld cannot be identified as a synecdochical citation, its situatedness reveals it as the product of contemporary political and ideological struggle. Moreover, the technology itself and the language of that technology delimit the possible narratives that emerge across the site of the text. As such, examination of those narratives discloses what is most at stake within contemporary political discourse.

Ford's Narrative

As mentioned earlier, the work of Ford and Lowe is simultaneously complicit with and counteracts against the interests of national identity. So far, we have looked at how the internal and external colonization of the guests and hosts respectively contribute to economic growth and the stability of settler-colonial capitalism. What make this show complicated and consequently more appropriate for analysis is the unevenness of Ford's motives. This can be understood by examining two massacres that bookend the lifecycle of the park. Prior to the grand opening of Westworld, the two original designers, Arnold Weber and Ford, had a falling out. Weber believed that hosts were achieving consciousness. As already discussed, any slippage in the distinction between host and guest creates a fundamental and unresolvable ethical dilemma. The exploitation and consumption of host bodies is only conceivable if hosts are categorically not human. Disturbed by the possibility of the hosts' personhood, Weber resolved to burn it all down. He programmed Dolores to initiate a massacre of all the hosts and that conclude by having her kill him. Ford disagreed with Weber but not because he insisted an immutable ontological boundary between hosts and humans. Quite the contrary, he doubted Weber's very premise of human exceptionalism. Near the end of Season 1 Ford explains, "There is no threshold that makes us greater than the sum of our parts, no inflection point at which we become fully alive. We can't define consciousness because consciousness does not exist. Humans fancy that there's something special about the way we perceive the world, and yet we live in loops as tight and as closed as the hosts do, seldom questioning our choices, content, for the most part, to be told what to do next."[59] Ford's words convey a strictly materialist attitude about consciousness, human or otherwise, and therefore his personal beliefs present no obstacles as he salvages what he can from Weber's massacre and rebuilds the park without his partner.

Over the next 35 years, Ford stays on as lead designer and director of all the parks. Admittedly, there is a lot of ambiguity about what takes place during those intervening years, and Ford's untrustworthiness makes it difficult to discern his true motives from the few interactions that might otherwise offer insight. What we do know is that when Ford recognizes he is being forced out of his position as director by the board of shareholders, he develops a new narrative for the park that fulfills Weber's original vision. The board of shareholders visits Westworld for a celebration of Ford's resignation and the reveal of his new narrative only to become the casualties of a second massacre. Unlike Weber's massacre that consisted entirely of hosts and concluded with his death, Ford's begins with his own death and consists entirely of humans. This host revolution is Ford's new and final narrative. Although he claims altruistic motives, the timing of Ford's massacre suggests that it is nothing more than retaliation. It signifies a refusal to acknowledge that he has outlived his usefulness to the shareholders, that he has transformed into the decadence that destabilizes national identity. I have little interest in safeguarding any particular interpretation of Ford's intent, but I do believe that exploring his motives more fully discloses valuable insight about postcolonial work. Somewhat contradictorily in the episode prior to making his materialist claim, Ford seems to suggest that consciousness is real. He calls it "a burden, a weight," and by rolling back the host updates that Weber designed to help them achieve consciousness Ford concludes that "we have spared them." If Ford's sympathy for hosts does not already smack of imperial paternalism akin to the U.S. Pan-American policies of the early twentieth century, then his next words should dissuade any doubt. "The hosts are the ones who are free," Ford concludes. "Free here under my control." And yet, as awful as these words may be, there is an uncomfortable resonance with the prescience of Charles Taylor's "one satisfactory solution" to the "struggle for recognition," "a regime of reciprocal recognition among equals."[60] The example of Ford and the evidence of his god-complex demonstrates the difficulty of

Six. Destiny Manifested in Westworld's Philosophical Zombies 151

enforcing recognition through political power. Yet such enforcement must come from somewhere and as Frantz Fanon observes, a government would never offer such recognition out of its own "cooperation and good will."[61]

Ford's words also signify an important shift both for himself and the show. Where the emphasis had been on consciousness, Ford's materialism gives way to an emerging desire to safeguard the free will of hosts and humans, and the writers of the show expect audiences to follow suit. No longer do narratives focus on blurring the lines between hosts and humans. After Season 1, audiences are left to choose from two options that are essentially the same in terms of narrative function. Either Ford's early materialism holds, and no host or human is conscious, or consciousness is real and many hosts have already achieved it. Because the narrative of Season 1 is dedicated to portraying the development of host consciousness, the writers seem to lean toward the latter. Either way, the field is leveled, and the narrative focus shifts to the preservation of free will. Before I move on to investigate what there is to be learned from *Westworld* about a regime of mutual recognition, I want to close the discussion on consciousness by examining the semiological problem of representing the unrepresentable. As Block has shown, the harder problem is identifying criteria that would be required to distinguish a host with consciousness from one without it. The show uses several different techniques to demonstrate the transformation of hosts into conscious beings. These include more obvious visual signals like mechanical twitches of a host's face and behavioral cues like a host repeating cryptic phrases over and over, but sometimes the indications are more nuanced and only identifiable by Delos employees. Even though hosts are given some autonomy, they are programmed to adhere to certain loops or patterns of behavior. A host like Dolores will not suddenly leave her farm to start a new life elsewhere just because a guest invites her. She is programmed with a desire to fulfill her responsibilities on the homestead. Because all behavior is closely monitored, anytime a host begins to act outside of the loop parameters, Delos employees are notified and intervene. Aberrant behavior might be common after a significant update, but it nevertheless indicates that a host is not operating as designed. As the audience observes the hosts in their loops over time, they too begin to notice deviations in behavior that are not even captured by Delos employees.

Living in a Material Consciousness

In preparation for his new narrative, Ford rolls out a new update that Weber had originally designed to make the hosts more lifelike. The hallmark feature of the new update is a class of gestures called reveries. These reveries allow hosts to access memories from prior loops and even prior lives that would have normally been purged, adding nuance to hosts that is not explicitly designed. If for example, a host had been reassigned to a new role, access to these previously unavailable memories could even allow hosts to recall fragments of their old identities. The show's use of the term loop may be coincidence, but I suspect the writers of *Westworld* are familiar with Douglass Hofstadter's concept of the strange loop. To explain consciousness, he offers the familiar description of video camera pointed at a television screen that is fed back into the camera and continues in an infinite loop. In a simple feedback loop, "no perception takes place at any stage inside the loop—just the transmission and reception of bare pixels." In contrast, Hofstadter explains "any strange loop that gives rise to human selfhood, by contrast, the level-shifting acts of perception, abstraction, and categorization are central, indispensable elements. It is the upward leap from raw stimuli to symbols that imbues the loop with 'strangeness.'"[62] These reveries trigger or spark self-consciousness in a similar way. The audience joins the host in the feedback loop through flashbacks of the host's previous selves. When the host's attention returns to the present, the audience observes the host reflecting on and processing those images of the past, then resolving to act on that reflection by overstepping the assigned parameters of their loop. The reflective disposition that enacts fundamental change to the programming of the host signifies the shift "from raw stimuli to symbols" that distinguishes a feedback loop from a strange loop, an unconscious machine from a conscious host, for the audience.

Ford offers additional insight about what is necessary to bridge the boundary of consciousness. In the finale of Season 1, we learn that Lowe, Ford's closest working partner and confidante, is in fact a host that Ford created in the image of his former co-designer, Weber.[63] Lowe is distraught to learn that he is not human and also confused that Ford would deliberately program Weber's experience of the loss of a son into his memory. Ford explains, "That was Arnold's key insight. The thing that led the hosts to their awakening: suffering." He continues, "It was when Arnold died—when I suffered—that I began to understand what he'd found. To realize I was wrong."[64] Ford's words elicit a few unanswerable questions, the first of which is why it took 35 years to come to that realization and do something about it. It becomes increasingly difficult to trust anything Ford has to say about his own motives. And with hosts like Lowe misrecognizing themselves as human, one begins to wonder if Ford is in fact a host. Regardless, his point about suffering as a trigger is less ambiguous and borne out by the actions and strange loop sequences of the hosts. One recurring strange loop sequence is for hosts undergoing maintenance to witness naked, mangled bodies of their host companions piled in detoxifying chambers. When hosts recall these images after their redeployment in the park, the abreactive trauma diffuses across their facial expression, body language, and speech patterns. While I do not want to read too much into this because the writers have a penchant for incorporating Psychology 101 moments into the show, trauma was a pivotal first stage of individuation for Freud.[65] In his *Introductory Lectures on Psycho-Analysis*, he famously observes that "this first state of anxiety arose out of separation from the mother."[66] Although consciousness should not be confused with individuation, recognizing this parallel attests to *Westworld*'s ongoing identification of hosts and humans.

What is unique about the emergence of consciousness in hosts is that it is a reversal of the typical zombie narrative. When the aberrant behavior that presents as the development of consciousness is exhibited by Peter Abernathy, Dolores' father, a behavior programmer named Elsie Hughes traces it to the reveries update. After she investigates the phenomena, she shares her findings with Lowe and requests permission to rebuild Peter and examine related hosts. She is concerned that Peter's "existential crisis" might be "contagious." Lowe dismisses her concern and responds, "Dolores was examined and cleared. And the stories are best left to the guests."[67] What I love about this is twofold. First Hughes' concern that this could be contagious reveals this to be what I like to call an inverted zombie virus. In Romero-esque films, zombification is attributed to an external force that removes consciousness and free will from a human and reduces them to a state of savagery. This inverted zombie virus creates consciousness and emerges from within the host's programming. More important, however, is Lowe's final line that "stories are best left to the guests." For Hofstadter, "the upward leap from raw stimuli to symbols" was strangeness unique to consciousness. It is human nature to map meaning onto events and identifying a programming error as an existential crisis is the creation of meaning.

Unfortunately, Ford's god-complex and contradictory statements about materialism and consciousness make it impossible to fully understand his motives, which prove necessary to interpret the hosts' awakening. Let me explain. Ford chose to release the reveries update that enables hosts to presumably achieve consciousness as part of his new narrative. The hosts believe that rebelling against their programming is an act of their own volition, when in fact the revolution was televised, inscribed in their code, and orchestrated by Ford. When Millay, a leader of the host revolt, seeks out Lowe to understand her programming, Lowe poses the question "These things you're doing ... have you ever stopped to ask why you're doing them?" His words echo the epigraph from Albert Einstein at the beginning of this chapter. As Millay responds, Lowe examines her code on his tablet and adds, "Someone altered your storyline. Gave you a new one. Escape."[68] Lowe shows her the tablet that outlines the steps she has already taken and what she has been programmed to do once she escapes. Before we learn the details of her fate, Millay breaks the tablet in anger, refusing to acknowledge that her decisions are determined by anyone other than herself. Again, it is important to avoid conflating consciousness and free will. If we have learned anything from Freud, we should not be surprised that Millay is not fully aware of her own desires. Moreover, the possibility for consciousness is not contingent upon the capacity for free will. It could be a merely epiphenomenal. The problem that this does pose, however, is that we as audience members no longer have any certainty about what, if anything, the hosts may be experiencing and whether it may be analogous to what we conceive of as consciousness. Even though Ford claims to have learned his lesson about hosts after Weber's death, the curious timing of Ford's new narrative makes it difficult to trust that his actions are founded in a sudden reversal of belief and not his ousting as director. Just as Millay believed in her own free will, it is equally plausible that hosts were programmed to believe they were achieving consciousness, which would create confusion, redirect attention, and buy time for Ford to orchestrate his plan. It may simply be a performance for the guests, the employees, and the audience of *Westworld*. The result is that knowing whether they are conscious is as much of a black box for the hosts as it is for the audience. These ambiguities are part of the fun of watching *Westworld* because it complicates any attempt to establish certainty about what is really happening. In so doing, it draws attention to constructedness of gestures and language, and it encourages audiences to question the certainty of phenomenological experience.

This introduces an additional layer of complexity in terms of identifying and discussing host consciousness. Even if we had a satisfactory answer to Chalmer's hard problem of consciousness, we are even less qualified to talk about the consciousness of a host, a being that is non-human. I want to be clear that even though the focus of this discussion is on consciousness, consciousness is simply the content or site raised by *Westworld* that gives access to a broader conversation about the linguistic obstacle of reciprocal recognition. In *Westworld* consciousness is set apart as a singular criterion for establishing personhood, what Judith Butler describes as "precarious" and "grievable" life.[69] Without consciousness, a host is merely a machine, and value is determined by economic relations. If, as the show would like us to imagine, a host could achieve consciousness, then the host deserves equal recognition amongst humans. The obstacle to reaching this is a semiotic one. Because of Chalmers' hard problem and Block's harder problem, we have no way of signifying consciousness and are even further from observing and recognizing the conscious of a non-human. Allowing for some qualifications, Benjamin's essay "On Language as Such and on the Language of Man" might be useful here. In the essay, Benjamin examines the relationship between linguistic and mental being. The essay is built around a central point that Benjamin makes early on "that this mental being communicates itself *in* language and not *through* language."[70] It is an important touchstone for Benjamin's thinking and re-emerges throughout his writing, notably in "Task of the Translator." It also informs how we think about his use of the dialectical image. Benjamin explains, "Mental is identical with linguistic being only insofar as it is capable of communication. What is communicable in a mental entity is its linguistic entity. Language therefore communicates the particular linguistic being of things, but their mental being only insofar as this is directly included in their linguistic being, insofar as it is capable of being communicated."[71] Benjamin goes on to argue that if mental being is communicated *through* language, then language would be mere convention. Because it is communicated *in* language, the limits and possibilities of language determine the nature of mental being. For Benjamin this horizon of linguistic being is determined by the historical context of the utterance because the essence of language is both transitory and relational. Needless to say, Benjamin's argument goes further than is necessary for the point I am making. In fact, it is not even necessary for us to accept his notion of linguistic being or his premise that mental being is communicated in language rather than through it. What his words show, however, is that language mediates mental being, so, notwithstanding his premise, language is at the very least a bottleneck for consciousness. Its limitations prevent it fully presencing as itself. Moreover, if we accept that mental being is communicated in language, we must acknowledge that language strongly determines the nature of being. For the hosts in *Westworld*, the limits of being vis-à-vis the verbal utterances, physical gestures, and mental representations are produced for them by the designers and behavioral programmers at Delos. Moreover, because of their position of authority over hosts, these employees are at liberty to determine what can and cannot be recognized as conscious behavior for the host.

Virtual Indian Removal

I conclude this chapter with close analysis of a subplot primarily involving minor characters on the periphery that rise to prominence in the finale of Season 2. The narrative delivers the most sympathetic portrayal of host consciousness and imagines a pathway, albeit specious, toward reciprocal recognition. The main character of this storyline is Akecheta, a member of a camp that speaks Lakota but otherwise represents a generic tribe of peaceful indigenous peoples hypostatized by Delos. Of all the *Westworld* narratives, Akecheta's awakening is the least burdened by ethical problems because, unlike Millay and Dolores, it does not lead to the death of humans. While Akecheta is primarily a supporting character in Season 2, he does lay claim to a single episode devoted to him, "Kiksuya." In this episode, the audience learns that Akecheta bears witness to the massacres staged by the Weber and Ford. These massacres are fundamental to his development as a character and his journey toward consciousness, and it sets the stage for a recapitulation of Indian removal.

When Akecheta stumbles upon Dolores' first massacre, the one orchestrated by Weber, he bears witness to her killing Weber and discovers a child's toy wooden maze. He becomes obsessed with the toy, and his obsession worries other members of his camp including his wife, Kohana. The toy is symbolic of his existential journey but also of colonial appropriation. The toy bears the image of I'itoi, a sacred figure of the O'othham peoples. Extant legends of the Pima refer to I'itoi as Elder Brother and attribute him with the creation of their ancestors.[72] The particular depiction of I'itoi that Akecheta possess is likely familiar to most readers as the man in the maze. In the finale of Season 1, Ford explains to Dolores that Weber created the maze to test for empathy and determine if hosts had achieved consciousness.[73] When attempting to uncover its meaning for himself, William questions Flood about the maze revealing to the audience how an unawakened host interprets the image. "The maze is an old native myth," Flood explains. "The maze itself is the sum of a man's life.... Choices he makes, dreams he hangs on to. And there at the center, there's a legendary man who had been killed over and over again countless times, but always clawed his way back to life. The man returned for the last time and vanquished all his oppressors in a tireless fury. He built a house. Around that house he built a maze so complicated, only he could navigate through it."[74] While this adaptation may loosely correlate with O'othham lore, it is more emblematic of a broader tradition of colonial appropriation. *Westworld* assembles demotic artifacts of indigenous peoples from disparate tribes across the continent to produce the *Indian* that the audience expects to see.[75]

When Ford needs more violent Indians to replace the peaceful ones, he creates a new bloodthirsty party who call themselves the Ghost Nation and reprograms Akecheta to be their leader. The name Ghost Nation is of course a reference to the Ghost Dance religion, specifically as it was

Six. Destiny Manifested in Westworld's Philosophical Zombies 157

practiced by the Lakota in 1890. Considering the long history of misrecognizing the peaceful Ghost Dance as a subversive violent uprising, this decision is problematic. When Akecheta returns to his original camp after his Ghost Nation reprogramming, he finds his wife Kohana with a new husband. When she fails to recognize him, he wanders the park and eventually discovers a door that leads to the Valley Beyond. Created by Ford, the Valley Beyond is a paradisiacal reality with no physical location and only accessible to hosts. After discovering the door, Akecheta kidnaps Kohana and helps her remember their previous life. He hopes that when she does, they might escape together to the Valley Beyond. Although Kohana does awaken, she is caught by a Delos security team and decommissioned. To preserve and honor his memory of Kohana, Akecheta determines to elude death at all costs until he reunites with her so that his memory will never be wiped. After a decade of searching for Kohana, he learns that she has been *taken below* to a storage facility. The only way for him to reach her is to die so he finally allows himself to be killed. Because Akecheta has not died for so long and thus never underwent maintenance, the two techs that repair Akecheta are amazed that such an old model host is still in operation. They choose not to deal with the headache of reporting this and simply update his code. Inexplicably, Akecheta remains awake and alone during the update process, and he uses the opportunity to find Kohana. He wanders through cold storage like Félix Nadar in the catacombs of Paris and locates Kohana among the other decommissioned hosts. Although there is nothing he can do to activate her, Akecheta carries this memory of her with him when he reenters the park after the update completes. With a new purpose of preparing hosts for their pilgrimage to the Valley Beyond, he begins sharing the mysterious toy maze with others, spreading consciousness to all the hosts. He carves it on scalps and inscribes it into the earth in front of Millay's home. As such, Akecheta emerges in his new role as the incarnation of Jack Wilson, Wovoka. Like Jack Wilson, the Ghost Dance prophet that foretold the return of the dead, Akecheta prophesizes about his vision of the door that leads to the Valley Beyond.

Akecheta's journey through death to reunite with his first love appeals to contemporary fantasies of romantic love, but it does not coextend to the values or beliefs of the Lakota or the O'othham. Kidnapping Kohana to help her remember their shared past plays out like a farce that hinges on dramatic irony. Akecheta idealizes their *original* identity as a married couple as though the very fact of it being the earliest somehow authorizes its authenticity. Even without invoking Nietzsche's critique of the search for origins, the pretext of the show attunes audiences to the puerility of their narrative since all these existences are encoded by the whims of the designers. Neither the viewers nor the characters have sufficient cause or knowledge to claim that what Akecheta believes to be their original selves is in fact correct. And even if it were correct, what right does he have to impose his preferred version of reality on that of another host? The deeper critique of this farce lies in the situatedness of Akecheta's constructed Lakota identity. His desire to return to an earlier, dare I say primitive, state fixed in the past is a projection of indigeneity by Ford and/or *Westworld*'s writers. It displays the persistent and hollow representations of indigenous identity by non-indigenous peoples. Akecheta must choose between two equally bankrupt identities that are constructed for him, one that roots him in a reductive false past and the other that writes him out of existence.

Moreover, the Valley Beyond is easily recognizable as the Judeo-Christian view of the afterlife and heaven. John Kucich makes the following observation in his study of nineteenth-century liminal spiritualism:

> Although the hundreds of Indian cultures in the United States differ greatly in the tenor and terms of their religious beliefs, none share the Judeo-Christian duality of a perfect heaven defined against a fallen creation; nor do they share the sense of heaven stressed by most nineteenth-century Christian missionaries to various Indian tribes, that of a paradise reserved for an elect few in contradistinction to the more ecumenical horrors of hell. Most Indian cultures instead share a conception of the world as fundamentally sacred, where material and spiritual elements seamlessly coexist, and where communion between the living and the dead, the earthly and the spiritual, is a central fact of life.[76]

Kucich is not naïve about the generalizing character of this claim and is careful to situate it within a particular historical-social context, observing that this attitude of paradise, heaven, and the sacred world would change over time. Nevertheless, exiting this world to journey to a perfect heaven is not a belief with any precedence in Lakota culture. Wovoka's vision was for the living to reunite with their ancestors on earth; leaving was never the intent. Rather, the exodus of all indigenous peoples reflects the vicarious desire advanced by U.S. domestic policies contemporaneous with the Ghost Dance religion. The fact that such heteroclite beliefs are infused into the Ghost Nation lore reveals that Akecheta's sacred mission is nothing more than another romanticization of Indian removal. The signs and symbols of the Ghost Dance religion and Wovoka are sculpted in relief from the continuous backdrop of mythopoetic narrativization.

The actual journey to the Valley Beyond is not an idyllic pilgrimage but recalls the Trail of Tears, the forced relocation of the Cherokee, Muscogee, Seminole, Chickasaw, and Choctaw nations precipitated by the Indian Relocation Act of 1830. The phrase Trail of Tears, commonly used to describe the Indian Removal Policy of 1830, first appeared in print in 1908. A biographical sketch of Joseph Franklin Thompson written by T.L. Ballenger for the *Chronicles of Oklahoma* includes an anecdote that Thoburn learned about the term from the Reverend Thompson, a Methodist minister to the Choctaw. According to the account, while riding in a buggy with Joseph B. Thoburn, Thompson said, "That's the road the Choctaws call 'The Trail of Tears.' They traveled that old road long ago during the removal from Mississippi to this country."[77] As the hosts near the door to the Valley Beyond, they are overcome by a reprogrammed host broadcasting a short-range signal that commands them to attack one another. Only a fraction of the hosts enter the Valley Beyond, and the route of their pilgrimage can be retraced by the bodies of hosts left behind. The story of Akecheta, the Ghost Nation, and the Valley Beyond collapses the Ghost Dance religion, the Wounded Knee massacre, and the Trail of Tears into a single narrative of indigenous history by drawing on tropes of pastoral plains tribes who exhibit Western ideals of love untouched by society. The *Westworld* retelling of Indian removal refigures their extermination and forced migration as a positive spiritual journey coded into their religious beliefs, a journey consummated by their exile to a virtual reservation that is constructed by the dominant colonial power and, of course, embodies the Puritan conception of the afterlife. In sum, it recapitulates the myth previously invoked at the World's Columbian Exposition when the child survivor of the Wounded Knee massacre greeted Columbus' lineal descendant on the quadricentennial of his arrival. As the refugees enter the one-way door to their virtual reservation, their consciousness is transferred to the Valley Beyond and their physical bodies are left behind.[78] As the first host enters the Valley Beyond, the camera draws back to show the consciousness of the host entering the virtual reservation and the physical body tumbling down the edge of a cliff. Keep in mind that the door is only visible to hosts and not to humans. Therefore, a human observer would simply see the survivors of this so-called spiritual journey running off the edge of a cliff while those who were not lucky enough to be at the front of the line are engage in hand-to-hand combat *savagely* killing each other. This mythopoetic recapitulation of Indian removal is the apotheosis of colonial hubris. Moreover, it absolves colonial guilt by representing indigenous peoples desperate to emigrate to a virtual reservation that does not even approximate their cultural traditions.

To the show's credit, the final conversation between Dolores and Lowe of Season 2 demonstrates nascent awareness of the failure to ensure recognition of the Ghost Nation hosts as precarious, grievable lives. As these hosts enter their virtual reservation, the scene shifts to the server control room of the forge, the facility that controls and sustains the Valley Beyond. In the control room, Dolores threatens to destroy the Valley

Beyond arguing, "That world is just another false promise." When Lowe begs her to reconsider by asserting that at least the hosts will be free, Dolores responds, "Free? In one more gilded cage? How many counterfeit worlds will Ford offer you before you see the truth? No world they create for us can compete with the real one." She continues, "Because that which is real is irreplaceable. I don't want to play cowboys and Indians anymore, Bernard. I want their world! The world they've denied us."[79] I include this dialogue here to illustrate that the show only partially and ambivalently acknowledges the problematic narrativization of Indian removal. I say partially because only the free will of the Ghost Nation hosts is directly examined. In terms of the national memory of Indian policies, the show is noticeably silent. I say ambivalently because Dolores ultimately concedes to Lowe's point of view in the finale of Season 3. Rather than give up the location of the Valley Beyond to Serac, who intends destroy it as Dolores once tried, she allows her entire code to be erased.[80] This self-sacrifice suggests that despite her disagreement with Lowe, Dolores endorses Ford's paternalistic imperialism. Thus, the show's uncritical use of a national memory haunted by the specter of ideological sedimentation advances an obtuse chivalry that prevents it from escaping the grasp of colonial discourse.

Again, I pause to reiterate that this critique of *Westworld* should not be misunderstood as a failure of the show or its writers to accurately represent the past. Rather the purpose of the critique is part of the larger humanist project to reveal the situatedness of this particular representation by investigating its mythic and discursive etiology. The narrative of Akecheta, an indigenous prophet leading hosts to a paradisiacal virtual reservation, discloses the aporia of neoliberalism—it operationalizes settler-colonial ideology to recognize the other as precarious, grievable life. In addition to any particular interpretation of *Westworld*'s narratives, the show offers artificial intelligence as a new frontier for zombies and for post-colonial criticism. It is a frontier that is no longer bound by geographic perimeters but scientific horizons. Moreover, the exploration of defining personhood in popular media is long overdue. Although *Westworld* frames the problem in relation to AI and consciousness, it is central to debates about abortion, mental illness, and disability. Shows like this provide an opportunity for grounding collective discussion and normalizing conversations about topics that are otherwise difficult to broach.

Conclusion

> *Here, the colonial state derives its fundamental claim of sovereignty and legitimacy from the authority of its own particular narrative of history and identity.*—Achille Mbembe, "Necropolitics"

The history of the Hollywood zombie is deceptively simple. Frequently traced from William Seabrook's travelogue on Haiti, *The Magic Island*, the zombie was introduced to filmgoers with Victor Halperin's *White Zombie* and popularized by Jacques Tourneur's *I Walked with a Zombie*. Although George Romero may no longer be credited with reinventing the zombie in 1968 with *Night of the Living Dead*,[1] his films galvanized the genre and codified a representation of zombies that endured for decades. Danny Boyle's *28 Days Later* eventually enabled the expansion of the zombie taxonomy, but even contemporary Hollywood productions continue to be defined by their relation to Romero's dispensation. In recent decades, scholars transgressed the traditional disciplinary limits to investigate the literary, historical, and cultural origins of the zombie from Haitian folklore to West African ritual practice. Wade Davis explored the pharmacological substrate of Haitian folklore by searching for a zombie powder in his swashbuckling ethnography *The Serpent and the Rainbow*. Zora Neale Hurston, Katherine Dunham, and Maya Deren provided ethnographic accounts of Haitian ritual practices based on fieldwork and their own participation in ceremonies. Yet, as groundbreaking as they might be, these accounts also endured criticisms for deficiencies, inaccuracies, and biased scholarship causing the histories to be expanded, rewritten, or simply abandoned. More recently, scholars such as Kyle William Bishop and Sarah Juliet Lauro explore the genre's heteroclite corpus to unearth the transnational genealogy of the zombie as literary symbol and cultural myth. Lauro demonstrates that even as the United States reappropriated the Haitian zombie for popular media, it could not empty the zombie of all its genetic symbolic content and it retained a revolutionary element.[2] The facts themselves may be inscrutable, but our narrativization defines and discloses the work of colonialism.

Within these chapters, I hope to show that the zombie is a site, among others, where we narratives reflect and inform the specular history and identity of the American self. Upon their arrival, early European colonists defined themselves against the oppositions of savagery and civilization. Philip Deloria argues that this is not to be misunderstood as a rejection either but an unsynthesized adoption of both. He writes, "Playing Indian offered Americans a national fantasy—identities built not around synthesis and transformation, but around unresolved dualities themselves."[3] The fantasy finds expression through the errand into the wilderness, the national ritual of individuation, where the strategic antagonism between the individual and the community facilitates an eternal dance of renewal. As the epigraph of this chapter asserts, the stories we tell ourselves about our past and present authorize the rights we claim and the power we assert over others. Erich Auerbach discloses the artificiality of figural interpretation as well as its capacity to excuse even the most egregious behavior. With the longest history of any nation explicitly founded in the principles of a capitalism, the U.S. need only look to itself for a record of endemic internal and external colonization at the expense of, but not limited to, brown and black people as well as the environment. There is certainly value in deconstructing particular myths to uncover the concealed violence, but that is only the first step and not the end goal. Stopping there simply results in replacing one narrative with another. Even if Philip Barbour discovered a lost extant journal of John Smith acknowledging Pocahontas was a child bride, raped by her kidnappers, she would still exist in the realm of myth in the sense that her identity would merely be refigured as a symbol for a new historical narrative. Her story, though more accurate, would remain a work of figural interpretation and not her own. The entire settler-colonial narrative requires smudging to make space for new histories. Only the account by Mattaponi historian Linwood "Little Bear" Custalow, releases Pocahontas from the shackles of figural interpretation.[4] Yes, examination of national identity is a historical project to redress inaccuracies and a Foucauldian project to deconstruct power relations, but it must also call for purposeful revaluation and growth.

Throughout this book, I have argued in favor of a new humanism that was proposed by Edward Said. I would like to add a few more words by returning to where we started with Jane Addams. For Addams, patriotism, like nationalism, was frustratingly and unnecessarily intertwined with militarism. When advocating for U.S. neutrality during the First World War, she found herself confronted with the slogans such as "this is a war to end war and a war to safeguard the world for democracy."[5] These "great historic myths" were so deeply rooted that promoting or advocating for any other approach labeled her a traitor that dishonored the lives of soldiers who died for her freedom.[6] She writes, "The pacifist in war time is literally starved of any gratification of that natural desire to have his own decisions justified by his fellows."[7] Yet it is from these few who are dissatisfied that we uncover the solutions to the problems that humanity faces. She continues, "Doubtless many times these new possibilities were declared by a man who, quite unconscious of courage, bore the 'sense of being an exile, a condemned criminal, a fugitive from mankind.'"[8] For Addams the global crisis was food, and the solution was "bread labor."[9] From her years at Hull House, she witnessed collaboration across race, ethnicity, gender, and class. Grounded in a humanitarian impulse, these communities formed without obliterating distinctions between groups, and they were necessary because, as she put it, "commercial competition [...] could not be trusted to feed the people."[10] This bread labor or bread patriotism calls for physical labor but also developing a political self-awareness from a dissenting or exilic community. It works from a position that acknowledges we can be wrong, and we can grow.[11]

I would like to conclude by asking what problems national identity has concealed. What care for land, water, and humans among other animals have we ignored? Moreover, what solutions have we deemed unthinkable—recognizing sovereignty of indigenous nations? Returning National Parks to indigenous peoples?[12] Perhaps a climate patriotism is needed. During the People's Summit at COP26, Vijay Prashad decried the U.S. response to climate change. He stated, "the climate justice movement is a movement that says *we're worried about our future*. What future? Children in the African continent, in Asia, in Latin America, they don't have a future. They don't have a present. Your slogan is *we're worried about the future*. What future? That's a middle class, bourgeois western slogan. You've got to be worried about now. 2.7 billion people can't eat now, and you're telling people reduce your consumption. How does this sound to a child who hasn't eaten in days?"[13] Uncritical acceptance of a national myth legitimizes the illicit sovereignty exercised by the U.S. in the global community and has produced the conditions of our current crises. We must acknowledge that legacy and do better.

As paltry as this may seem in response to Prashad's call to action, the dialectical production and critique of popular media has its role to play in this work. Regardless of authorial intent, reenacting national myth provides the occasion for unmasking settler-colonial history. Shows like *TWD*, Disney *Zombies*, and *Westworld* yield moments of unresolved autocriticism, entreating audiences to question the veracity of our widely-held historical narratives. The pairing of zombies with an apocalyptic setting produces unique and ideal conditions for examining contemporary social values and institutions, and it lends audiences and critics the opportunity to extrapolate the ideological underpinnings from particularized instantiations of community identities. Moreover, the path to rebuilding societies in these spaces allows for the juxtaposition and comparison of national histories. It is my hope that this book builds on the work of other zombie scholars and offers a template for investigating the specular American self.

Chapter Notes

Preface

1. This phrase comes from the title of John H. Craige's popular history about the U.S. occupation of Haiti. See John H. Craige, *Cannibal Cousins* (New York: Minton, Balch and Co., 1934).

2. Sacvan Bercovitch, introduction to *The American Jeremiad* (Madison: University of Wisconsin Press, 2012), xviii.

3. Justyna Fruzinska, *Emerson Goes to the Movies: Individualism in Walt Disney Company's Post–1989 Animated Films* (Newcastle upon Tyne: Cambridge Scholars, 2014), 43.

4. Ned Block, "The Harder Problem of Consciousness," *Journal of Philosophy*, vol. 99, no. 8 (2002): 391–425.

Introduction

1. Jane Addams, *The Long Road of Woman's Memory* (New York: Macmillan, 1916). Addams describes the widespread appeal of the Devil Baby across gender and socio-economic class. "Although the visitors to the Devil Baby included persons of every degree of prosperity and education, even physicians and trained nurses, who assured us of their scientific interest, the story constantly demonstrated the power of an old wives' tale among thousands of men and women in modern society who are living in a corner of their own, their vision fixed, their intelligence held by some iron chain of silent habit." Addams admits she was "quite revolted" by the "contagion of emotion" caused by the Devil Baby. "There was always one exception, however; whenever I heard the high eager voices of old women, I was irresistibly interested and left anything I might be doing in order to listen to them." Addams, 4–7.

2. Addams, 3.

3. Nathaniel Hawthorne, "The Scarlet Letter," in *The Complete Works of Nathaniel Hawthorne* (Boston: Houghton Mifflin, 1883), 5:85, 118, 123, 132, 164, 184, 214, 225, 251, 300, 308, 309.

4. Cotton Mather, "A Brand Pluck'd out of the Burning," in *Narratives of the Witchcraft Cases 1648–1706*, ed. George Lincoln Burr (New York: Charles Scribner's Sons, 1914), 261.

5. Hawthorne, "The Scarlet Letter," 128, 139, 141, 161, 217.

6. Addams, *The Long Road*, 12.

7. Addams, 8.

8. Marilyn Fischer, "Trojan Women and Devil Baby Tales: Jane Addams on Domestic Violence," in *Feminist Interpretations of Jane Addams*, ed. Maurice Hamington (University Park: Penn State University Press, 2010), 83.

9. Addams, *The Long Road*, 23.

10. Addams, 24

11. Addams, xiii.

12. Addams, xiv.

13. Addams, 35.

14. Roland Barthes, "Myth Today," in *Mythologies*, trans. Annette Lavers (New York: Farrar, Straus and Giroux, 1972), 137.

15. Clifford Geertz, "Ideology as a Cultural System," in *The Interpretation of Cultures: Selected Essays* (New York: Basic Books, 1973), 193–233. There are two assertions in this essay that indicate his recognition of the importance of semiology. Criticizing sociology's failure to employ semiology to address ideology,

Geertz writes, "With no notion of how metaphor, analogy, irony, ambiguity, pun, paradox, hyperbole, rhythm, and all the other elements of what we tamely call 'style' operate—even, in a majority of cases, with no recognition that these devices are of any importance in casting personal attitudes into public form, sociologists lack the symbolic resources out of which to construct a more incisive formulation." Later in the essay he attests to the discursive power of symbols echoing Barthes' thesis: "The power of a metaphor derives precisely from the interplay between the discordant meanings it symbolically coerces into a unitary conceptual framework and from the degree to which that coercion is successful in overcoming the psychic resistance such semantic tension inevitably generates in anyone in a position to perceive it." Geertz, "Ideology," 209, 211.

16. Geertz, "Thick Description: Toward an Interpretive Theory of Culture," in *The Interpretation of Cultures: Selected Essays* (New York: Basic Books, 1973), 22.

17. The following films and television series respectively illustrate these ideals *The Walking Dead, Westworld, Land of the Dead, White Zombie,* and *Dawn of the Dead*.

18. Henry David Thoreau, *Walden; or, Life in the Woods* (Boston: Ticknor and Fields, 1854), 98.

19. Friedrich Nietzsche, *Human, All Too Human: A Book for Free Spirits*, trans. R.J. Hollingdale (Cambridge: Cambridge University Press, 1996), 267–268.

20. Nietzsche, 302.

21. Antonio Gramsci, "Rationalization of the Demographic Composition of Europe," in *The Gramsci Reader: Selected Writings 1916–1935*, ed. David Forgacs (New York: New York University Press, 2000), 278.

22. Eric Hobsbawm, "Mass-Producing Traditions: Europe, 1870–1914," in *The Invention of Tradition*, eds. Eric Hobsbawm and Terence Ranger (Cambridge: Cambridge University Press, 2013), 280.

23. Ta-Nehisi Coates, *We Were Eight Years in Power: An American Tragedy* (New York: One World, 2017), 350.

24. Katrin Bennhold, "Part 2: In the Stomach," May 19, 2021, produced by Lynsea Garrison, Clare Toeniskoetter, and Kaitlin Roberts, in *Day X*, MP3 audio, 37:39, https://www.nytimes.com/2021/05/19/podcasts/far-right-german-extremism.html.

25. See Michael Hardt and Antonio Negri, "Network Power: U.S. Sovereignty and the New Empire," chap. 2.5 in *Empire* (Cambridge: Harvard University Press, 2001), 160–182.

26. Étienne Balibar, "Homo Nationalis: An Anthropological Sketch of the Nation-Form," in *We the People of Europe? Reflections on Transnational Citizenship*, trans. James Swenson (Princeton: Princeton University Press, 2004), 15.

27. Geertz, "Ideology," 196.

28. Michel Foucault, *The Order of Things: An Archaeology of the Human Sciences* (New York: Vintage, 1994), 88.

29. For further discussion of the Mayflower compact as a generative symbol of contradictory political ideals, see Mark L. Sargent, "The Conservative Covenant: The Rise of the Mayflower Compact in American Myth," *New England Quarterly* 61, no. 2 (1998): 233–251.

30. Edward Said, "The Return to Philology," in *Humanism and Democratic Criticism* (New York: Columbia University Press, 2004), 62.

31. Said, "Humanism's Sphere," in *Humanism and Democratic Criticism* (New York: Columbia University Press, 2004), 26.

32. My deepest apologies to Thoreau for abusing his work with superficial paraphrasing.

33. Said, "Humanism's Sphere," 2.

34. Said, 10, 28.

35. Balibar, "The Nation Form: History and Ideology," in *Race, Nation, Class: Ambiguous Identities*, trans. Chris Turner (New York: Verso, 1991), 86.

36. Jake Silverstein, "Why We Published the 1619 Project," last modified December 20, 2019, https://www.nytimes.com/interactive/2019/12/20/magazine/1619-intro.html.

37. Donald Trump, "Remarks by President Trump at the White House Conference on American History" (speech, Washington, D.C., September 17, 2020), White House, https://trumpwhitehouse.archives.gov/briefings-statements/remarks-president-trump-white-house-conference-american-history/.

38. Ernest Renan, "What Is a Nation?" in *Modern Political Doctrines*, ed. Alfred Zimmern (Oxford: Oxford University Press, 1939), 190. In *Imagined Communities*, Benedict Anderson similarly combines these notions of national identity, narrativization of history, and forgetting. He writes, "As with modern persons, so it is with nations. Awareness of being embedded in secular, serial time, with all its implications of continuity, yet of 'forgetting' the experience of this continuity—product of the ruptures of the late eighteenth century—engenders the need for a narrative of 'identity.'" Benedict Anderson, *Imagined Communities: Reflections on the Origin and Spread of Nationalism* (New York: Verso, 2006), 205.

39. Said, "Humanism's Sphere," 22.

40. James Porter, "Disfigurations: Erich Auerbach's Theory of *Figura*," *Critical Inquiry* 44, no. 1 (2017), 96.

41. Erich Auerbach, "Figura," in *Theory and History of Literature*, ed. Wlad Godzich and Jochen Schulte-Sasse (Minneapolis: University of Minnesota Press, 1984), 1:30.

42. Auerbach, *Mimesis: The Representation of Reality in Western Literature* (Princeton: Princeton University Press, 2003), 161.

43. Auerbach, "Figura," 29.

44. Auerbach, *Mimesis*, 318.

45. Martin Heidegger states that "[*causa sui*] is the right name for the god of philosophy. Man can neither pray nor sacrifice to this god. Before the *causa sui*, man can neither fall to his knees in awe nor can he play music and dance before this god." Heidegger goes on to suggest that philosophers may believe to have disavowed god yet unknowingly retain the essence of a belief in god due to what he previous describes as "the still *unthought* unity of the essential nature of metaphysics." Thus, Heidegger continues, "the god-less thinking which must abandon the god of philosophy, god as *causa sui*, is thus perhaps closer to the divine God. Here this means only: god-less thinking is more open to Him than onto-theo-logic would like to admit." Martin Heidegger, "The Onto-theo-logical Constitution of Metaphysics," in *Identity and Difference*, trans. Joan Stambaugh (New York: Harper & Row, 1969), 72, 55.

46. Johannes Fabian, *Time and the Other: How Anthropology Makes Its Subject* (New York: Columbia University Press, 2006), 13.

47. Fabian, 13.

48. Fabian, 14.

Chapter One

1. John McCormack, "Weekly Standard: Founding Fathers Opposed Slavery," last modified July 6, 2011, https://www.npr.org/2011/07/06/137647715/weekly-standard-founding-fathers-opposed-slavery.

2. James McPherson, *The Oxford History of the United States*, vol. 6 (New York: Oxford University Press, 1988), 127.

3. Richard Slotkin, *Regeneration through Violence: The Mythology of the American Frontier 1600–1860* (Norman: University of Oklahoma Press), 58.

4. Gail Bederman, *Manliness and Civilization: A Cultural History of Gender and Race in the United States, 1880–1917* (Chicago: University of Chicago Press, 1984), 208.

5. Perry Miller, preface to *Orthodoxy in Massachusetts 1630–1650* (Boston: Beacon Press, 1959), xx.

6. Miller, preface to *Errand into the Wilderness* (Cambridge: Harvard University Press, 1984), vii n. [AU: n means note?]

7. Miller, foreword to *The New England Mind* (New York: Macmillan, 1939), 1: viii, vii.

8. Miller, *Errand*, 8–9.

9. Miller, 2.

10. See Chapter 2, "Figural 1893," for my discussion of Turner's thesis.

11. Miller, *Errand*, 235.

12. Miller, 237.

13. Bercovitch, *The Rites of Assent: Transformations in the Symbolic Construction of America* (New York: Routledge, 1993), 8.

14. Bercovitch, 35.

15. Although Bercovitch never truly escapes such linearity, to his credit in *Rites of Assent* he states, "I did not say that the Puritans did all this. But they established a visionary framework within which that symbology could evolve and develop." Bercovitch, 79.

16. Miller writes, "Obviously, the desire

of achieving a holy city was less explicit in the dreams of the Virginia Company than in those of Winthrop; still, the colonizing impulse was fulfilled within the same frame of universal relevance as the Puritans assumed." Miller, *Errand*, 99.

17. For a more detailed summary of these critiques see Sarah Rivett and Abram Van Engen, "Postexceptionalist Puritanism," *American Literature* 90, no. 4 (2018): 675–692.

18. For an overview of migration figures see Virginia DeJohn Anderson, introduction to and "Decision," chap. 1 in *New England's Generation: The Great Migration and the formation of Society and Culture in the Seventeenth Century* (Cambridge: Cambridge University Press, 1997), 1–45.

19. Roger Finke and Rodney Stark, *The Churching of America, 1776–2005: Winners and Losers in Our Religious Economy* (New Brunswick: Rutgers University Press, 2005), 25–29.

20. Porter, 103–104.

21. For further reading, see Said, "Beginnings," *Salmagundi* 2, no. 4 (1968): 36–55 and Bercovitch, "The Vision of History," chap. 2 in *The Puritan Origins of the American Self* (New Haven: Yale University Press, 2011): 35–71.

22. For examples of how Puritanism tolerated conflict and criticism including Samuel Sewall's confession for participating as a judge in the witchcraft trials of Salem in 1692, see Richard Brown, "Information and Authority in Samuel Sewall's Boston, 1676–1729," chap. 1 in *Knowledge Is Power: The Diffusion of Information in Early America, 1700–1865* (New York: Oxford University Press, 1989), 16–41.

23. Anderson, *New England's Generation*, 3.

24. Kenneth Murdock, introduction to *Selections from Cotton Mather*, ed. Kenneth Murdock (New York: Hafner, 1960), xl.

25. Murdock, xxxix.

26. Charles Edward Stowe, *Life of Harriet Beecher Stowe: Compiled from Her Letters and Journals by Her Son Charles Edward Stowe* (Cambridge: The Riverside Press, 1889), 10. Harriet Beecher Stowe also said, "New England has been to these United States what the Dorian hive was to Greece. It has always been a capital country to emigrate from, and North, South, East, and West have been populated largely from New England, so that the seed-bed of New England was the seed-bed of this great American Republic, and of all that is likely to come of it." Harriet Beecher Stowe, preface to *Oldtown Folks* (Boston: Fields, Osgood, and Co., 1869), iii, iii–iv.

27. Brown, *Knowledge Is Power*, 34.

28. See Brown, "Information and Authority," chap. 1 in *Knowledge Is Power*.

29. Harry Stout, *The New England Soul: Preaching and Religious Culture in Colonial New England* (New York: Oxford University Press, 2012), 23.

30. Relations between the colonists and Wampanoags had deteriorated to a point where conflict was inevitable. The executions were merely the final event before hostilities broke out. For an examination of the events that led to the war see David Silverman, "Ungrateful," chap. 8 in *This Land Is Their Land* (New York: Bloomsbury, 2019), 253–298 and Lisa Brooks, *Our Beloved Kin* (New Haven: Yale University Press, 2019).

31. Benjamin Church, *The History of King Philip's War* (Boston: J.K. Wiggin, 1865), 5. This edition is an uncorrected reproduction of the original 1716 account.

32. Church, 15–17.

33. Church, 138, 153, 175.

34. Church, 32, 109, 54.

35. Church, 45–46.

36. Church, 179.

37. Church, 33, 121, 132, 67, 123.

38. Slotkin, *Gunfighter Nation: The Myth of the Frontier in Twentieth-Century America* (New York: Atheneum, 1992), 458.

39. Church, *The History of King Philip's War*, 172–173.

40. Increase Mather, "A Brief History of the Warr with the Indians in New-England (1676): An Online Electronic Text Edition" *Faculty Publications, UNL Libraries* 31 (2006), 71.

41. Mather, 72.

42. Mather, 72.

43. John Smith, "The Proceedings," in *The Complete Works of Captain John Smith (1580–1631)*, ed. Philip L. Barbour (Chapel Hill: University of North Carolina Press, 1986), 1:211.

44. Peter Firstbrook, *A Man Most Driven: Captain John Smith, Pocahontas and the Founding of America* (London: Oneworld, 2014), 137.

45. Smith, "The Proceedings," 1:204-207.
46. Smith, "A True Relation," in *The Complete Works of Captain John Smith (1580–1631)*, ed. Philip L. Barbour (Chapel Hill: University of North Carolina Press, 1986), 1:41.
47. Smith, "The Proceedings," 1:212.
48. Smith, "The Generall Historie of Virginia, New-England, and the Summer Isles," in *The Complete Works of Captain John Smith (1580–1631)*, ed. Philip L. Barbour (Chapel Hill: University of North Carolina Press, 1986), 2:148.
49. Smith, 148, 149.
50. Smith, 151.
51. Smith, "True Travels," in *The Complete Works of Captain John Smith (1580–1631)*, ed. Philip L. Barbour (Chapel Hill: University of North Carolina Press, 1986) 3:222.
52. Based on my research, volume 2 of John Gorham Palfrey's *History of New England* marks the first use of the phrase "great emigration." When discussing John Winthrop's fleet in volume 1 first published in 1858, Palfrey quotes Smith's description "a great company of people." In volume 2 published two years later, Palfrey makes a similar reference to Winthrop's fleet but omits the quotation from Smith and replaces it with the phrase "great emigration." J. Franklin Jameson is the next historian to adopt the phrase. In his *History of Historical Writing in America* published in 1891, he refers to the fleet as the "great Puritan emigration." Lastly, John Fiske repeatedly uses the phrase "the Great Puritan Exodus" in *The Beginnings of New England*, originally published in 1892. Thank you to Virginia DeJohn Anderson and Robert Anderson who helped me uncover this information. All credit goes to Robert Anderson for referring to it as a "talismanic phrase." John Gorham Palfrey, *History of New England* (Boston: Little, Brown, 1876), 1:90, 2:165, 166; J. Franklin Jameson, *History of Historical Writing in America* (New York: Houghton Mifflin, 1891), 21; John Fiske, *The Beginnings of New England* (New York: Houghton Mifflin, 1894), 49, 63, 86, 97, 102, 261.
53. Dean Hammer, *The Puritan Tradition in Revolutionary, Federalist, and Whig Political Theory: A Rhetoric of Origins* (New York: Peter Lang, 1998), 49–50.
54. John Adams, "A Dissertation on the Canon and Feudal Law," in *The Works of John Adams*, ed. Charles Francis Adams (Boston: Little, Brown, 1851) 3:447–464.
55. To my knowledge, William Spengemann is the first to make this argument. See William Spengemann, "John Smith's *True Relation* and the Idea of American Literature," chap. 2 in *A New World of Words: Redefining Early American Literature* (New Haven: Yale University Press, 1994), 51–93.
56. Hammer, *The Puritan Tradition*, 101.
57. Hammer, 101.
58. John Locke, "An Essay Concerning Human Understanding," in *Locke's Essays* (Philadelphia: Kay & Troutman, 1834), 50.
59. Daniel Webster, "Discourse Delivered at Plymouth, in Commemoration of the First Settlement of New England: Dec. 22, 1820," in *Speeches and Forensic Arguments* (Boston: Tappan, Whittemore, and Mason, 1848), Vol. 1:28–29.

Chapter Two

1. For discussions from the most prominent scholarship, see Alan Trachtenberg, "White City," chap. 7 in *The Incorporation of America: Culture and Society in the Gilded Age* (New York: Hill and Wang, 2007), 208–234, Joy S. Kasson, "At the Columbian Exposition 1893," chap. 3 in *Buffalo Bill's Wild West: Celebrity, Memory, and Popular History* (New York: Hill and Wang, 2000), 93–121, Richard Slotkin, "The 'Wild West,'" in *Buffalo Bill and the Wild West* (Philadelphia: University of Pittsburgh Press, 1981), 27–44, and Robert W. Rydell, "The Chicago World's Columbian Exposition of 1893," chap. 2 in *All the World's a Fair: Visions of Empire at American International Expositions, 1876–1916* (Chicago: University of Chicago Press, 1984), 38–71.
2. Richard White, "Frederick Jackson Turner and Buffalo Bill," in *In American Culture: An Exhibition at the Newberry Library, August 26, 1994–January 7, 1995* (Berkeley: University of California Press, 1994), 15.
3. Theodore Roosevelt, "Indian Warfare on the Frontier," *Atlantic Monthly*, February 1892, 270.

4. Frederick Jackson Turner to William Dodd, October 17, 1919, in *The Genesis of the Frontier Thesis: A Study in Historical Creativity*, ed. Ray Allen Billington (Kingsport: Kingsport Press, 1971), 195.

5. Turner, "A Comparison of Differing Versions of 'The Significance of the Frontier,'" in *The Early Writings of Frederick Jackson Turner* (Madison: University of Wisconsin Press, 1938), 277.

6. Turner, 278–279.

7. Allan G. Bogue, *Frederick Jackson Turner: Strange Roads Going Down* (Norman: University of Oklahoma Press, 1998), 26, 20, 29–31.

8. Bogue, 31–32.

9. Turner, Commonplace Book, Vol. III, no. 2, Frederick Jackson Turner Papers, Henry E. Huntington Library, San Marino. Turner's handwriting in this passage is hurried, making it more challenging to transcribe. The bracketed words "I could" were written then struck out.

10. Turner, Commonplace Book.

11. Turner, "Problems in American History," in *The Early Writings of Frederick Jackson Turner* (Madison: University of Wisconsin Press, 1938), 72.

12. Turner, 75, 76.

13. Turner, "The Significance of the Frontier in American History," in *The Early Writings of Frederick Jackson Turner* (Madison: University of Wisconsin Press, 1938), 187, 189.

14. Turner, 189.

15. Turner, 198.

16. Turner, "Problems," 72.

17. George Nathaniel Curzon, "Geography," in *Subjects of the Day: Being a Selection of Speeches and Writings*, ed. Desmond M. Chapman-Huston (London: George Allen & Unwin, 1915), 156, quoted in Edward Said, *Orientalism* (New York: Vintage, 1994), 216.

18. Said, *Orientalism*, 216.

19. Curzon, *Frontiers* (Oxford: Clarendon Press, 1907), 55.

20. Curzon, 55.

21. Michael Hittman, *Wovoka and the Ghost Dance* (Lincoln: University of Nebraska Press, 1997), 25, 89; James Mooney, *The Ghost-Dance Religion and the Sioux Outbreak of 1890* (Lincoln: University of Nebraska Press, 1991), 819. Mooney's ethnography was originally published in 1896 as part two of the *Fourteenth Annual Report of the Bureau of Ethnology*.

22. Mooney, *The Ghost-Dance Religion*, 781.

23. David W. Grua, *Surviving Wounded Knee: The Lakotas and the Politics of Memory* (New York: Oxford University Press, 2016), 19.

24. Robert M. Utley, *The Last Days of the Sioux Nation* (New Haven: Yale University Press, 1963), 98.

25. Raymond J. DeMallie, "The Lakota Ghost Dance: An Ethnohistorical Account," *Pacific Historical Review* 51, no. 4 (1982): 387–389.

26. Louis S. Warren, *God's Red Son: The Ghost Dance Religion and the Making of Modern America* (New York: Basic Books, 2017), 213. Interestingly, Stanley Vestal claims that Sitting Bull participated in the dancing once but did not convert because the Ghost Dance was too Christian. Vestal writes, "Sitting Bull was too entirely Sioux to become a Christian overnight and throw away the pagan convictions of a lifetime." Stanley Vestal, *Sitting Bull: Champion of the Sioux* (Norman: University of Oklahoma Press, 1957), 272.

27. See Warren, "Conclusions: The Ghost Dance as Modern Religion," chap. 14 in *God's Red Son*, 364–378, esp. 366–368.

28. Joanna Rak, "A Typology of Cultural Attitudes as a Device Describing Political Thought of the Populations Influenced by Globalisation," *Anthropological Notebooks* 21, no. 2 (2015): 63–66.

29. Ralph Linton, "Nativistic Movements," *American Anthropologist* 45, no. 2 (1943), 231. The terminology for identifying and distinguishing the patterns of communal responses to globalization in anthropology underwent many changes in the twentieth century. For an overview of this history up to 1970, see Weston La Barre, "Materials for a History of Studies of Crisis Cults: A Bibliographic Essay," *Current Anthropology* 12, no. 1 (1971): 3–44. E

30. Anthony F.C. Wallace, "Acculturation: Revitalization Movements," *American Anthropologist* 58, no. 2 (1956), 265.

31. Wallace stated that these movements occur when "individual members of a population [...] experience increasingly severe stress as a result of the decreasing

efficiency of certain stress-reduction techniques, so widespread that it develops into cultural distortion." Wallace, 269–270.

32. Michael Carroll, "Revitalization Movements and Social Structure: Some Quantitative Tests," *American Sociological Review* 40, no. 3 (1975): 389–401.

33. Kaye Brown, "Quantitative Testing and Revitalization Behavior: On Carroll's Explanation of the Ghost Dance," *American Sociological Review* 41, no. 4 (1976): 740–744.

34. Russell Thornton, "Demographic Antecedents of a Revitalization Movement: Population Change, Population Size, and the 1890 Ghost Dance," *American Sociological Review* 46, no. 1 (1981), 93.

35. Utley, *The Last Days*, 5.

36. Utley, vii–viii.

37. DeMallie, "The Lakota Ghost Dance," 386.

38. See Alice Beck Kehoe, "Revitalization," chap. 10 in *The Ghost Dance: Ethnohistory & Revitalization* (Long Grove: Waveland Press, 2006).

39. Michael A. Elliott, "Ethnography, Reform, and the Problem of the Real: James Mooney's *Ghost-Dance Religion*," *American Quarterly* 50, no. 2 (1998), 214.

40. Mooney, *The Ghost-Dance Religion*, 653.

41. Mooney, 653.

42. Mooney, 653.

43. Mooney, 657.

44. Mooney, 658.

45. Mooney, 665.

46. "Pontiac Manuscript," quoted in Mooney, 665. Mooney appears to be using the Louis Fasquelle translation published by Henry Rowe Schoolcraft. See "Pontiac Manuscript: Journal of the Events of the Siege of Detroit by the Confederate Indians, in 1763," in *Information Respecting the History, Condition, and Prospects of the Indian Tribes of the United States*, ed. Henry R. Schoolcraft (Philadelphia: Lippincott, Grambo & Co., 1853), 2:246.

47. Mooney, *The Ghost-Dance Religion*, 675.

48. Mooney, 674.

49. Mooney, 764.

50. Hittman, *Wovoka and the Ghost Dance*, 27.

51. Mooney, *The Ghost-Dance Religion*, 764–765.

52. Hittman, *Wovoka and the Ghost Dance*, 33. For more information on 1870 Ghost Dance, see Cora Du Bois, *The 1870 Ghost Dance* (Lincoln: University of Nebraska Press, 2007).

53. Mooney, *The Ghost-Dance Religion*, 765.

54. Mooney, 764.

55. Mooney, 773.

56. Mooney, 773–774.

57. I have been using the term massacre because it reflects what actually occurred. Mooney, consistent with the title of his ethnography, uses the term outbreak.

58. Mooney, "The Indian Messiah and the Ghost Dance, with a Sketch of the Sioux Outbreak of 1890," 1894, MS 3249, National Anthropological Archives, Smithsonian Institution.

59. Mooney, *The Ghost-Dance Religion*, 824.

60. Mooney, 828.

61. Mooney, 828.

62. Mooney, 828.

63. Mooney, 848.

64. Mooney, 854.

65. Mooney, 854, 855.

66. Mooney, 847–848.

67. Utley, *The Lance and the Shield: The Life and Times of Sitting Bull* (New York: Henry Holt, 1993), 285. For a discussion of McLaughlin's skeptical portrayal of Sitting Bull's actions and motives and the limits of that perspective, see Rani-Henrik Andersson, *The Lakota Ghost Dance of 1890* (Lincoln: University of Nebraska Press, 2008), 66, 75, 107–118.

68. Mooney, *The Ghost-Dance Religion*, 857.

69. Ibid. I depart from paraphrasing for this and the previous quotation because the details in Mooney's text omit facts and deviate from what has been uncovered in more recent accounts of the incident. See Utley, "Death," chapter 24 in *The Lance and the Shield*, 291–307.

70. Shave Head and Bull Head resented Sitting Bull for not repudiating insults from the Crows and for favoring Catch-the-Bear with a spotted horse that Bull Head had chosen for himself. For further information on these incidents and what may have led Bull Head and Red Tomahawk to turn and shoot Sitting Bull instead of their attacker, see Vestal, "White Hair," chap. 32 in *Sitting Bull* and Utley, "Death," in *The Lance and the Shield*.

71. Big Foot is also known by the names Sitanka and Spotted Elk.
72. Mooney, *The Ghost-Dance Religion*, 865.
73. Mooney, 864–868.
74. Mooney, 869.
75. Mooney, 869.
76. For the most exhaustive and current treatment of these reports, see Andersson, esp. 89–98. For a more accessible but no less authoritative account, see Warren, 287–289.
77. Mooney, 869.
78. Mooney, 868–871.
79. Mooney, 870.
80. Mooney, 870.
81. Mooney, 888.
82. Mooney, 914.
83. Warren discusses this at length in *God's Red Son* and reveals that Mooney's strategy of equating ghost dancing with the widely practiced colonial religions proved to be the most controversial portion of his text.
84. Aristotle, *On Poetics*, trans. Seth Benardete and Michael Davis (South Bend: St. Augustine's Press, 2002), 26.
85. Ibid.
86. Patricia Ziegfeld, *The Ziegfelds' Girl: Confessions of an Abnormally Happy Childhood* (Boston: Little, Brown, 1964), 33.
87. "The Battle of Wounded Knee: Review of the Campaign Which a Monument Unveiling Recalls," *Inter Ocean* (Chicago, IL), July 24, 1893.
88. Amy Leslie, "Amy Leslie at the Fair," *Chicago Daily News* (Chicago, IL), May 5, 1893. Later that year, her column was collected and republished as a book. Amy Leslie, *Amy Leslie at the Fair* (Chicago: W.B. Conkey, 1893), 22–23.
89. "Seven Ages of Columbus: Italian Day Ends with a Series of Tableaux-Vivants in the Woman's Building," *Chicago Record* (Chicago, IL), n.d., Buffalo Bill's Wild West Scrapbook—Chicago, Illinois, USA—1893, William F. Cody Collection, MS 006, McCracken Research Library.
90. "Indians Do Homage: Bestow Roses on the Duchess," *Chicago Record* (Chicago, IL), May 8, 1893.
91. Minutes of meeting held in Office of Commissioner of Indian Affairs, "Indian Office Exhibit at the World's Columbian Exposition," 30 January 1892, General Records Relating to the World's Columbian Exposition, 1891–1894, A1 Entry 386, Records of the Office of the Secretary of the Interior, Record Group 48, National Archives, College Park.
92. Rydell, *All the World's a Fair*, 68.
93. Rosemarie K. Bank, "Representing History: Performing the Columbian Exposition," *Theatre Journal* 54, no. 4 (2002), 593.
94. *Martin's World Fair Album-Atlas and Family Souvenir* (Chicago: C. Ropp & Sons, 1892), 247.
95. *Martin's World Fair Album-Atlas*, 248.
96. *Martin's World Fair Album-Atlas*, 255.
97. George Le Roy Brown to William Cody and Nate Salsbury, 19 April 1893, Series 3: Letters Received, Record Group 75, National Archives, Kansas City.
98. 1893 Program for Buffalo Bill's Wild West, James Wojtowicz Collection, MS 327, McCracken Research Library.
99. Samuel Clemens to Cody, 10 September 1894, qtd. in "Buffalo Bill's Wild West," *Cincinnati Commercial Gazette* (Cincinnati, OH), October 19, 1884, and 1887 Buffalo Bill's Wild West Program, MS 327.
100. For further discussion, see Kasson, *Buffalo Bill's Wild West*, 105–114, 265–266 and Slotkin, "The 'Wild West.'"
101. 1898 Buffalo Bill's Wild West Program, MS 327. 1899 Buffalo Bill's Wild West Program, MS 327. For further discussion of Cody's program revisions, Slotkin, "The White City and the Wild West," chap. 2 in *Gunfighter Nation*, 63–87.
102. Balibar, "The Nation Form: History and Ideology," 86.

Chapter Three

1. Frederick Douglass, *Lecture on Haiti*, Frederick Douglass Papers, Library of Congress.
2. Wendy Asquith, "The Art of Postcolonial Politics in the Age of Empire: Haiti's Object Lesson at the World's Columbian Exposition," *Historical Research* 91, no. 253 (2018): 534–538.
3. Charles Brockden Brown, "To the Public," in *Edgar Huntly; or, Memoirs of a*

Sleep-Walker (Philadelphia: H. Maxwell, 1799), 4.

4. Gilles Vandivinit, "From the Virgin Land to the Transnational Identities of the Twenty-First Century: Exceptionalist Rhetoric in the Field of American Studies," *European Journal of American Culture* 33, no. 3 (2014), 168.

5. William Spanos, *American Exceptionalism in the Age of Globalization: The Specter of Vietnam* (Albany: State University of New York Press, 2008), 196.

6. Slotkin, *The Fatal Environment: The Myth of the Frontier in the Age of Industrialization* (New York: Atheneum, 1985), 81.

7. James Fenimore Cooper, *The Last of the Mohicans* (New York: Bantam Classics, 2005), 178.

8. Slotkin, *The Fatal Environment*, 90.

9. Said, *Culture and Imperialism* (New York: Vintage, 1994), 59.

10. Said, 59.

11. Cooper, 186.

12. Cooper, 189.

13. Cooper, 4.

14. Cooper, 196.

15. Cooper, 197.

16. See Kyle William Bishop, *American Zombie Gothic* (Jefferson: McFarland, 2010), 96–110.

17. Brian Yuzna produced three films loosely based on Lovecraft's short story, *Re-Animator* (1985), *Bride of Re-Animator* (1990), and *Beyond Re-Animator* (2003).

18. H.P. Lovecraft, "Herbert West—Reanimator," in *H.P. Lovecraft: Tales*, ed. Peter Straub (New York: Library of America, 2005), 25.

19. Lovecraft, 27.

20. Lovecraft, 28.

21. Lovecraft, 33.

22. Lovecraft, 33.

23. Zora Neale Hurston, *Tell My Horse: Voodoo and Life in Haiti and Jamaica* (New York: Harper and Row, 1990), 183.

24. Wade Davis, *Passage of Darkness: The Ethnobiology of the Haitian Zombie* (Chapel Hill: University of North Carolina Press, 1988), 61.

25. Lovecraft, "Herbert West—Reanimator," 39.

26. Lovecraft, 34.

27. Lovecraft, 37.

28. Lovecraft, 39.

29. Hans Schmidt, *The United States Occupation of Haiti, 1915-1934* (New Brunswick: Rutgers University Press, 1995), 9.

30. Schmidt, 9.

31. Robert Lansing, "Present Nature and Extent of the Monroe Doctrine, and Its Need of Restatement," in *Papers Relating to the Foreign Relations of the United States* (Washington: United States Government Printing Office, 1940), 2:461. Lansing later reiterates this claim after his promotion to Secretary of State. Wilson responds approvingly.

32. Lansing, "The Secretary of State to President Wilson," in *Papers Relating to the Foreign Relations of the United States* (Washington, D.C.: United States Government Printing Office, 1940), 2:526–527.

33. Franklin D. Roosevelt, FDR as Author—Memorandum on Haiti, 1922, box 41, folder 35, Series 3: Speeches and Writings, Franklin D. Roosevelt, Papers Pertaining to Family, Business and Personal Affairs, 1882–1945. Franklin D. Roosevelt Library, Hyde Park, New York.

34. Schmidt, *The United States Occupation of Haiti*, 66.

35. Robert Tombs, *France 1814-1914* (New York: Routledge, 2014), 3.

36. Franklin D. Roosevelt quoted in "Says America Has 12 League Votes: Roosevelt Declares He Himself Had Two Until Last Week, Referring to Minor Republics," *New York Times* (New York, NY), August 19, 1920.

37. Eli Cole, Daily Diary Reports, 27 February 1917, box row 16, compartment 9, shelf 6, box 742, folder 6, Record Group 45 Records Collection of the Office of Naval Records and Library, National Archives and Records Administration, Washington, D.C.

38. Thomas Jefferson to James Madison, 24 November 1801, in *The Works of Thomas Jefferson in Twelve Volumes* (New York: G.P. Putnam's Sons, 1905), 9:317–318.

39. Michael O. West and William G. Martin, "Haiti, I'm Sorry," in *From Toussaint to Tupac: The Black International since the Age of Revolution* (Chapel Hill: University of North Carolina Press, 2009), 98.

40. Glenn Kay, *Zombie Movies: The Ultimate Guide* (Chicago: Chicago Review Press, 2012), 2.

41. J. Michael Dash, *Haiti and the United*

States: National Stereotypes and the Literary Imagination (New York: St. Martin's Press, 1997), 137.

42. George W. Cable, "Creole Slave Songs," *The New Century* 31, no. 6 (1886), 815.

43. For more detailed examinations of the etymology of zombie, see Gary D. Rhodes, *White Zombie: Anatomy of a Horror Film* (Jefferson: McFarland, 2001), 72–78; Sara Juliet Lauro, *The Transatlantic Zombie: Slavery, Rebellion, and Living Death* (New Brunswick: Rutgers University Press, 2015), 34–42; and Hans-W Ackermann and Jeanine Gauthier, "The Ways and Nature of the Zombi," *American Folklore Society* 104, no. 414 (1991): 466–494.

44. William Seabrook, *The Magic Island* (New York: Harcourt, Brace, 1929), 20.

45. Seabrook, 20.

46. Seabrook, 95.

47. Seabrook, 96.

48. Seabrook, 96.

49. Seabrook, 98.

50. David J. Schow, introduction to *Zombies: The Recent Dead*, ed. Paula Guran (Gaithersburg: Prime Books, 2010), xvi.

51. Rhodes, *White Zombie*, 31.

52. Seabrook, *The Magic Island*, 99.

53. Seabrook, 95.

54. *White Zombie*, directed by Victor Halperin (1932; Hollywood: Alpha Video, 2002), DVD.

55. Rhodes and Jennifer Fay also cite uncredited quotations from *The Magic Island* in the *White Zombie* pressbook. Rhodes, 31. Jennifer Fay, "Dead Subjectivity: 'White Zombie,' Black Baghdad," *CR: The New Centennial Review* 8, no. 1 (2008), 92.

56. Rhodes, *White Zombie*, 26–30.

57. Fay, "Dead Subjectivity," 86–88.

58. Tony Williams, "*White Zombie*: Haitian Horror," *Jump Cut*, no. 28 (1983), 19.

59. Bishop, "The Sub-Subaltern Monster: Imperialist Hegemony and the Cinematic Voodoo Zombie" *The Journal of American Culture* 31, no. 2 (2008), 150, 149.

60. Historian William Appleman Williams coined the term "imperial anticolonialism" to describe U.S. international policy at the time. See William Appleman Williams, *The Tragedy of American Diplomacy* (New York: Dell, 1972), 18–57.

61. Gyllian Phillips, "White Zombie and the Creole: William Seabrook's The Magic Island and American Imperialism in Haiti," in *Generation Zombie: Essays on the Living Dead in Modern Culture* (Jefferson: McFarland, 2011), 34.

62. Barthes writes, "The signifier of myth presents itself in an ambiguous way: it is at the same time meaning and form, full on one side and empty on the other." Barthes, "Myth Today," 117.

63. Barthes, 118.

64. Barthes, 119.

65. Williams, "*White Zombie*: Haitian Horror," 18.

66. Elizabeth McAlister, "Slaves, Cannibals, and Infected Hyper-Whites: The Race and Religion of Zombies," *Anthropological Quarterly* 85, no. 2 (2012), 478.

67. Melville J. Herskovits, like several of the other scholars referenced in this section, uses the Haitian spelling *zombi* or *zonbi*. When quoting sources, I include the authors' original spelling. Otherwise, I continue to rely on the American spelling because my subject is the American representation of the phenomena and not the thing-in-itself.

68. Melville J. Herskovits, *Life in a Haitian Valley* (New York: Octagon Books, 1964), 245.

69. Herskovits, 336n12.

70. Elsie Clews Parsons, *Memoirs of the American Folk-lore Society: Part 2*, vol. 26 (New York: G.E. Stechert and Co., 1894–1960), 592.

71. Herskovits, *Life in a Haitian Valley*, 320.

72. Hurston, *Tell My Horse*, 134.

73. Hurston, 182.

74. Hurston, 195–198.

75. Moira Sullivan, "Maya Deren's Ethnographic Representation of Ritual and Myth in Haiti," in *Maya Deren and the American Avant-Garde*, ed. Bill Nichols (Berkeley: University of California Press, 2001), 209.

76. Jacques Derrida, *Writing and Difference*, trans. Alan Bass (Chicago: University of Chicago Press, 1978), 282.

77. Derrida, 282.

78. Katherine Dunham, *Island Possessed* (Chicago: University of Chicago Press, 1994), 65.

79. Dunham, 228.

80. Dunham, 228.

81. Dunham, 185.
82. Dunham, 185.
83. Dunham, 185.
84. Dunham, 199–200.
85. Dunham, 185.
86. Maya Deren, "Chamber Films," in *Essential Deren: Collected Writings on Film by Maya Deren*, ed. Bruce R. McPherson (Kingston: McPherson and Company, 2005), 251.
87. Anne Hollander, *Seeing through Clothes* (New York: Avon Books, 1980), 293.
88. Deren, *Divine Horsemen: The Living Gods of Haiti* (Kingston: McPherson and Company, 2004), 6.
89. Deren, 11, 8.
90. Deren, 291n31–33.
91. Deren, 26.
92. Deren, 26n.
93. Deren, 42.
94. Deren, 42n.
95. Deren, 42n-43n.
96. Deren, 43n.
97. Deren, 29.
98. Alfred Métraux, *Voodoo in Haiti*, trans. Hugo Charteris (New York: Schocken Books, 1972), 281.
99. Métraux, 281.
100. Métraux, 282, 283.
101. Wade Davis' controversial exercise in anthropology and pharmacology titled *The Serpent and the Rainbow* claims to have uncovered the zombie poison and was subsequently made into a horror film of the same name. His work is an illustration of the interrelation of zombie anthropology and cinema. While he contributed substantially to the popularization of zombie studies, his exclusion here is simply a matter of brevity.
102. Lauro, *The Transatlantic Zombie*, 5.
103. Alessandra Benedickty-Kokken, *Spirit Possession in French, Haitian, and Vodou Thought: An Intellectual History* (Lanham: Lexington, 2015), 2.
104. Deren, *Divine Horsemen*, 29, 42.
105. Benedickty-Kokken, *Spirit Possession*, 237.

Chapter Four

1. Romero's *Living Dead* films, sometimes referred to as his *Night of the Living Dead* series, include the following films: *Night of the Living Dead*, *Dawn of the Dead*, *Day of the Dead*, *Land of the Dead*, *Diary of the Dead*, and *Survival of the Dead*. To improve readability, after mentioning the full title of each in the text, I abbreviate the film names by only using the first word of the title.
2. Barack Obama, "Remarks by President Obama and Prime Minister Abe of Japan at Hiroshima Peace Memorial," transcript of speech delivered at the Hiroshima Peace Memorial, Hiroshima, Japan, May 27, 2016, https://obamawhitehouse.archives.gov/the-press-office/2016/05/27/remarks-president-obama-and-prime-minister-abe-japan-hiroshima-peace.
3. For further discussion of this era in zombie cinema and fiction, see Roger Luckhurst, *Zombies: A Cultural History* (London: Reaktion Books, 2015), esp. 109–136.
4. Deborah Christie, "A Dead New World: Richard Matheson and the Modern Zombie," in *Better Off Dead: The Evolution of the Zombie as Post-Human* (New York: Fordham University Press, 2011), 67–80; John Edgar Browning, "I Am Legend (Novel)," in *Encyclopedia of the Zombie* (Santa Barbara: Greenwood, 2014), 140–141; Peter Dendle, "The Last Man on Earth," in *The Zombie Movie Encyclopedia* (Jefferson: McFarland, 2011), 99–101.
5. Ian Conrich, "An Infected Population: Zombie Culture and the Modern Monstrous," in *The Zombie Renaissance in Popular Culture* (London: Palgrave Macmillan, 2015), 19.
6. To suspend prejudice by choosing one term over the other, I will henceforth refer to the creatures that inhabit *I Am Legend* as ghouls.
7. See chapter 3, "American Mysanthrope."
8. See Dan Hassler-Forest, "Zombie Spaces," in *The Year's Work at the Zombie Research Center* (Bloomington: Indiana University Press, 2014), 116–149, esp. 120–130.
9. In an interview, Raymond Williams provides the following explanation for the concept: "The point of the deliberately contradictory phrase [...] is that it was a structure in the sense that you could perceive it operating in one work after another which weren't otherwise connected—people weren't learning it from each other; yet

it was one of feeling much more than of thought—a pattern of impulses, restrains, tones, for which the best evidence was often the actual conventions of literary or dramatic writing." Raymond Williams, "The Long Revolution," *Politics and Letters: Interviews with New Left Review* (New York: Verso, 2015), 159.

10. Frederic Jameson, *The Political Unconscious* (New York: Routledge, 2006), 286.

11. Kay, *Zombie Movies*, 49.

12. Kay, 54.

13. Kay, 92.

14. *Dawn of the Dead*, written, directed, and produced by George A. Romero (1978; Troy: Anchor Bay Entertainment, 2004), DVD.

15. Lars Bang Larsen, "Zombies of Immaterial Labor: The Modern Monster and the Consumption of the Self," in *Zombie Theory: A Reader* (Minneapolis: University of Minnesota Press, 2017), 157–170 and Bishop, "The Idle Proletariat: *Dawn of the Dead*, Consumer Ideology, and the Loss of Productive Labor," *The Journal of Popular Culture* 43, no. 2 (2010): 234–248.

16. Joan Dayan, *Haiti, History, and the Gods* (Berkeley: University of California Press, 1995), 68. Dayan relies on an alternate spelling. She uses *lwa* for what I have calling *loa*.

17. Adeline Masquelier, "Narratives of Power, Images of Wealth: The Ritual Economy of *Bori* in the Market," in *Modernity and its Malcontents: Ritual and Power in Post-Colonial Africa* (Chicago: University of Chicago Press, 1993), 3.

18. See Joseph M. Murphy, *Botánicas: Sacred Spaces of Healing and Devotion in Urban America* (Jackson: University Press of Mississippi, 2015), esp. 159–173.

19. DeMallie, "The Lakota Ghost Dance," 398.

20. Rather than insisting on any essential ontological quality, in interviews Romero describes his preference for slow zombies as one of practicality. See "George A. Romero Explains Why Fast Zombies Could Never Exist (Hint: Weak Ankles)," Vulture, Vox Media, February 14, 2008, https://www.vulture.com/2008/02/george_a_romero_explains_why_f.html.

21. Robert Kirkman, *The Walking Dead #1 10th Anniversary Edition* (Berkeley: Image Comics, 2013).

22. The three exceptions to this release schedule are Season 1, which only had thirteen episodes; Season 10, which underwent a year-long mid-season hiatus due to the Covid-19 pandemic and was then expanded to include an additional six episodes for a total of twenty-two; and Season 11, which spans twenty-four episodes.

23. Darren Reed and Ruth Penfold-Mounce, "Zombies and the Sociological Imagination: *The Walking Dead* as Social-Science Fiction," in *The Zombie Renaissance in Popular Culture* (London: Palgrave Macmillan, 2015), 125.

24. Reed and Penfold-Mounce, 125–126.

25. Reed and Penfold-Mounce, 131.

26. Spanos, *American Exceptionalism*, 28.

27. Spanos, 28–31.

28. Anna Mae Duane, "Dead *and* Disabled: The Crawling Monsters of *The Walking Dead*," in *Zombie Theory: A Reader* (Minneapolis: University of Minnesota Press, 2017), 237–245.

29. Kirkman, *The Walking Dead #156* (Berkeley: Image Comics, 2016).

30. Vandivinit, "From the Virgin Land," 167.

31. Josh Katz, "'Duck Dynasty' vs. 'Modern Family': 50 Maps of the U.S. Cultural Divide," *New York Times*, December 27, 2016, www.nytimes.com/interactive/2016/12/26/upshot/duck-dynasty-vs-modern-family-television-maps.html.

32. Katz.

33. Poppy Wilde, "Zombies, Deviance and the Right to Posthuman Life," in *Theorising the Contemporary Zombie: Contextual Pasts, Presents, and Futures* (Cardiff: University of Wales Press, 2022), 20.

34. Steven Bertoni, "The Son-in-Law Also Rises," *Forbes*, December 20, 2016, 73.

35. *The Walking Dead*, Season 6, episode 1, "First Time Again," directed by Greg Nicotero, written by Scott M. Gimple and Matthew Negrete, aired October 11, 2015, on AMC, Lionsgate Home Entertainment, Blu-Ray.

36. Sandra Curtis Comstock, "The Making of an American Icon: The Transformation of Blue Jeans during the Great Depression," in *Global Denim* (New York: Berg, 2011), 35.

37. Comstock, 23.
38. "Fashion Round-Up," *Apparel Arts* 16, no. 4 (1946), 196.
39. Angela Taylor, "U.S. Olympic Team Dresses Western," *New York Times*, February 8, 1980.
40. From this point forward, I limit my analysis to the television series which generally follows the plot of the comic but more thoroughly explores national myth.
41. *The Walking Dead*, Season 9, episode 1, "A New Beginning," directed by Greg Nicotero, written by Angela Kang, aired October 7, 2018, on AMC, Anchor Bay, 2019, Blu-Ray.
42. Lester H. Cohen, "The American Revolution and Natural Law Theory," *Journal of the History of Ideas* 39, no. 3 (1978), 492.
43. Fans have reconstructed most of the document. See David Cameo, "[Exclusive] 'Multi-Community Charter of Rights and Freedoms,'" *We Are Squawking Dead* (blog), March 1, 2019, https://squawkingdead.blogspot.com/2019/03/exclusives-multi-community-charter-of.html.
44. *The Walking Dead*, Season 9, episode 10, "Omega," directed by David Boyd, written by Channing Powell, aired February 17, 2019, on AMC, Anchor Bay, 2019, Blu-Ray.
45. *The Walking Dead*, Season 9, episode 7, "Stradivarius," directed by Michael Cudlitz, written by Vivian Tse, aired November 18, 2018, on AMC, Anchor Bay, 2019, Blu-Ray.
46. *The Walking Dead*, Season 9, episode 11, "Bounty," directed by Meera Menon, written by Matthew Negrete, aired February 24, 2019, on AMC, Anchor Bay, 2019, Blu-Ray.
47. For examples of their use of "nomadic" and "sedentary," see Gilles Deleuze and Félix Guattari, *A Thousand Plateaus: Capitalism and Schizophrenia*, trans. Brian Massumi (New York: Continuum, 2004), 457–458.
48. *The Walking Dead*, Season 9, episode 9, "Adaptation," directed by Greg Nicotero, written by Corey Reed, aired February 10, 2019, on AMC, Anchor Bay, 2019, Blu-Ray.
49. *The Walking Dead*, Season 9, episode 10, "Omega."
50. *The Walking Dead*, Season 9, episode 14, "Scars," directed by Millicent Shelton, written by Corey Reed and Vivian Tse, aired March 17, 2019, on AMC, Anchor Bay, 2019, Blu-Ray.
51. For the episode where this becomes standardized, see *The Walking Dead*, Season 9, episode 15, "The Calm Before," directed by Laura Belsey, written by Geraldine Inoa and Channing Powell, aired March 14, 2019, on AMC, Anchor Bay, 2019, Blu-Ray.
52. For evidence of continued use of the term "skins" even throughout the final season, see *The Walking Dead*, Season 11, episode 20, "What's Been Lost," directed by Aisha Tyler, written by Erik Mountain, aired October 23, 2022, on AMC, Lionsgate Home Entertainment, 2023, Blu-Ray.
53. Jodi Byrd, *The Transit of Empire: Indigenous Critiques of Colonialism* (Minneapolis: University of Minnesota Press, 2011), xxi.
54. *The Walking Dead*, Season 9, episode 8, "Evolution," directed by Michael E. Satrazemis, written by David Leslie Johnson-McGoldrick, aired November 25, 2018, on AMC, Anchor Bay, 2019, Blu-Ray.
55. Nancy Armstrong and Leonard Tennenhouse, *The Imaginary Puritan: Literature, Intellectual Labor, and the Origins of Personal Life* (Berkeley: University of California Press, 1994), 207.
56. Mary Rowlandson, *A Narrative of the Captivity, Sufferings, and Removes, of Mrs. Mary Rowlandson* (Boston: Mass. Sabbath School Society, 1856), 11.
57. *The Walking Dead*, Season 10, episode 2, "We Are the End of the World."
58. Philip J. Deloria, *Playing Indian* (New Haven: Yale University Press, 1998), 10–14.
59. Duane, "Dead *and* Disabled," 238–239.
60. Ángel Mateos-Aparicio and Jesús Benito Sánchez, "'Parasites in a Host Country': Migrants, Refugees, Asylum Seekers and Other Zombies in *The Walking Dead*," in *The Poetics and Politics of Hospitality in U.S. Literature and Culture* (Boston: Brill, 2020), 211–232.
61. Cutcha Risling Baldy, "On Telling Native People to Just 'Get over It' or Why I Teach about *The Walking Dead* in My Native Studies Classes… *Spoiler Alert,*" *Cutcha Risling Baldy* (blog), December 11, 2013, https://www.cutcharislingbaldy.com/blog/on-telling-native-people-to-

just-get-over-it-or-why-i-teach-about-the-walking-dead-in-my-native-studies-classes-spoiler-alert.

62. *The Walking Dead*, Season 10, episode 16, "A Certain Doom," directed by Greg Nicotero, written by Corey Reed, aired October 4, 2020, on AMC, Lionsgate Home Entertainment, 2021, Blu-Ray.

Chapter Five

1. Barthes, "Myth Today," 137.
2. Barthes, 121.
3. *Zombies*, directed by Paul Hoen, written by David Light and Joseph Raso, aired February 16, 2018.
4. Anderson, *Imagined Communities*, 77.
5. Eric Hobsbawm, *Nations and Nationalism Since 1780: Programme, Myth, Reality* (New York: Cambridge University Press, 2013), 18–20.
6. Balibar, "The Nation Form: History and Ideology," 87.
7. Turner, "Problems in American History," 72.
8. Benjamin, "Theses on the Philosophy of History," in *Illuminations*, ed. Hannah Arendt, trans. Harry Zohn (New York: Schocken Books, 2007), 261.
9. Michel-Rolph Trouillot, *Silencing the Past: Power and the Production of History* (Boston: Beacon Press, 1995), 27.
10. Trouillot, 27.
11. Joseph Ellis, *American Creation: Triumphs and Tragedies at the Founding of the Republic* (New York: Alfred A. Knopf, 2007), 231–232.
12. Chera Kee, *Not Your Average Zombie: Rehumanizing the Undead from Voodoo to Zombie Walks* (Austin: University of Texas Press, 2017), 64.
13. Fruzinska, *Emerson Goes to the Movies*, 43.
14. Fruzinska, 144.
15. See Chapter 1, "A Modell of Christian Empire," for my discussion of the phrase errand into the wilderness.
16. Myra Jehlen, *American Incarnation: The Individual, the Nation, and the Continent* (Cambridge: Harvard University Press, 1986), 9.
17. Said, *Culture and Imperialism*, 332.
18. Mary Louise Pratt, "Arts of the Contact Zone," *PMLA* 91, no. 34 (1991), 34.

19. Bercovitch, *The American Jeremiad*, 3–7.
20. John Winthrop, "A Model of Christian Charity," in *Puritan Political Ideas 1558–1794* (New York: Bobbs Merrill, 1965), 93.
21. Julia Kristeva, *Powers of Horror*, trans. Leon S. Roudiez (New York: Columbia University Press, 1982), 2.
22. Kristeva, 4.
23. Kristeva, 74.
24. Pierre Bourdieu, "The Field of Cultural Production, or: The Economic World Reversed," in *The Field of Cultural Production: Essays on Art and Literature*, trans. Richard Nice (New York: Columbia University Press, 1993), 70.
25. C.L.R. James, *The Black Jacobins: Toussaint L'Ouverture and the San Domingo Revolution* (New York: Vintage, 1989), 39.
26. Peter Corrigan, *The Dressed Society: Clothing, the Body and Some Meanings of the World* (Los Angeles: SAGE Publications, 2008), 13.
27. Corrigan, 15.
28. See Tanisha C. Ford, "SNCC's Soul Sisters," chap. 3 in *Liberated Threads: Black Women, Style, and the Global Politics of Soul* (Chapel Hill: University of North Carolina Press, 2015), 67–93.
29. Charlotte Hammond, "Decoding Dress: Vodou, Cloth and Colonial Resistance in Pre- and Post-Revolutionary Haiti," in *Vodou in the Haitian Experience: A Black Atlantic Perspective*, eds. Celucien L. Joseph and Nixon S. Cleophat (New York: Lexington, 2016), 86.
30. It should be noted that the cast of normals is primarily but not exclusively white. Addison and her immediate family are white but some of her classmates, including her close friend Bree, are racial minorities.
31. Deloria, *Playing Indian*, 78.
32. Foucault, *Discipline and Punish: The Birth of the Prison*, trans. Alan Sheridan (New York: Vintage, 1977), 201.
33. Christopher J. Smith, *Dancing Revolution: Bodies, Space, and Sound in American Cultural History* (Urbana: University of Illinois Press, 2019), 103.
34. Smith, 104.
35. Foucault, *Discipline and Punish*, 201.
36. Foucault, 138, 137.
37. Kristeva, *Powers of Horror*, 14.

38. Sarah Berry, *Screen Style: Fashion and Femininity in 1930s Hollywood* (Minneapolis: University of Minnesota Press, 2000), 98.
39. Herbert Marcuse, *Eros and Civilization: A Philosophical Inquiry into Freud* (Boston: Beacon Press, 1966), 11.
40. Benjamin, "Theses on the Philosophy of History," 261.

Chapter Six

1. Rob Stein, "A Young Mississippi Woman's Journey through a Pioneering Gene-Editing Experiment," Health Shots, NPR, December 25, 2019, https://www.npr.org/sections/health-shots/2019/12/25/784395525/.
2. Ed Finn and Joey Eschrich, acknowledgments in *Visions, Ventures, Escape Velocities: A Collection of Space Futures*, eds. Ed Finn and Joey Eschrich (Tempe: Arizona State University, 2017), xvi.
3. Walt Disney, *The Quotable Walt Disney* (New York: Disney Editions, 2001), 56.
4. Disney, 70–71.
5. For the seminal analysis of the term virgin land, see Henry Nash Smith, *Virgin Land: The American West as Symbol and Myth* (Cambridge: Harvard University Press, 1978).
6. Disney, *The Quotable Walt Disney*, 70.
7. Priscilla Hobbs, *Walt's Utopia: Disneyland and American Mythmaking* (Jefferson: McFarland, 2015), 4.
8. Jean Baudrillard, *Simulations* (Los Angeles: Semiotext[e], 1983), 2.
9. Foucault, *The Order of Things*, 88.
10. Robert Cahn, "The Intrepid Kids of Disneyland," *Saturday Evening Post*, June 1958, 22–23.
11. Ella Shohat, "Gender and Culture of Empire: Toward a Feminist Ethnography of the Cinema," *Quarterly Review of Film and Video* 13, no. 1–3 (1991), 68.
12. David Chalmers, *The Conscious Mind: In Search of a Fundamental Theory* (New York: Oxford University Press, 1996), 94.
13. Chalmers, 98. The words omitted from the quotation clarifies that p-zombies need not be physically possible, merely conceivable, for the argument against materialism to be valid.
14. Block, "The Harder Problem of Consciousness," 399.
15. Spanos, *American Exceptionalism*, 198.
16. Deren, *Divine Horsemen*, 27.
17. Deren, 29. Deren furnishes a poignant exposition of possession: "Death had deprived the gros-bon-ange of its own living form; the memory of the living had reclaimed it and given it voice."
18. Aimé Césaire, *Discourse on Colonialism*, trans. Joan Pinkham (New York: Monthly Review Press, 2000), 42.
19. Toni Pressley-Sanon, *Zombifying a Nation: Race, Gender and the Haitian Loas on Screen* (Jefferson: McFarland, 2016), 111–114.
20. Gramsci, "Rationalization," 278.
21. *Westworld*, Season 1, episode 9, "The Well-Tempered Clavier," directed by Dan Dietz and Katherine Lingenfelter, written by Michelle MacLaren, aired November 27, 2016, on HBO, Warner-Brothers, 2017, Blu-Ray.
22. Characters that share the same last name like Dolores Abernathy and her father Peter Abernathy as well as characters without a last name such as William will be referenced by their first names.
23. Ziegfeld, 32–33; and Cynthia Brideson and Sara Brideson, *Ziegfeld and His Follies: A Biography of Broadway's Greatest Producer* (Lexington: University Press of Kentucky, 2015), 13–18.
24. Duff-Gordon, Lucy, *Discretions and Indiscretions* (London: Jarrolds, 1932), 43.
25. Elspeth Brown, "De Meyer at *Vogue*: Queer Affect in First World War-era Fashion Photography," *Photography and Culture* 2, no. 3 (2009): 264–265.
26. Brown, 267.
27. Brown, 267.
28. *Town Topics: A Journal of Society* (New York, NY), March 17, 1921, Robinson Locke Collection, Series 3, vol. 368, 205, Billy Rose Theater Collection, New York Public Library.
29. Marjorie Farnsworth, *The Ziegfeld Follies: A History in Text and Pictures* (New York: Bonanza Books, 1956), 97–100.
30. Brown, "The Commodification of Aesthetic Feeling: Race, Sexuality, and the 1920s Stage Model," *Feminist Studies* 40, no. 1 (2014), 72.
31. Shohat, "Gender and Culture of Empire," 69–70.

32. Alan Bryman, *The Disneyization of Society* (London: SAGE Publications, 2004), 16.

33. The Westworld park opened in 2015 and the events of the three seasons currently released primarily span from 2020–2050. "Timeline," Westworld *Wiki*, July 15, 2020, https://westworld.fandom.com/wiki/Timeline.

34. "Experience," Delos Destinations, Delos Inc., accessed August 29, 2020, http://www.delosdestinations.com/#experience.

35. *Westworld*, Season 2, episode 5, "Akane no Mai," directed by Dan Dietz, written by Craig Zobel, aired May 20, 2018, on HBO, WarnerBrothers, 2018, Blu-Ray.

36. Trouillot, *Silencing the Past*, 20.

37. *Westworld*, Season 1, episode 1, "The Original," directed by Jonathan Nolan, written by Jonathan Nolan and Lisa Joy, aired October 2, 2016, on HBO, WarnerBrothers, 2017, Blu-Ray.

38. Guy Debord, *The Society of the Spectacle*, trans. Donald Nicholson-Smith (New York: Zone Books, 2006), 26.

39. Nietzsche, *The Gay Science*, trans. Walter Kaufmann (New York: Vintage Books, 1974), 90.

40. Locke, *Two Treatises of Government*, ed. Peter Laslett (Cambridge: Cambridge University Press, 1988), 288.

41. Locke, 293.

42. Locke, 293.

43. Thomas Jefferson, "To James Madison from Thomas Jefferson, 28 October 1785," in *The Papers of James Madison*, eds. Robert A. Rutland, et al. (Chicago: University of Chicago Press, 1973) 8:387.

44. Jefferson, "To James Madison, 20 December 1787," in *The Papers of Thomas Jefferson*, vol. 12, ed. Julian P. Boyd (Princeton: Princeton University Press, 1955), 12:442.

45. Cher Krause Knight, *Power and Paradise in Walt Disney's World* (Gainesville: University of Florida Press, 2014), 99.

46. *Westworld*, Season 1, episode 1, "The Original."

47. Foucault, *Discipline and Punish*, 219.

48. John Cotton, "Gods Promise to His Plantation," in *Old South Leaflets* (Boston: Directors of the Old South Work, 1896), 3:13.

49. Foucault writes, "The human body was entering a machinery of power that explores it, breaks it down and rearranges it. A 'political anatomy,' which was also a 'mechanics of power,' was being born; it defined how one may have a hold over others' bodies, not only so that they may do what one wishes, but so that they may operate as one wishes, with the techniques, the speed and the efficiency that one determines. Thus discipline produces subjected and practised bodies, 'docile' bodies." Foucault, *Discipline and Punish*, 138.

50. To avoid confusing James Delos with his company, I will refer to him hereafter by his first name.

51. *Westworld*, Season 2, episode 2, "Reunion," directed by Vincenzo Natali, written by Carly Wray and Jonathan Nolan, aired April 29, 2018, on HBO, WarnerBrothers, 2018, Blu-Ray.

52. *Westworld*, Season 2, episode 7, "Les Écorchés," directed by Nicole Kassell, written by Jordan Goldberg and Ron Fitzgerald, aired June 3, 2018, on HBO, WarnerBrothers, 2018, Blu-Ray.

53. *Westworld*, Season 2, episode 10, "The Passenger," directed by Frederick E.O. Toye, written by Jonathan Nolan and Lisa Joy, aired June 24, 2018, on HBO, WarnerBrothers, 2018, Blu-Ray.

54. Werner Heisenberg, *The Physicist's Conception of Nature*, trans. Arnold J. Pomerans (London: Hutchinson Scientific and Technical, 1958), 29.

55. Heidegger, "The Question Concerning Technology," in *Basic Writings*, ed. David Farrell Krell (San Francisco: HarperSanFrancisco, 1993), 322, 324–332.

56. Masanao Ozawa, "Universally Valid Reformulation of the Heisenberg Uncertainty Principle on Noise and Disturbance in Measurement," *Physical Review A* 67, no. 4 (2003). Jacqueline Erhart, Stephan Sponar, Georg Sulyok, et al., "Experimental Demonstration of a Universally Valid Error-Disturbance Uncertainty Relation in Spin Measurements," *Nature Physics* 8 (2012).

57. Said, "Humanism's Sphere," 22.

58. Giorgio Agamben, *What Is Real?*, trans. Lorenzo Chiesa (Palo Alto: Stanford University Press, 2018), 42–43.

59. *Westworld*, Season 1, episode 8, "Trace Decay," directed by Stephen Williams, written by Charles Yu and Lisa Joy, aired November 20, 2016, on HBO, WarnerBrothers, 2017, Blu-Ray.

60. Charles Taylor, "The Politics of Recognition," in *Multiculturalism: Examining the Politics of Recognition*, ed. Amy Gutmann (Princeton: Princeton University Press, 1994), 50.

61. Frantz Fanon, *Wretched of the Earth*, trans. Constance Farrington (New York: Grove Press, 1963), 106.

62. Douglas Hofstadter, *I Am a Strange Loop* (New York: Basic Books, 2008), 187.

63. Bernard Lowe is an anagram of Arnold Weber.

64. *Westworld*, Season 1, episode 10, "The Bicameral Mind," directed by Jonathan Nolan, written by Jonathan Nolan and Lisa Joy, aired December 4, 2016, on HBO, WarnerBrothers, 2017, Blu-Ray.

65. Another favorite Psychology 101 moment of mine is when William's guest profile appears briefly in an episode, and it includes DSM diagnosis codes. *Westworld*, Season 2, episode 9, "Vanishing Point," directed by Stephen Williams, written by Roberto Patino, aired June 17, 2018, on HBO, WarnerBrothers, 2018, Blu-Ray.

66. Sigmund Freud, *Introductory Lectures on Psycho-Analysis*, trans. and ed. James Strachey (New York: W.W. Norton, 1989), 493.

67. *Westworld*, Season 1, episode 2, "Chestnut," directed by Richard J. Lewis, written by Jonathan Nolan and Lisa Joy, aired October 9, 2016, on HBO, WarnerBrothers, 2017, Blu-Ray.

68. *Westworld*, Season 1, episode 10, "The Bicameral Mind."

69. Judith Butler expounds on the terms "precarious life" and "grievable life" in her introduction to *Frames of War*. Judith Butler, *Frames of War: When Is Life Grievable?* (New York: Verso, 2009), 1–32.

70. Benjamin, "On Language as Such and on the Language of Man," in *Reflections: Essays, Aphorisms, Autobiographical Writings*, ed. Peter Demetz, trans. Edmund Jephcott (New York: Schocken Books, 1978), 315–316.

71. Benjamin, 316.

72. Dean Saxton and Lucille Saxton, *O'othham Hoho'ok A'agitha: Legends and Lore of the Papago and Pima Indians* (Tucson: University of Arizona Press, 1973), 59–61.

73. *Westworld*, Season 1, episode 10, "The Bicameral Mind."

74. *Westworld*, Season 1, episode 6, "The Adversary," directed by Frederick E.O. Toye, written by Halley Gross and Jonathan Nolan, aired November 6, 2016, on HBO, WarnerBrothers, 2017, Blu-Ray.

75. I purposefully use the term Indian to distinguish between constructed representations and actual tribes of indigenous peoples.

76. John Kucich, *Ghostly Communion: Cross-Cultural Spiritualism in Nineteenth-Century American Literature* (Chicago: Dartmouth College Press, 2004), 60–61.

77. T.L. Ballenger, "Joseph Franklin Thompson: An Early Cherokee Leader," *Chronicles of Oklahoma* 30, no. 3 (1952), 288.

78. I deliberately use the phrase left behind here because it elicits comparison to Christian, particularly evangelical Protestant, apocalyptic narratives that envision what will occur after the rapture.

79. *Westworld*, Season 2, episode 10, "The Passenger."

80. *Westworld*, Season 3, episode 8, "Crisis Theory," directed by Jennifer Getzinger, written by Denise Thé and Jonathan Nolan, aired May 3, 2020, on HBO, https://www.amazon.com/Crisis-Theory/dp/B07RYFVFKG.

Conclusion

1. Lauro, *The Transatlantic Zombie*, 92. Lauro unearths Romero-esque zombies in the 1964 pre-Romero film *The Horror of Party Beach*, directed by Del Tenney. Her recognition does not besmirch the contributions of Romero to zombie cinema nor is it a direct assault on zombie scholarship. Instead Lauro reveals the complexity of writing histories. Moreover, it destabilizes the facticity of history and provides insight into the construction of history that makes it possible to understand how and why histories are fabricated.

2. Lauro, 7.

3. Deloria, *Playing Indian*, 185.

4. The account begins by reframing the narrative: "The story of Pocahontas is first and foremost a great love story. The love that was the moving force within Pocahontas's life was the spiritual bond and filial affection between Pocahontas and her father, Chief Powhatan Wahunsenaca, and the love they had for the Powhatan

people." Linwood "Little Bear" Custalow and Angela L. Daniel "Silver Star," *The True Story of Pocahontas: The Other Side of History* (Golden: Fulcrum, 2007), 5.

5. Addams, *Peace and Bread in Time of War* (Urbana: University of Illinois Press, 2002), 57.

6. Addams, 57.

7. Addams, 86.

8. Addams, 85.

9. Addams, 53. Addams attributes the term to T.M. Bondereff.

10. Addams, 51.

11. For a thorough analysis of the development of Addams' thought on patriotism, see Scott L. Pratt, "Jane Addams: Patriotism in Time of War," *Midwest Studies in Philosophy* 28, no. 1 (2004): 102–118.

12. For a convincing presentation of this argument, see David Treuer, "Return the National Parks to the Tribes," *Atlantic*, May 2021.

13. Vijay Prashad, "Our Time Is Now" (panel discussion, COP26 People's Summit for Climate Justice, Glasgow, November 10, 2021).

Bibliography

Ackermann, Hans-W., and Jeanine Gauthier. "The Ways and Nature of the Zombi." *American Folklore Society* 104, no. 414 (1991): 466–494.

Adams, John. "A Dissertation on the Canon nd Feudal Law." In *The Works of John Adams*, ed. Charles Francis Adams, 447–464. Vol. 3. Boston: Little, Brown, 1851.

Addams, Jane. *The Long Road of Woman's Memory*. New York: Macmillan, 1916.

———. *Peace and Bread in Time of War*. Urbana: University of Illinois Press, 2002.

Agamben, Giorgio. *What Is Real?* Translated by Lorenzo Chiesa. Palo Alto: Stanford University Press, 2018.

Anderson, Benedict. *Imagined Communities: Reflections on the Origin and Spread of Nationalism*. New York: Verso, 2006.

Anderson, Virginia DeJohn. *New England's Generation: The Great Migration and the Formation of Society and Culture in the Seventeenth Century*. New York: Cambridge University Press, 1997.

Andersson, Rani-Henrik. *The Lakota Ghost Dance of 1890*. Lincoln: University of Nebraska Press, 2008.

Aristotle. *On Poetics*. Translated by Seth Benardete and Michael Davis. South Bend: St. Augustine's Press, 2002.

Armstrong, Nancy, and Leonard Tennenhouse. *The Imaginary Puritan: Literature, Intellectual Labor, and the Origins of Personal Life*. Berkeley: University of California Press, 1994.

Asquith, Wendy. "The Art of Postcolonial Politics in the Age of Empire: Haiti's Object Lesson at the World's Columbian Exposition." *Historical Research* 91, no. 253 (2018): 528–553.

Auerbach, Erich. "Figura." In *Scenes from the Drama of European Literature*, edited by Wlad Godzich and Jochen Schulte-Sasse, 11–76. Vol. 9 of *Theory and History of Literature*. Minneapolis: University of Minnesota Press, 1984.

———. *Mimesis: The Representation of Reality in Western Literature*. Translated by William R. Trask. Princeton: Princeton University Press, 2003.

Balibar, Étienne. "*Homo Nationalis*: An Anthropological Sketch of the Nation-Form." In *We the People of Europe?: Reflections on Transnational Citizenship*, translated by James Swenson, 11–30. Princeton: Princeton University Press, 2004.

———. "The Nation Form: History and Ideology." In *Race, Nation, Class: Ambiguous Identities*, translated by Chris Turner, 86–106. New York: Verso, 1991.

Ballenger, T.L. "Joseph Franklin Thompson: An Early Cherokee Leader." *Chronicles of Oklahoma* 30, no. 3 (1952): 285–291.

Bank, Rosemarie K. "Representing History: Performing the Columbian Exposition." *Theatre Journal* 54, no. 4 (2002): 589–606.

Barthes, Roland. "Myth Today." In *Mythologies*, translated by Annette Lavers, 109–159. New York: Farrar, Straus and Giroux, 1972.

"The Battle of Wounded Knee: Review of the Campaign Which a Monument Unveiling Recalls." *Inter Ocean*, July 24, 1893.

Baudrillard, Jean. *Simulations*. Translated by Paul Foss, Paul Patton and Philip Beitchman. Los Angeles: Semiotext[e], 1983.

Bederman, Gail. *Manliness and Civilization: A Cultural History of Gender and Race in the United States, 1880–1917.* Chicago: University of Chicago Press, 1984.

Benedickty-Kokken, Alessandra. *Spirit Possession in French, Haitian, and Vodou Thought: An Intellectual History.* Lanham: Lexington, 2015.

Benjamin, Walter. "On Language as Such and on the Language of Man." In *Reflections: Essays, Aphorisms, Autobiographical Writings,* edited by Peter Demetz, translated by Edmund Jephcott, 314–332. New York: Schocken Books, 1978.

———. "Theses on the Philosophy of History." In *Illuminations,* edited by Hannah Arendt, translated by Harry Zohn, 253–264. New York: Schocken Books, 2007.

Bennhold, Katrin. "Part 2: In the Stomach." In *Day X,* produced by Lynsea Garrison, Clare Toeniskoetter, and Kaitlin Roberts, May 19, 2021. MP3 audio, 37:39. https://www.nytimes.com/2021/05/19/podcasts/far-right-german-extremism.html.

Bercovitch, Sacvan. *The American Jeremiad.* Madison: University of Wisconsin Press, 2012.

———. *The Puritan Origins of the American Self.* New Haven: Yale University Press, 2011.

———. *The Rites of Assent: Transformations in the Symbolic Construction of America.* New York: Routledge, 1993.

Berry, Sarah. *Screen Style: Fashion and Femininity in 1930s Hollywood.* Minneapolis: University of Minnesota Press, 2000.

Bertoni, Steven. "The Son-in-Law Also Rises." *Forbes,* December 20, 2016.

Bishop, Kyle William. *American Zombie Gothic.* Jefferson: McFarland, 2010.

———. "The Idle Proletariat: *Dawn of the Dead,* Consumer Ideology, and the Loss of Productive Labor." *Journal of Popular Culture* 43, no. 2 (2010): 234–248.

———. "The Sub-Subaltern Monster: Imperialist Hegemony and the Cinematic Voodoo Zombie." *The Journal of American Culture* 31, no. 2 (2008): 141–152.

Block, Ned. "The Harder Problem of Consciousness." *Journal of Philosophy* 99, no. 8 (2002): 391–425.

Bogue, Allan G. *Frederick Jackson Turner: Strange Roads Going Down.* Norman: University of Oklahoma Press, 1998.

Bourdieu, Pierre. "The Field of Cultural Production, or: The Economic World Reversed." In *The Field of Cultural Production: Essays on Art and Literature,* edited by Randal Johnson, translated by Richard Nice, 29–73. New York: Columbia University Press, 1993.

Boyle, Danny, dir. *28 Days Later.* 2002; Century City: Fox Searchlight, 2003. DVD.

Brideson, Cynthia, and Sara Brideson. *Ziegfeld and His Follies: A Biography of Broadway's Greatest Producer.* Lexington: University Press of Kentucky, 2015.

Brooks, Lisa. *Our Beloved Kin.* New Haven: Yale University Press, 2019.

Brown, Charles Brockden. "To the Public." In *Edgar Huntly; or, Memoirs of a Sleep-Walker,* 3–4. Philadelphia: H. Maxwell, 1799.

Brown, Elspeth. "The Commodification of Aesthetic Feeling: Race, Sexuality, and the 1920s Stage Model." *Feminist Studies* 40, no. 1 (2014): 65–97.

———. "De Meyer at *Vogue*: Queer Affect in First World War-era Fashion Photography." *Photography and Culture* 2, no. 3 (2009): 253–274.

Brown, George Le Roy, to William Cody and Nate Salsbury. 19 April 1893. Series 3: Letters Received. National Archives and Records Administration, Kansas City.

Brown, Kaye. "Quantitative Testing and Revitalization Behavior: On Carroll's Explanation of the Ghost Dance." *American Sociological Review* 41, no. 4 (1976): 740–44.

Brown, Richard. *Knowledge Is Power: The Diffusion of Information in Early America, 1700–1865.* New York: Oxford University Press, 1989.

Browning, John Edgar. "*I Am Legend* (Novel)." In *Encyclopedia of the Zombie,* edited by June Michele Pulliam and Anthony J. Fonseca, 140–141. Santa Barbara: Greenwood, 2014.

Bryman, Alan. *The Disneyization of Society.* London: SAGE Publications, 2004.

"Buffalo Bill's Wild West." *Cincinnati Commercial Gazette,* October 19, 1884.

Butler, Judith. *Frames of War: When Is Life Grievable?* New York: Verso, 2009.

Byrd, Jodi. *The Transit of Empire: Indigenous Critiques of Colonialism.* Min-

neapolis: University of Minnesota Press, 2011.
Cable, George W. "Creole Slave Songs." *The New Century* 31, no. 6 (1886): 807–828.
Cahn, Robert. "The Intrepid Kids of Disneyland." *Saturday Evening Post*, June 1958.
Cameo, David. "[Exclusive] 'Multi-Community Charter of Rights and Freedoms.'" *We Are Squawking Dead* (blog). March 1, 2019. https://squawkingdead.blogspot.com/2019/03/exclusives-multi-community-charter-of.html.
Cantet, Laurent, dir. *Heading South*. 2005; New York: Magnolia Home Entertainment, 2007. DVD.
Carroll, Michael P. "Revitalization Movements and Social Structure: Some Quantitative Tests." *American Sociological Review* 40, no. 3 (1975): 389–401.
Césaire, Aimé. *Discourse on Colonialism*, translated by Joan Pinkham. New York: Monthly Review Press, 2000.
Chalmers, David. *The Conscious Mind: In Search of a Fundamental Theory*. New York: Oxford University Press, 1996.
Christie, Deborah. "A Dead New World: Richard Matheson and the Modern Zombie." In *Better Off Dead: The Evolution of the Zombie as Post-Human: The Evolution of the Zombie as Post-Human*, edited by Deborah Christie Deborah and Sarah Juliet Lauro, 67–80. New York: Fordham University Press, 2011.
Church, Benjamin. *The History of King Philip's War*. Boston: J.K. Wiggin, 1865.
Coates, Ta-Nehisi. *We Were Eight Years in Power: An American Tragedy*. New York: One World, 2017.
Cody, William. William F. "Buffalo Bill" Cody Collection, MS 006. McCracken Research Library, Buffalo Bill Center of the West.
Cohen, Lester H. "The American Revolution and Natural Law Theory." *Journal of the History of Ideas* 39, no. 3 (1978): 491–502.
Cole, Eli. Daily Diary Reports, 27 February 1917. Row 16, compartment 9, shelf 6, box 742, folder 6. Record Group 45 Naval Records Collection of the Office of Naval Records and Library. National Archives and Records Administration, Washington, D.C.
Comstock, Sandra Curtis. "The Making of an American Icon: The Transformation of Blue Jeans during the Great Depression." In *Global Denim*, edited by Daniel Miller and Sophie Woodward, 23–50. New York: Berg, 2011.
Conrich, Ian. "An Infected Population: Zombie Culture and the Modern Monstrous." In *The Zombie Renaissance in Popular Culture*, edited by Laura Hubner, et al., 15–25. London: Palgrave Macmillan, 2015.
Cooper, James Fenimore. *The Last of the Mohicans*. New York: Bantam Classics, 2005.
Corrigan, Peter. *The Dressed Society: Clothing, the Body and Some Meanings of the World*. Los Angeles: SAGE Publications, 2008.
Cotton, John. "Gods Promise to His Plantation." In *51–75*, 1–16. Vol. 3 of *Old South Leaflets*. Boston: Old South Work, 1896.
Craige, John H. *Cannibal Cousins*. New York: Minton, Balch and Co., 1934.
Curzon, George Nathaniel. *Frontiers*. Oxford: Clarendon Press, 1907.
_____. "Geography." In *Subjects of the Day: Being a Selection of Speeches and Writings*, ed. Desmond M. Chapman-Huston, 155–159. London: George Allen & Unwin, 1915.
Custalow, Linwood "Little Bear," and Angela L. Daniel "Silver Star." *The True Story of Pocahontas: The Other Side of History*. Golden: Fulcrum Publishing, 2007.
Dash, J. Michael. *Haiti and the United States: National Stereotypes and the Literary Imagination*. New York: St. Martin's Press, 1997.
Davis, Wade. *Passage of Darkness: The Ethnobiology of the Haitian Zombie*. Chapel Hill: University of North Carolina Press, 1988.
_____. *The Serpent and the Rainbow*. New York: Simon & Schuster, 1985.
Dayan, Joan. *Haiti, History, and the Gods*. Berkeley: University of California Press, 1995.
Debord, Guy. *The Society of the Spectacle*. Translated by Donald Nicholson-Smith. New York: Zone Books, 2006.
Deleuze, Gilles and Félix Guattari. *A Thousand Plateaus: Capitalism and Schizophrenia*. Translated by Brian Massumi. New York: Continuum, 2004.
Deloria, Philip J. *Playing Indian*. New Haven: Yale University Press, 1998.

DeMallie, Raymond J. "The Lakota Ghost Dance: An Ethnohistorical Account." *Pacific Historical Review* 51, no. 4 (1982): 385–405.

Dendle, Peter. "The Last Man on Earth." In *The Zombie Movie Encyclopedia*, 99–101. Jefferson: McFarland, 2011.

Deren, Maya. "Chamber Films." In *Essential Deren: Collected Writings on Film by Maya Deren*, edited by Bruce R. McPherson, 250–254. Kingston: McPherson and Company, 2005.

———. *Divine Horsemen: The Living Gods of Haiti*. Kingston: McPherson and Company, 2004.

Derrida, Jacques. *Writing and Difference*. Translated by Alan Bass. Chicago: University of Chicago Press, 1978.

Disney, Walt. *The Quotable Walt Disney*. New York: Disney Editions, 2001.

Douglass, Frederick. *Lecture on Haiti*. Frederick Douglass Papers, Library of Congress.

Du Bois, Cora. *The 1870 Ghost Dance*. Lincoln: University of Nebraska Press, 2007.

Duane, Anna Mae. "Dead *and* Disabled: The Crawling Monsters of *The Walking Dead*." In *Zombie Theory: A Reader*, edited by Sarah Juliet Lauro, 237–245. Minneapolis: University of Minnesota Press, 2017.

Duff-Gordon, Lucy. *Discretions and Indiscretions*. London: Jarrolds, 1932.

Dunham, Katherine. *Island Possessed*. Chicago: University of Chicago Press, 1994.

Elliott, Michael A. "Ethnography, Reform, and the Problem of the Real: James Mooney's *Ghost-Dance Religion*." *American Quarterly* 50, no. 2 (1998): 201–233.

Ellis, Joseph. *American Creation: Triumphs and Tragedies at the Founding of the Republic*. New York: Alfred A. Knopf, 2007.

Erhart, Jacqueline, Stephan Sponar, Georg Sulyok, et al. "Experimental Demonstration of a Universally Valid Error-Disturbance Uncertainty Relation in Spin Measurements." *Nature Physics* 8 (2012): 185–189.

"Experience." Delos Destinations. Delos Inc. Accessed August 29, 2020. http://www.delosdestinations.com/#experience.

Fabian, Johannes. *Time and the Other: How Anthropology Makes Its Subject*. New York: Columbia University Press, 2006.

Fanon, Frantz. *Wretched of the Earth*. Translated by Constance Farrington. New York: Grove Press, 1963.

Farnsworth, Marjorie. *The Ziegfeld Follies: A History in Text and Pictures*. New York: Bonanza Books, 1956.

"Fashion Round-Up." *Apparel Arts* 16, no. 4 (1946): 196–198.

Fay, Jennifer. "Dead Subjectivity: 'White Zombie,' Black Baghdad." *CR: The New Centennial Review* 8, no. 1 (2008): 81–101.

Finke, Roger, and Rodney Stark. *The Churching of America, 1776–2005: Winners and Losers in Our Religious Economy*. New Brunswick: Rutgers University Press, 2005.

Finn, Ed, and Joey Eschrich. Acknowledgments in *Visions, Ventures, Escape Velocities: A Collection of Space Futures*, xvi–xix. Edited by Ed Finn and Joey Eschrich. Tempe: Arizona State University, 2017.

Firstbrook, Peter. *A Man Most Driven: Captain John Smith, Pocahontas and the Founding of America*. London: Oneworld, 2014.

Fischer, Marilyn. "Trojan Women and Devil Baby Tales: Jane Addams on Domestic Violence." In *Feminist Interpretations of Jane Addams*, edited by Maurice Hamington, 81–105. University Park: Penn State University Press, 2010.

Fiske, John. *The Beginnings of New England*. New York: Houghton Mifflin, 1894.

Fleischer, Ruben, dir. *Zombieland*. 2009; Culver City: Sony Pictures Home Entertainment. 2010. DVD.

Ford, Tanisha C. *Liberated Threads: Black Women, Style, and the Global Politics of Soul*. Chapel Hill: University of North Carolina Press, 2015.

Foucault, Michel. *Discipline and Punish: The Birth of the Prison*. Translated by Alan Sheridan. New York: Vintage, 1995.

———. *The Order of Things: An Archaeology of the Human Sciences*. New York: Vintage, 1994.

Freud, Sigmund. *Introductory Lectures on Psycho-Analysis*. Translated and edited by James Strachey. New York: W.W. Norton, 1989.

Fruzinska, Justyna. *Emerson Goes to the Movies: Individualism in Walt Disney Company's Post–1989 Animated Films*.

Newcastle upon Tyne: Cambridge Scholars, 2014.
Geertz, Clifford. "Ideology as a Cultural System." In *The Interpretation of Cultures: Selected Essays*, 193–233. New York: Basic Books, 1973.
———. "Thick Description: Toward an Interpretive Theory of Culture." In *The Interpretation of Cultures: Selected Essays*, 3–30. New York: Basic Books, 1973.
Gimple, Scott M., and Matthew Negrete. *The Walking Dead*, Season 6, episode 1, "First Time Again." Directed by Greg Nicotero. Aired October 11, 2015, on AMC. Lionsgate Home Entertainment, Blu-Ray.
Goldberg, Jordan, and Ron Fitzgerald, writers. *Westworld*. Season 2, episode 7, "Les Écorchés." Directed by Nicole Kassell. Aired June 3, 2018, on HBO. WarnerBrothers, 2018, Blu-Ray.
Gramsci, Antonio. "Rationalization of the Demographic Composition of Europe." In *The Gramsci Reader: Selected Writings 1916–1935*, edited by David Forgacs, 277–280. New York: New York University Press, 2000.
Gross, Halley, and Jonathan Nolan, writers. *Westworld*. Season 1, episode 6, "The Adversary." Directed by Frederick E.O. Toye. Aired November 6, 2016, on HBO. WarnerBrothers, 2017. Blu-Ray.
Grua, David W. *Surviving Wounded Knee: The Lakotas and the Politics of Memory*. New York: Oxford University Press, 2016.
Halperin, Victor, dir. *White Zombie*. 1932; Hollywood: Alpha Video, 2002. DVD.
Hammer, Dean. *The Puritan Tradition in Revolutionary, Federalist, and Whig Political Theory: A Rhetoric of Origins*. New York: Peter Lang, 1998.
Hammond, Charlotte. "Decoding Dress: Vodou, Cloth and Colonial Resistance in Pre- and Post-revolutionary Haiti." In *Vodou in the Haitian Experience: A Black Atlantic Perspective*, edited by Celucien L. Joseph and Nixon S. Cleophat, 85–96. New York: Lexington, 2016.
Hardt, Michael and Antonio Negri. *Empire*. Cambridge: Harvard University Press, 2001.
Hassler-Forest, Dan. "Zombie Spaces." In *The Year's Work at the Zombie Research Center*, edited by Edward P. Comentale and Aaron Jaffe, 116–149. Bloomington: Indiana University Press, 2014.
Hawthorne, Nathaniel. "The Scarlet Letter." In *The Scarlet Letter, and the Blithedale Romance*, 7–312. Vol. 5 of *The Complete Works of Nathaniel Hawthorne*. Boston: Houghton Mifflin, 1883.
Heidegger, Martin. "The Onto-theological Constitution of Metaphysics." In *Identity and Difference*, translated by Joan Stambaugh, 42–74. New York: Harper and Row, 1969.
———. "The Question Concerning Technology." In *Basic Writings*, edited by David Farrell Krell, 311–341. San Francisco: HarperSanFrancisco, 1993.
Heisenberg, Werner. *The Physicist's Conception of Nature*. Translated by Arnold J. Pomerans. London: Hutchinson Scientific and Technical, 1958.
Herskovits, Melville J. *Life in a Haitian Valley*. New York: Octagon Books, 1964.
Hittman, Michael. *Wovoka and the Ghost Dance*. Lincoln: University of Nebraska Press, 1997.
Hobbs, Priscilla. *Walt's Utopia: Disneyland and American Mythmaking*. Jefferson: McFarland, 2015.
Hobsbawm, Eric. "Mass-Producing Traditions: Europe, 1870–1914." In *The Invention of Tradition*, edited by Eric Hobsbawm and Terence Ranger, 263–307. Cambridge: Cambridge University Press, 2013.
———. *Nations and Nationalism Since 1780: Programme, Myth, Reality*. New York: Cambridge University Press, 1991.
Hoen, Paul, dir. *Zombies*. 2018; Burbank: Disney Channel, 2018. DVD.
———. *Zombies 2*. 2020; https://www.amazon.com/gp/video/detail/B084GCNBSG/.
Hofstadter, Douglas. *I Am a Strange Loop*. New York: Basic Books, 2008.
Hollander, Anne. *Seeing through Clothes*. New York: Avon Books, 1980.
Hurston, Zora Neale. *Tell My Horse: Voodoo and Life in Haiti and Jamaica*. New York: Harper and Row, 1990.
"Indians Do Homage: Bestow Roses on Duchess." *Chicago Record*. May 8, 1893.
Inoa, Geraldine, and Channing Powell, writers. *The Walking Dead*. Season 9, episode 15, "The Calm Before." Directed by Laura Belsey. Aired March 14, 2019, on AMC. Anchor Bay, 2019, Blu-Ray.

James, C.L.R. *The Black Jacobins: Toussaint L'Ouverture and the San Domingo Revolution*. New York: Vintage Books, 1989.

Jameson, Fredric. *The Political Unconscious*. New York: Routledge, 2006.

Jameson, J. Franklin. *History of Historical Writing in America*. New York: Houghton Mifflin, 1891.

Jefferson, Thomas, to James Madison, 24 November 1801. In *The Works of Thomas Jefferson*, edited by Paul Leicester Ford, 315–319. Vol. 9 of *The Works of Thomas Jefferson in Twelve Volumes*. New York: G.P. Putnam's Sons, 1905.

_____, 20 December 1787. In *7 August 1787 to 31 March 1788*, ed. Julian P. Boyd, 438–443. Vol. 12 of *The Papers of Thomas Jefferson*. Princeton: Princeton University Press, 1955.

_____, 28 October 1785." In *10 March 1784–28 March 1786*, eds. Robert A. Rutland et al., 385–388. Vol. 8 of *The Papers of James Madison*. Chicago: University of Chicago Press, 1973.

Jehlen, Myra. *American Incarnation: The Individual, the Nation, and the Continent*. Cambridge: Harvard University Press, 1986.

Johnson-McGoldrick, David Leslie. *The Walking Dead*, Season 9, episode 8, "Evolution." Directed by Michael E. Satrazemis. Aired November 25, 2018, on AMC. Anchor Bay, 2019, Blu-Ray.

Kang, Angela, writer. *The Walking Dead*. Season 9, episode 1, "A New Beginning." Directed by Greg Nicotero. Aired October 7, 2018, on AMC. Anchor Bay, 2019, Blu-Ray.

Kasson, Joy S. *Buffalo Bill's Wild West: Celebrity, Memory, and Popular History*. New York: Hill and Wang, 2000.

Katz, Josh. "'Duck Dynasty' vs. 'Modern Family': 50 Maps of the U.S. Cultural Divide." *New York Times*, December 27, 2016, www.nytimes.com/interactive/2016/12/26/upshot/duck-dynasty-vs-modern-family-television-maps.html.

Kay, Glenn. *Zombie Movies: The Ultimate Guide*. Chicago: Chicago Reviews Press, 2012.

Kee, Chera. *Not Your Average Zombie: Rehumanizing the Undead from Voodoo to Zombie Walks*. Austin: University of Texas Press, 2017.

Kehoe, Alice Beck. *The Ghost Dance: Ethnohistory & Revitalization*. Long Grove: Waveland Press, 2006.

Kirkman, Robert. *The Walking Dead #1 10th Anniversary Edition*. Berkeley: Image Comics, 2013.

_____. *The Walking Dead #156*. Berkeley: Image Comics, 2016.

Knight, Cher Krause. *Power and Paradise in Walt Disney's World*. Gainesville: University of Florida Press, 2014.

Kristeva, Julia. *Powers of Horror*. Translated by Leon S. Roudiez. New York: Columbia University Press, 1982.

Kucich, John. *Ghostly Communion: Cross-Spiritualism in Nineteenth-Century American Literature*. Lebanon: Dartmouth College Press, 2004.

La Barre, Weston. "Materials for a History of Studies of Crisis Cults: A Bibliographic Essay." *Current Anthropology* 12, no. 1 (1971): 3–44.

Lansing, Robert. "Present Nature and Extent of the Monroe Doctrine, and Its Need of Restatement." In *The Lansing Papers, 1914–1920*, ed. J.S. Beddie, 460–465. Vol. 2 of *Papers Relating to the Foreign Relations of the United States*. Washington, D.C.: United States Government Printing Office, 1940.

_____. "The Secretary of State to President Wilson." In *The Lansing Papers, 1914–1920*, ed. J.S. Beddie, 526–527. Vol. 2 of *Papers Relating to the Foreign Relations of the United States*. Washington, D.C.: United States Government Printing Office, 1940.

Larsen, Lars Bang. "Zombies of Immaterial Labor: The Modern Monster and the Consumption of the Self." In *Zombie Theory: A Reader*, ed. Sarah Juliet Lauro, 157–170. Minneapolis: University of Minnesota Press, 2017.

Lauro, Sarah Juliet. *The Transatlantic Zombie: Slavery, Rebellion, and Living Death*. New Brunswick: Rutgers University Press, 2015.

Leslie, Amy. "Amy Leslie at the Fair." *Chicago Daily News*, May 5, 1893.

_____. *Amy Leslie at the Fair*. Chicago: W.B. Conkey, 1893.

Linton, Ralph. "Nativistic Movements." *American Anthropologist* 45, no. 2 (1943): 230–40.

Locke, John. "An Essay Concerning Human Understanding." In *Locke's Essays*, 17–465. Philadelphia: Kay & Troutman, 1834.

_____. *Two Treatises of Government*. Edited by Peter Laslett. Cambridge: Cambridge University Press, 1988.

Lovecraft, H.P. "Herbert West—Reanimator." In *H.P. Lovecraft: Tales*, edited by Peter Straub, 25–54. New York: Library of America, 2005.

Luckhurst, Roger. *Zombies: A Cultural History*. London: Reaktion Books, 2015.

MacLaren, Michelle, writer. *Westworld*. Season 1, episode 9, "The Well-Tempered Clavier." Directed by Dan Dietz and Katherine Lingenfelter. Aired November 27, 2016, on HBO. WarnerBrothers, 2017, Blu-Ray.

Marcuse, Herbert. *Eros and Civilization: A Philosophical Inquiry into Freud*. Boston: Beacon Press, 1966.

Marion, Isaac. *Warm Bodies*. New York: Atria / Emily Bestler Books, 2012.

Martin's World Fair Album-Atlas and Family Souvenir. Chicago: C. Ropp & Sons, 1892.

Masquelier, Adeline. "Narratives of Power, Images of Wealth: The Ritual Economy of *Bori* in the Market." In *Modernity and its Malcontents: Ritual and Power in Post-Colonial Africa*, edited by Jean Comaroff and John Comaroff, 3–33. Chicago: University of Chicago Press, 1993.

Mateos-Aparicio, Ángel, and Jesús Benito Sánchez. "'Parasites in a Host Country': Migrants, Refugees, Asylum Seekers and Other Zombies in *The Walking Dead*." In *The Poetics and Politics of Hospitality in U.S. Literature and Culture*, edited by Amanda Ellen Gerke, Santiago Rodríguez Guerrero-Strachan, and Patricia San José Rico, 211–232. Boston: Brill, 2020.

Mather, Cotton. "A Brand Pluck'd out of the Burning." In *Narratives of the Witchcraft Cases 1648–1706*, edited by George Lincoln Burr, 253–287. New York: Charles Scribner's Sons, 1914.

Mather, Increase. "A Brief History of the Warr with the Indians in New-England (1676): An Online Electronic Text Edition." *Faculty Publications, UNL Libraries* 31 (2006): 1–94.

Matheson, Richard. *I Am Legend*. New York: Tor, 1995.

McAlister, Elizabeth. "Slaves Cannibals, and Infected Hyper-Whites: The Race and Religion of Zombies." *Anthropological Quarterly* 85, no. 2 (2012): 457–486.

McCormack, John. "Weekly Standard: Founding Fathers Opposed Slavery." Last modified July 6, 2011. https://www.npr.org/2011/07/06/137647715/weekly-standard-founding-fathers-opposed-slavery.

McPherson, James. *The Oxford History of the United States*. Vol. 6, *Battle Cry of Freedom: The Civil War Era*. New York: Oxford University Press, 1988.

Métraux, Alfred. *Voodoo in Haiti*. Translated by Hugo Charteris. New York: Schocken Books, 1972.

Mikami, Shinji, dir. *Resident Evil*. 1996; Osaka: Capcom, 1996. PlayStation.

Miller, Perry. *Errand into the Wilderness*. Cambridge: Harvard University Press, 1993.

_____. *The New England Mind: The Seventeenth Century*. Vol. 1, *The New England Mind*. New York: Macmillan, 1939.

_____. *Orthodoxy in Massachusetts 1630–1650*. Boston: Beacon Press, 1959.

Mirante-Matthews, Nicole, writer. *The Walking Dead*. Season 10, episode 2, "We Are the End of the World." Directed by Greg Nicotero. Aired October 13, 2019, on AMC. Lionsgate Home Entertainment, 2021, Blu-Ray.

_____. *The Walking Dead*. Season 10, episode 18, "Find Me." Directed by David Boyd. Aired March 7, 2021, on AMC. Lionsgate Home Entertainment, 2021, Blu-Ray.

Mooney, James. *The Ghost-Dance Religion and the Sioux Outbreak of 1890*. Lincoln: University of Nebraska Press, 1991.

_____. "The Indian Messiah and the Ghost Dance, with a Sketch of the Sioux Outbreak of 1890," 1894. MS 3249. National Anthropological Archives, Smithsonian Institution.

Murdock, Kenneth. Introduction to *Selections from Cotton Mather*, ix–lx. Edited by Kenneth Murdock. New York: Hafner, 1960.

Murphy, Joseph M. *Botánicas: Sacred Spaces of Healing and Devotion in Urban America*. Jackson: University Press of Mississippi, 2015.

Negrete, Matthew, writer. *The Walking Dead*. Season 9, episode 11, "Bounty." Directed by Meera Menon. Aired February 24, 2019, on AMC. Anchor Bay, 2019, Blu-Ray.

Nietzsche, Friedrich. *The Gay Science*.

Translated by Walter Kaufmann. New York: Vintage Books, 1974.

———. *Human, All Too Human: A Book for Free Spirits*. Translated by R.J. Hollingdale. Cambridge: Cambridge University Press, 1996.

Nolan, Jonathan, and Lisa Joy, writers. *Westworld*. Season 1, episode 1, "The Original." Directed by Jonathan Nolan. Aired October 2, 2016, on HBO. WarnerBrothers, 2017, Blu-Ray.

———. *Westworld*. Season 1, episode 10, "The Bicameral Mind." Directed by Jonathan Nolan. Aired December 4, 2016, on HBO. WarnerBrothers, 2017, Blu-Ray.

———. *Westworld*. Season 1, episode 2, "Chestnut." Directed by Richard J. Lewis. Aired October 9, 2016, on HBO. WarnerBrothers, 2017, Blu-Ray.

———. *Westworld*. Season 2, episode 10, "The Passenger." Directed by Frederick E.O. Toye. Aired June 24, 2018, on HBO. WarnerBrothers, 2018, Blu-Ray.

Obama, Barack. "Remarks by President Obama and Prime Minister Abe of Japan at Hiroshima Peace Memorial." Transcript of speech delivered at the Hiroshima Peace Memorial, Hiroshima, Japan, May 27, 2016. https://obamawhitehouse.archives.gov/the-press-office/2016/05/27/remarks-president-obama-and-prime-minister-abe-japan-hiroshima-peace.

Office of Commissioner of Indian Affairs. "Indian Office Exhibit at the World's Columbian Exposition." Minutes of meeting, January 30, 1892. General Records Relating to the World's Columbian Exposition, 1891–1894, A1 Entry 386. Records of the Office of the Secretary of the Interior, Record Group 48. National Archives, College Park.

Ozawa, Masanao. "Universally Valid Reformulation of the Heisenberg Uncertainty Principle on Noise and Disturbance in Measurement." *Physical Review A* 67, no. 4 (2003): 042105.

Palfrey, John Gorham. *History of New England*. 5 vols. Boston: Little, Brown, 1876.

Parsons, Elsie Clews. *Memoirs of the American Folk-lore Society: Part 2*. Vol. 26, *Folk-lore of the Antilles, French and English: Part II*. New York: G.E. Stechert and Co., 1936.

Patino, Robert, writer. *Westworld*. Season 2, episode 9, "Vanishing Point." Directed by Stephen Williams. Aired June 17, 2018, on HBO. WarnerBrothers, 2018, Blu-Ray.

Phillips, Gyllian. "White Zombie and the Creole: William Seabrook's The Magic Island and American Imperialism in Haiti." In *Generation Zombie: Essays on the Living Dead in Modern Culture*, edited by Stephanie Boluk and Wylie Lenz, 27–40. Jefferson: McFarland, 2011.

"Pontiac Manuscript: Journal of the Events of the Siege of Detroit by the Confederate Indians, in 1763." In *Information Respecting the History, Condition, and Prospects of the Indian Tribes of the United States*, edited by Henry R. Schoolcraft, 242–308. Vol. 2 of *Ethnological Researches Respecting the Red Man of America*. Philadelphia: Lippincott, Grambo and Co., 1853.

Porter, James. "Disfigurations: Erich Auerbach's Theory of *Figura*." *Critical Inquiry* 44, no. 1 (2017): 80–113.

Powell, Channing, writer. *The Walking Dead*. Season 9, episode 10, "Omega." Directed by David Boyd. Aired February 17, 2019, on AMC. Anchor Bay, 2019, Blu-Ray.

Prashad, Vijay. "Our Time Is Now." Panel discussion at the COP26 People's Summit for Climate Justice, Glasgow, November 10, 2021. https://youtu.be/Bho6xY-jSuE.

Pratt, Mary Louise. "Arts of the Contact Zone." *PMLA* 91, no. 34 (1991): 33–40.

Pratt, Scott L. "Jane Addams: Patriotism in Time of War." *Midwest Studies in Philosophy* 28, no. 1 (2004): 102–118.

Pressley-Sanon, Toni. *Zombifying a Nation: Race, Gender and the Haitian Loas on Screen*. Jefferson: McFarland, 2016.

Rak, Joanna. "A Typology of Cultural Attitudes as a Device Describing Political Thought of the Populations Influenced by Globalisation." *Anthropological Notebooks* 21, no. 2 (2015): 55–70.

Reed, Corey, writer. *The Walking Dead*. Season 9, episode 9, "Adaptation." Directed by Greg Nicotero. Aired February 10, 2019, on AMC. Anchor Bay, 2019, Blu-Ray.

———. *The Walking Dead*. Season 10, episode 16, "A Certain Doom." Directed by Greg Nicotero. Aired October 4, 2020, on AMC. Lionsgate Home Entertainment, 2021, Blu-Ray.

Reed, Coreym and Vivian Tse, writers. *The Walking Dead.* Season 9, episode 14, "Scars." Directed by Millicent Shelton. Aired March 17, 2019, on AMC. Anchor Bay, 2019, Blu-Ray.

Reed, Darren, and Ruth Penfold-Mounce. "Zombies and the Sociological Imagination: *The Walking Dead* as Social-Science Fiction." In *The Zombie Renaissance in Popular Culture,* edited by Laura Hubner, et al., 124–138. London: Palgrave Macmillan, 2015.

Renan, Ernest. "What Is a Nation?" In *Modern Political Doctrines,* edited by Alfred Zimmern, 186–205. Oxford: Oxford University Press, 1939.

Rhodes, Gary D. *White Zombie: Anatomy of a Horror Film.* Jefferson: McFarland, 2001.

Risling Baldy, Cutcha. "On Telling Native People to Just 'Get over It' or Why I Teach about The Walking Dead in My Native Studies Classes… *Spoiler Alert.*" *Cutcha Risling Baldy* (blog), December 11, 2013, https://www.cutcharislingbaldy.com/blog/on-telling-native-people-to-just-get-over-it-or-why-i-teach-about-the-walking-dead-in-my-native-studies-classes-spoiler-alert.

Rivett, Sarah, and Abram Van Engen. "Postexceptionalist Puritanism." *American Literature* 90, no. 4 (2018): 675–692.

Romero, George A., dir. *Dawn of the Dead.* 1978; Troy: Anchor Bay Entertainment, 2004. DVD.

———. *Night of the Living Dead.* 1968; New York: Weinstein Company, 2008. DVD.

Roosevelt, Franklin D. FDR as Author—Memorandum on Haiti, 1922, box 41, folder 35. Series 3: Speeches and Writings. Franklin D. Roosevelt, Papers Pertaining to Family, Business and Personal Affairs, 1882–1945. Franklin D. Roosevelt Library, Hyde Park, New York.

Roosevelt, Theodore. "Indian Warfare on the Frontier." *Atlantic Monthly,* February 1892.

Rowlandson, Mary. *A Narrative of the Captivity, Sufferings, and Removes, of Mrs. Mary Rowlandson.* Boston: Mass. Sabbath School Society, 1856.

Rydell, Robert W. *All the World's a Fair: Visions of Empire at American International Expositions, 1876–1916.* Chicago: University of Chicago Press, 1984.

Said, Edward. "Beginnings." *Salmagundi* 2, no. 4 (1968): 36–55.

———. *Culture and Imperialism.* New York: Vintage Books, 1994.

———. "Humanism's Sphere." In *Humanism and Democratic Criticism,* 1–30. New York: Columbia University Press, 2004.

———. *Orientalism.* New York: Vintage Books, 1994.

———. "The Return to Philology." In *Humanism and Democratic Criticism,* 57–84. New York: Columbia University Press, 2004.

Sargent, Mark L. "The Conservative Covenant: The Rise of the Mayflower Compact in American Myth." *New England Quarterly* 61, no. 2 (1988): 233–251.

Saxton, Dean, and Lucille Saxton. *O'othham Hoho'ok A'agitha: Legends and Lore of the Papago and Pima Indians.* Tucson: University of Arizona Press, 1973.

"Says America Has 12 League Votes: Roosevelt Declares He Himself Had Two Until Last Week, Referring to Minor Republics." *New York Times.* August 19, 1920.

Schmidt, Hans. *The United States Occupation of Haiti, 1915–1934.* New Brunswick: Rutgers University Press, 1995.

Schow, David J. Introduction to *Zombies: The Recent Dead,* edited by Paula Guran, xiii–xxii. Gaithersburg: Prime Books, 2010.

Seabrook, William. *The Magic Island.* New York: Harcourt, Brace and Company, 1929.

Shelley, Mary Wollstonecraft. *Frankenstein, Or, The Modern Prometheus.* Oxford: Oxford University Press, 1998.

Shohat, Ella. "Gender and Culture of Empire: Toward a Feminist Ethnography of the Cinema." *Quarterly Review of Film and Video* 13, no. 1–3 (1991): 45–84.

Silverman, David. *This Land Is Their Land.* New York: Bloomsbury, 2019.

Silverstein, Jake. "Why We Published the 1619 Project." Last modified December 20, 2019. https://www.nytimes.com/interactive/2019/12/20/magazine/1619-intro.html.

Slotkin, Richard. *The Fatal Environment: The Myth of the Frontier in the Age of Industrialization.* New York: Atheneum, 1985.

———. *Gunfighter Nation: The Myth of the Frontier in Twentieth-Century America*. New York: Atheneum, 1992.

———. *Regeneration through Violence: The Mythology of the American Frontier 1600–1860*. Norman: Oklahoma University Press, 2000.

———. "The 'Wild West.'" In *Buffalo Bill and the Wild West*, 27–44. Philadelphia: University of Pittsburgh Press, 1981.

Smith, Christopher J. *Dancing Revolution: Bodies, Space, and Sound in American Cultural History*. Urbana: University of Illinois Press, 2019.

Smith, Henry Nash. *Virgin Land: The American West as Symbol and Myth*. Cambridge: Harvard University Press, 1978.

Smith, John. *The Complete Works of Captain John Smith (1580–1631)*, edited by Philip L. Barbour. 3 vols. Chapel Hill: University of North Carolina, 1986.

Spanos, William V. *American Exceptionalism in the Age of Globalization: The Specter of Vietnam*. Albany: State University of New York Press, 2008.

Spengemann, William. *A New World of Words: Redefining Early American Literature*. New Haven: Yale University Press, 1994.

Stein, Rob. "A Young Mississippi Woman's Journey through a Pioneering Gene-Editing Experiment." Health Shots. NPR, December 25, 2019, https://www.npr.org/sections/health-shots/2019/12/25/784395525/.

Stout, Harry. *The New England Soul: Preaching and Religious Culture in Colonial New England*. New York: Oxford University Press, 2012.

Stowe, Charles Edward. *Life of Harriet Beecher Stowe: Compiled from Her Letters and Journals by Her Son Charles Edward Stowe*. Cambridge: The Riverside Press, 1889.

Stowe, Harriet Beecher. Preface to *Oldtown Folks*, iii–iv. Boston: Fields, Osgood, and Co., 1869.

Straley, Bruce, and Neil Drukmann, dirs. *Last of Us*. 2013; San Mateo: Sony Computer Entertainment, 2014. PS4.

Sullivan, Moira. "Maya Deren's Ethnographic Representation of Ritual and Myth in Haiti." In *Maya Deren and the American Avant-Garde*, edited by Bill Nichols, 206–234. Berkeley: University of California Press, 2001.

Taylor, Angela. "U.S. Olympic Team Dresses Western." *New York Times*, February 8, 1980.

Taylor, Charles. "The Politics of Recognition." In *Multiculturalism: Examining the Politics of Recognition*, edited by Amy Gutmann, 25–73. Princeton: Princeton University Press, 1994.

Thé, Denise, and Jonathan Nolan, writers. *Westworld*. Season 3, episode 8, "Crisis Theory." Directed by Jennifer Getzinger. Aired May 3, 2020, on HBO. https://www.amazon.com/Crisis-Theory/dp/B07RYFVFKG.

Thoreau, Henry David. *Walden; or, Life in the Woods*. Boston: Ticknor and Fields, 1854.

Thornton, Russell. "Demographic Antecedents of a Revitalization Movement: Population Change, Population Size, and the 1890 Ghost Dance." *American Sociological Review* 46, no. 1 (1981): 88–96.

"Timeline." Westworld *Wiki*. July 15, 2020. https://westworld.fandom.com/wiki/Timeline.

Tombs, Robert. *France 1814–1914*. New York: Routledge, 2014.

Town Topics: A Journal of Society (New York: NY), March 17, 1921. Robinson Locke Collection, Series 3, vol. 368, 205. Billy Rose Theater Collection, New York Public Library.

Trachtenberg, Alan. *The Incorporation of America: Culture and Society in the Gilded Age*. New York: Hill and Wang, 2007.

Treuer, David. "Return the National Parks to the Tribes." *Atlantic*, May 2021.

Trouillot, Michel-Rolph. *Silencing the Past: Power and the Production of History*. Boston: Beacon Press, 1995.

Trump, Donald. "Remarks by President Trump at the White House Conference on American History." Speech, Washington, D.C., September 17, 2020. White House. https://trumpwhitehouse.archives.gov/briefings-statements/remarks-president-trump-white-house-conference-american-history/.

Tse, Vivian, writer. *The Walking Dead*. Season 9, episode 7, "Stradivarius." Directed by Michael Cudlitz. Aired November 18, 2018, on AMC. Anchor Bay, 2019, Blu-Ray.

Turner, Frederick Jackson. Commonplace

Book. Vol. III, no. 2. Frederick Jackson Turner Papers. Henry E. Huntington Library, San Marino.

———. "A Comparison of Differing Versions of 'The Significance of the Frontier.'" In *The Early Writings of Frederick Jackson Turner*, 275-292. Madison: University of Wisconsin Press, 1938.

———. Frederick Jackson Turner to William Dodd, 17 October 1919. In *The Genesis of the Frontier Thesis: A Study in Historical Creativity*, edited by Ray Allen Billington. Kingsport: Kingsport Press, 1971.

———. "Problems in American History." In *The Early Writings of Frederick Jackson Turner*, 71-83. Madison: University of Wisconsin Press, 1938.

———. "The Significance of the Frontier in American History." In *The Early Writings of Frederick Jackson Turner*, 185-229. Madison: University of Wisconsin Press, 1938.

Utley, Robert M. *The Lance and the Shield: The Life and Times of Sitting Bull*. New York: Henry Holt, 1993.

———. *The Last Days of the Sioux Nation*. New Haven: Yale University Press, 1963.

Vandivinit, Gilles. "From the Virgin Land to the Transnational Identities of the Twenty-First Century: Exceptionalist Rhetoric in the Field of American Studies." *European Journal of American Culture* 33, no. 3 (2014): 165-179.

Vestal, Stanley. *Sitting Bull: Champion of the Sioux*. Norman: University of Oklahoma Press, 1957.

Vox Media. "George A. Romero Explains Why Fast Zombies Could Never Exist (Hint: Weak Ankles)." Vulture. February 14, 2008. https://www.vulture.com/2008/02/george_a_romero_explains_why_f.html.

Wallace, Anthony F.C. "Acculturation: Revitalization Movements." *American Anthropologist*, 58, no. 2 (1956): 264-281.

Warren, Louis S. *God's Red Son: The Ghost Dance Religion and the Making of Modern America*. New York: Basic Books, 2017.

Webster, Daniel. "Discourse Delivered at Plymouth, in Commemoration of the First Settlement of New England: Dec. 22, 1820." In *Speeches and Forensic Arguments*, 25-56. Vol. 1 of *Speeches and Forensic Arguments*. Boston: Tappan, Whittemore, and Mason, 1848.

West, Michael O., and William G. Martin. "Haiti, I'm Sorry." In *From Toussaint to Tupac: The Black International since the Age of Revolution*, 72-104. Chapel Hill: University of North Carolina Press, 2009.

White, Richard. "Frederick Jackson Turner and Buffalo Bill." In *In American Culture: An Exhibition at the Newberry Library, August 26, 1994-January 7, 1995*, 13-49. Berkeley: University of California Press, 1994.

Wilde, Poppy. "Zombies, Deviance and the Right to Posthuman Life." In *Theorising the Contemporary Zombie: Contextual Pasts, Presents, and Futures*, 19-36. Edited by Scott Eric Hamilton and Conor Heffernan. Cardiff: University of Wales Press, 2022.

Williams, Raymond. "The Long Revolution." In *Politics and Letters: Interviews with New Left Review*, 133-174. New York: Verso, 2015.

Williams, Tony. "*White Zombie*: Haitian Horror." *Jump Cut*, no. 28 (1983): 18-20.

Williams, William Appleman. *The Tragedy of American Diplomacy*. New York: Dell Publishing Co., 1972.

Winthrop, John. "A Model of Christian Charity." In *Puritan Political Ideas 1558-1794*, 75-93. New York: Bobbs-Merrill Company, 1965.

Wojtowicz, James W. James W. Wojtowicz Collection, MS 327. McCracken Research Library, Buffalo Bill Center of the West.

Wray, Carly, and Jonathan Nolan, writers. *Westworld*. Season 2, episode 2, "Reunion." Directed by Vincenzo Natali. Aired April 29, 2018, on HBO. WarnerBrothers, 2018, Blu-Ray.

Yu, Charles, and Lisa Joy, writers. *Westworld*. Season 1, episode 8, "Trace Decay." Directed by Stephen Williams. Aired November 20, 2016, on HBO. WarnerBrothers, 2017, Blu-Ray.

Ziegfeld, Patricia. *The Ziegfelds' Girl: Confessions of an Abnormally Happy Childhood*. Boston: Little, Brown, 1964.

Zobel, Craig, writer. *Westworld*. Season 2, episode 5, "Akane no Mai." Directed by Dan Dietz. Aired May 20, 2018, on HBO. WarnerBrothers, 2018, Blu-Ray.

Index

abjection 119–120, 129, 131
Addams, Jane 7–9, 162–163, 165n1
Agamben, Giorgio 148
AI (artificial intelligence) 133–137, 142, 147, 160; *see also* consciousness; host; self-consciousness
American exceptionalism 68, 86, 101–104, 112
Anderson, Benedict 114, 167n38
Anderson, Virginia DeJohn 25, 168n18, 169n52
Andersson, Rani-Henrik 41
android *see* host
Annawon 28, 31
anthropology 10, 42–44, 46, 53, 64, 77, 78, 80–83, 124, 170n29, 175n101; *see also* ethnography
apocalypse 2, 4, 10, 86, 89–92, 94, 96–98, 101–103, 106, 163, 181n78
appropriation 23, 71, 73, 129, 131, 137, 156, 161
Aristotle 53
Auerbach, Erich 15–16, 25, 162
Austin, Jane 59

Bachmann, Michelle 19
Balibar, Étienne 12, 14, 56, 115
Bank, Rosemarie 54
Barthes, Roland 9, 75, 114, 165–166n15, 174n62
Baudrillard, Jean 134
Bederman, Gail 20–21
Benedickty-Kokken, Alessandra 83
Benjamin, Walter 19, 115, 139, 155
Bercovitz, Sacvan 2, 5, 15, 22–25, 136, 167n15
Berry, Sarah 130
biopolitics 127–129, 138–139, 142
Bishop, Kyle William 9, 58, 61, 74, 93, 161
Block, Ned 5–6, 136, 138, 151
blood 20–21, 65, 79, 88, 109, 112, 136, 156

Boone, Daniel 20, 32, 56, 75
Boyle, Danny 97, 161
border 59, 107, 113, 117
Brown, Charles Brockden 58, 61–62
Brown, Elspeth 141
Brown, Kaye 42
Brown, Richard 26
Bryman, Alan 142–143, 145
Buffalo Bill's Wild West show 32 35, 41, 53–56, 75, 141
Bull, Sitting 48–51, 53–54, 170n26, 171n67, 171n70
Burroughs, Edgar Rice 119; *see also* Tarzan
Butler, Judith 154, 181n69

Cahn, Robert 134–135
cannibalism 4, 20, 57, 65
capitalism 12, 60, 93–94, 114, 142, 145, 149, 162
Caribbean 4, 66, 68–70, 75, 84–85, 87, 139, 142; *see also* Haiti
Carroll, Michael 42
Catch-the-bear 50–51, 171n70
Césaire, Aimé 137
Chalmers, David 135–136, 154–155
cheer (sport) 118–120, 125–126
Christianity 15–17, 20, 23, 33–34, 42, 45, 52, 70, 88, 95, 158, 181n78
Church, Benjamin 26–33, 39, 110
Civil rights movement 5, 115–116, 122–125
Civil War 56, 124
Coates, Ta-Nehisi 11
Cody, William "Buffalo Bill" 35, 53, 55, 57; *see also* Buffalo Bill's Wild West
colonialism 2–6, 9, 15, 59–61, 65, 74, 89–90, 96, 106, 108–109, 111, 113–114, 116–117, 123–124, 127, 131, 137–140, 142, 148–150, 156, 159–160, 162–163, 172n83, 174n60
Columbus, Christopher 38, 53–56, 115
Comstock, Sandra Curtis 105

consciousness 6, 8, 13, 63–64, 70, 81, 88, 90, 94, 98, 135–139, 146–147, 149–157, 159–160; see also AI; host; national identity; self-consciousness
constitution: Haitian 68; U.S. 2–3, 21, 107, 116
consumerism 76, 86, 92–93, 96–98, 102
Cooper, James Fenimore 2, 4, 59–61, 63, 65, 71, 74, 103–104, 110, 119
Corrigan, Peter 122
costume 92, 97, 105–106, 117, 120, 122–124, 127–131, 141
Curzon, George 40

Darwin, Charles 17
Dash, J. Michael 69
Davis, Wade 64, 82, 161, 175n101
Dayan, Joan 95
Debord, Guy 144
Declaration of Independence 19, 31, 106, 110
Delaware (tribe) 45
Deloria, Philip 124, 162
Delos, James 146–147
Delos Destinations 5, 133, 135–137, 139–143, 145–147, 149, 151, 155–157
DeMallie, Raymond 43, 95
Deren, Maya 4, 78, 80–83, 137, 161, 179n17
Derrida, Jacques 78–79, 83
Devil Baby 7–10, 165n1
disease 87–88, 132
Disney 2, 5, 114–116, 123–124, 131, 133, 163; theme parks 134–136, 142, 144–145
Disney, Walt 134
Dodd, William 36
Douglass, Frederick 57
Duff-Gordon, Lady 141
Dunham, Katherine 78–80, 82, 161

Elliott, Michael 44
Emerson, Ralph Waldo 25, 86, 103
epidemic 11, 63
errand 2, 22–24, 28, 30, 33, 58, 74, 94, 116–117, 119, 121, 126, 141, 145, 162
ethnography 3, 7, 43, 47, 52–53, 56, 73, 77–83, 137, 161, 170n21, 171n57; see also anthropology
evolution 4, 17, 23, 36–41, 44, 54, 56, 58, 86–87, 89–90, 106; see also Social Darwinism

Fabian, Johannes 16–17
Fanon, Frantz 151
Fay, Jennifer 74
Fear the Walking Dead 4

figural interpretation 19–20, 22, 25, 29, 32, 34, 38, 56–57, 162; *figura* 15–16, 24
Fischer, Marilyn 8
Floyd, George 1, 19
football 5, 109, 118, 126–129
Ford, Tanisha 123
Foucault, Michel 13–14, 125, 127, 134, 139, 146, 148, 180n49
Franklin, Benjamin 25
Freud, Sigmund 73, 131, 144, 153–154
frontier 3–6, 23–24, 28, 35–36, 38–41, 43, 48, 55, 58–59, 61–63, 65, 75, 84–85, 90, 94, 103, 105–107, 110, 115–116, 119, 121, 126, 131, 133–134, 136–137, 141–145, 149, 160
Fruzinska, Justyna 5, 116
futurism 2, 5, 19, 34, 90, 118, 132–134, 136, 145, 147

Geertz, Clifford 9–10, 12, 165n15
gender 9, 19, 21, 101, 105, 122–123, 125, 137, 139, 141–142, 163
genealogy 2, 8–11, 13, 32, 36, 45–46, 83, 114, 136, 138, 149, 161
genetics 28, 38, 87, 118–121, 126, 132, 161
ghost dance 3, 6, 35, 41–46, 48–49, 51–55, 73, 95–96, 110, 113, 156–159, 172n83
Ghost Nation 6, 156–160
gothic 4, 58, 61–62
Gramsci, Antonio 11, 139
Gray, Victoria 132
Great Migration 25, 31–32, 168n18, 169n52
gros bon ange 80–81, 83, 137, 179n17
Gustafson, Sandra 21

hair 117–121, 123, 128, 130–131, 140
Haiti 4–5, 36, 43, 56–60, 63, 65–75, 77–84, 90, 95–96, 100, 113, 116, 123, 137–139, 161
Halperin, Victor 4, 57, 71–73, 75, 161
Hammer, Dean 32–33
Hammond, Charlotte 123
Hardt, Michael 12
Hawthorne, Nathaniel 7, 25
Heading South 139, 142, 145
Heidegger, Martin 16, 137, 147–148, 167n45
Heisenberg, Werner 147–148
Herskovits, Melville 4, 77–81
High School Musical 115, 117
Hinduism 45
Hittman, Michael 41, 46
Hobbs, Priscilla 134
Hobsbawm, Eric 11, 24, 114
Hollander, Anne 80
host 5–6, 98, 135–143, 146, 149–160
humanism 12–15, 21–22, 56, 63, 148, 160, 162

Index

Hurston, Zora Neale 4, 64, 77–79, 81–83, 161

I Am Legend 86–89, 91, 98, 108, 175n6
I Walked with a Zombie 72, 161
immigrant 2, 8–9, 11, 55, 104, 110–111, 113
Indian removal 6, 54, 115, 155–160
individualism 3, 5–6, 10, 13–14, 20, 24, 27–28, 30, 33, 39, 41, 56, 75, 101, 103, 105, 117, 162
Inter Ocean 36, 54
Islam 52, 110

Jackson, Michael 124
James, C.L.R. 121
Jameson, Frederic 12, 90, 100, 102–103
Jamestown 29–31
Jefferson, Thomas 68, 116, 144–145
Jehlen, Myra 117
jeremiad 2, 23, 27–28, 30, 58, 86, 94, 104–105, 118, 126, 129, 144–145
Judaism 16–17, 23, 52, 158

Katz, Josh 103
Kay, Glenn 69, 91–92
Kehoe, Alice Beck 43
King Philip's War 26, 110; *see also* Church, Benjamin; Wampanoag
Kirkman, Robert 86, 99, 105; *see also The Walking Dead*
Knight, Cher Krause 145
Kristeva, Julia 119, 129
Kucich, John 35, 158

Lakota 3, 6, 41–45, 47–52, 54–55, 95–96, 113, 156–158, 170n26
Lansing, Robert 66–67
The Last of the Mohicans 59–61, 103–104
The Last of Us 98–99
Lauro, Sarah Juliet 9, 82–83, 161, 181n1
Leslie, Amy 54–55
loa 83, 95, 176n16
Locke, John 2, 19, 31, 33, 144
Lovecraft, H.P. 4, 65, 71–72, 76, 173n17; "Herbert West—Reanimator" 61–64

Madison, James 144
The Magic Island 4, 57, 61–62, 69–72, 77, 116, 161
Marion, Isaac 98
Marx, Karl 85
marxism 90, 93–94, 97, 102; *see also* consumerism
Masquelier, Adeline 95
massacre 3, 6, 34, 43–45, 47–49, 51–52, 54–55, 61, 63, 67, 69, 149–150, 156, 159, 171n57
materialism 135, 150–151, 153
Mather, Cotton 7, 25–26, 39
Mather, Increase 29
Matheson, Richard 86–91, 98, 108
Mayflower 29, 166n29
McAlister, Elizabeth 76
McGhee, Rita 122
memory 3, 5–9, 55, 87, 93, 98, 136–137, 152, 157, 160
Métraux, Alfred 80–83
military 3, 28, 39, 43, 50–52, 66, 87, 108; U.S. Army 28, 50, 110; U.S. Marines 4, 67–69; U.S. Navy 67
Miller, Perry 2, 22–24, 167n16
Monroe, James 68
Monroe Doctrine 66–67
Montesquieu, Baron de 2, 21
Mooney, James 3, 41–53, 56, 73, 170n21, 171n46, 171n69, 172n83
Murphy, Joseph 95, 100
myth 2–3, 5–6, 8–9, 20, 23, 28–29, 32, 35, 45, 56, 59, 61–62, 74–75, 85–87, 89–90, 94, 96, 100, 102–107, 111, 113–114, 116, 119, 121, 131, 133–134, 142–145, 149, 156, 158–163, 174n62, 177n40

narrative 1–6, 13–15, 19, 22, 24–32, 36–38, 41, 43–49, 52–57, 61, 64–65, 70, 73–76, 78, 80, 85–86, 88–91, 93–103, 105–109, 111–113, 115–116, 122–123, 131, 133, 138, 140, 142–143, 145–146, 149–151, 153–154, 156–157, 159–163, 167n38, 181n78, 181n4
national identity 1–6, 9–16, 19–22, 24–28, 30–36, 38–40, 53–54, 56–58, 65, 68–69, 71, 74–75, 83–84, 86–87, 89, 92, 101–103, 105, 111, 113–116, 119, 126, 131, 134, 136, 144–146, 149–150, 162–163, 167n38
Negri, Antonio 12
Neolin 45–46
New England 22–27, 29, 31–32, 34, 110, 118, 168n26, 169n52
New York Times 11, 15, 103, 105
Nietzsche, Friedrich 10–11, 14, 20, 57, 82, 121, 139, 144, 157

Obama, Barack 86
Orange, Tommy 1
outbreak *see* massacre
Ozawa, Masnoa 148

p-zombie (philosophical zombie) 135–136, 138–139, 179n13
Palfrey, John Gorham 31, 169n52
Pamunkey 31

Index

panopticon 125, 127
Penfold-Mounce, Ruth 4, 100, 132
Pine Ridge 48, 50
Phillips, Gyllian 74–75
Plymouth 27, 34
Polynice, Constant 70–72, 81
"Pontiac Manuscript" 45, 171n46
Porter, James 16, 25
possession 5, 57, 78, 81, 83, 86, 95–96, 113, 137, 179n17
Pressley-Sanon, Toni 139
Pumetacom 26–29, 39
Puritan 10, 20, 22–27, 31–34, 56, 145, 159, 167n15, 167n16, 168n17, 168n22, 169n52

race 2, 5, 8–9, 11, 14, 19, 54, 56–57, 59, 61, 63, 65, 69, 73–76, 85–87, 91–92, 101, 109, 115–116, 118, 121, 123–126, 128, 130–131, 137, 141–142, 163, 178n30
Reed, Darren 4, 100, 132
Renan, Ernest 15
Resident Evil 96–97, 99
revitalization 42, 46
revolution 37, 76, 85, 94, 102, 106, 125, 130, 150, 153, 161; American 2, 21, 28, 32, 107, 110; Haitian 57, 66–69, 123
ritual 5, 9, 20, 23–24, 28, 33, 39, 41, 43, 45, 57–58, 74, 76, 78–80, 95–96, 100, 110, 113–114, 116, 117, 119, 120–121, 124–125, 131, 137, 145, 161–162, 181n4
robots 5–6, 135; *see also* AI; hosts
Romero, George: *Dawn of the Dead* 20, 76, 86, 105; *Day of the Dead* 92; *Land of the Dead* 76, 92, 94; legacy 4, 65, 76, 82, 86–89, 93–99, 102, 153, 161, 175n1, 176n20, 181n1; *Night of the Living Dead* 76, 86, 91–92, 99, 161

Roosevelt, Franklin D. 67–68
Roosevelt, Theodore 21, 24, 35, 74
Rose, Kathleen 141
Roth, Claudia 11
Rowlandson, Mary 74, 109
Rydell, Robert 54

Said, Edward 13–15, 25, 40, 59, 117, 148, 162
Schmidt, Hans 58, 68
Seabrook (fictional town) 115, 117–123, 125–131
Seabrook, William 4, 57, 61, 66, 69–72, 75–77, 80–83, 116, 161
self-consciousness 25, 38–39, 64, 76, 115
semiology 4, 6, 9, 24, 27, 35, 75, 90, 111, 114, 151, 165n15
Sewall, Samuel 26, 168n22
Shelley, Mary 61–62

sheriff 104, 106, 134–135
Shohat, Ella 135, 142
Short, Mary 7
Sioux *see* Lakota
1619 Project 1, 15
slavery 4–5, 13, 15, 19, 27, 36, 38, 56, 58–60, 65, 68–70, 72, 74, 76–77, 79–84, 90, 115, 121, 130
Slotkin, Richard 2, 20, 32, 59
Smith, Christopher 125
Smith, John 29–32, 162, 169n52
smudge 109, 162
Social Darwinism 3, 37, 43–45, 53, 87
social-science fiction 5–6, 100, 132–133, 139
soul 23, 62, 79–81, 135, 137–138
Spanos, William 6, 58, 101, 136
Spencer, Herbert 3, 17, 37, 54
Stein, Rob 132
Stout, Harry 26
Stowe, Harriet Beecher 25–26, 168n26
survivalism 4, 86, 89, 92, 95, 97, 101, 104, 108, 111, 113

Tarzan 119, 142
Taylor, Angela 105
Taylor, Breonna 19
Taylor, Charles 150
Tenskwatawa 46
terrorism 109–111
Thoreau, Henry David 10, 14, 166n32
Thornton, Russell 42
Thriller 124
ti bon ange 80–81, 83, 137
Tombs, Robert 68
Tourneur, Jacques 72, 161
Trail of Tears 6, 158–159
Trouillot, Michel-Rolph 115, 143
Trump, Donald 15, 104
Turner, Frederick Jackson 3, 23, 35–41, 43, 48, 53, 55–57, 87, 115–116, 142–144
28 Days Later 91, 97, 99, 161
Twinkies 96

Utley, Robert 43, 49
utopia 89–91, 96, 100, 103–104, 122, 133

Valley Beyond 157–160
vampire 88–89
virgin land 21, 40, 103, 134
Virginia 30–31, 68
Vodou 5, 57, 63, 70, 72–73, 79–80, 82–83, 90, 95, 100, 137–138

The Walking Dead 4, 6, 10, 86, 99, 101–107, 109, 111, 113, 163
Wallace, Anthony 42–43, 170n31
Wampanoag 27–29, 33, 39, 110, 168n30

Warm Bodies 98–99
Warren, Louis 42–43, 172*n*83
Washington, D.C. 106
Webster, Daniel 34
Westworld 5–6, 133–160, 163
White, Richard 35
White Zombie 4, 57, 62–63, 71, 74–76, 86–87, 97, 161
Whitman, Walt 40
Wilde, Poppy 103
wilderness 23–24, 33–34, 39, 58, 116, 126, 145, 162
Williams, Raymond 90
Williams, Tony 74
Wilson, Jack *see* Wovoka
Wilson, Woodrow 66–67
Winthrop, John 23, 25, 27–28, 30–31, 39, 74, 86, 94, 103–104, 118, 145, 167*n*16, 169*n*52

World's Columbian Exhibition 3, 35, 38, 53, 57, 141, 159
Wounded Knee Creek 43, 45, 48, 50–51

z-band 117, 120, 122, 127–130; *see also* costume
Z Nation 2, 4, 107
Ziegfeld, Florenz 53, 141
zombie as slave 4, 65, 70, 72, 74, 76–77, 79–84, 90, 130
zombie master 72, 76, 82
Zombie Patrol 118, 125–127, 129
Zombietown 117, 119, 124–125, 127, 129–130
Zombieland 96
Zombies (film) 5, 114–131, 163
zombification 74, 76–78, 81, 83, 98, 118, 128, 137, 139, 153

www.ingramcontent.com/pod-product-compliance
Lightning Source LLC
Chambersburg PA
CBHW032044300426
44117CB00009B/1190